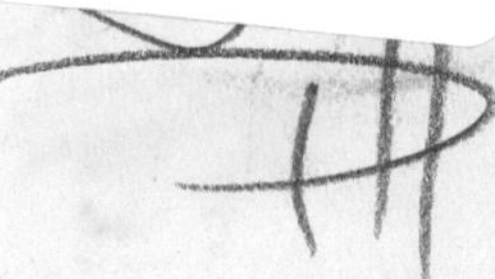

THE ENGLISH SCENE

1 Author and Publisher in the Eighteenth Century
From a print after H. Wigstead (1784)

THE ENGLISH SCENE

In the Works of Prose-Writers since 1700

Edited and Arranged by
F. ALAN WALBANK

With a Foreword by
SIR JOHN SQUIRE

Illustrated from Contemporary Pictures and Prints

Second Edition Revised

LONDON
B. T. BATSFORD LTD.
15 NORTH AUDLEY STREET, W.1
& MALVERN WELLS, WORCESTERSHIRE

First Published, May 1941
Second Edition Revised, 1944–45

MADE AND PRINTED IN GREAT BRITAIN
FOR THE PUBLISHERS, B. T. BATSFORD LTD., LONDON
BY WESTERN PRINTING SERVICES LTD., BRISTOL

FOREWORD

By

SIR JOHN SQUIRE

I DON'T know the author of this learned and delightful book, but my heart warmed to him for compiling it at a time when we are being forced to bare our reluctant teeth to half the world, are blacked out at night, and our remotest cottages and water-mills and meadows are overshadowed by Satan's wings. He has denied himself a great deal by omitting the poets, but had he included them he would have had less room for unfamiliar passages which would have been replaced by quotations excellent but known by heart. He has naturally included a few things (for no anthology pleases everybody on every page) which I could have spared; and I should have welcomed further extracts about our waterways (Mr. Robert Gibbings' latest book would have supplied them), something from John Nyren or more from Hilaire Belloc, who has celebrated our country and our coasts in prose which no living man has excelled. But there is a treasury here of enduring things recorded in enduring prose: the endlessly living England, obstinate under all superficial change, persisting from the Roman day until our own. Here are the immemorial lite of the village, the fights of our country life for survival, not treated in a sentimental way but with an eye on economics (for every man must be fed) as well as an eye on the "loveliest village of the plain" and the alders drooping over the stream and the hounds pouring over hedges, and the noise of ball against bat on the green, and Stokes Poges tower and the holly and the mistletoe.

It is natural that such a book should be produced now. "Home, what a perfect place," wrote Edward Wyndham Tennant, just before he was killed, from a broken garden at Laventie where a sprig of daphne still bloomed. Most of the soldier poets of the last war wrote about home in that way; they valued it more than they ever had because it was in danger. Like the rest of us they had probably grumbled about the defilement of England in peace-time. When they were away from it and its whole way of life was imperilled they realized that it was still the kindliest and loveliest thing in this world. So it still is; so, in all these pages, it is shown to be; and a book like this should encourage us all to fight to the death and to rebuild it, excelling our fathers, after this ghastly conflict is over.

For looking on this whole record of love and melancholy about things passing I choose to end on what is called "A Note of Hope." This very day on which I write a Methodist lawyer, who happens to be Chancellor of the Exchequer—and whose grandson, if he has one, may very well be an orthodox, rustic squire or even peer—has produced a Budget which, on the face of it, looks as though it may kill the last remains of traditional rural England. A person with £50,000 a year will have, after his taxes have been levied, about £5,000 a year, out of which he will have to pay his rates, for the education of his children to lead and serve, and (subject to complications, if he is a countryman), repairs to fences, release of tenants' rent and (though this seems now impossible) insurance against death-duties, which are well enough when the "estate" consists of stocks and shares, but very ill when the "estate" is a real estate in the country and farms and farmers have to be sold to syndicates or speculators to fill the maw of a "State," manned and dominated by professional politicians who let us into wars, allow agriculture to die, and trust to the rest of us to save their faces and necks when the crises which they have precipitated come upon us. The old privilege of farmers to have their income-tax assessed on their rent rather on their profits (which give them headaches to work out, they being mostly men of their hands and not highly "educated" in the urban and clerkly sense) has been taken away from them. On paper the dukes, the squires, the yeomen, the tenant farmers, and all their collaborators and servants ought to "go west" because of this new financial strain. But, without wishing to be too Micawberish, and although unable to see the precise way out, I can't help thinking that, however direly persecuted, they will somehow survive. For, basically, our whole people—including the exiled East-Enders who still dress their window-boxes in their bombed parishes—want them to survive and know that they are the real England.

"In isolated districts, no doubt," runs one sentence in this book, "the English squire lives on." That is (cf. Burke's *Landed Gentry*) too gloomy a view. "By Elizabeth's time," runs another sentence, "land had become a business proposition"; that is true in a sense, but the business agriculturists of her day became the Cavaliers of the next day; the land and the people on it, the church, the manor, the crops, the cottage-gardens exercised a pull even upon the grandsons of usurers. There was a Venetian Envoy to England in the reign of Henry VII (I think) who reported on this country as having the best roads, inns and parish churches in the world, but added that the English were an extraordinary people because the moment one of them had made his fortune (*anglice* "pile") the only thing he thought about was retiring into a house in the country. Our present author, celebrating the obstinate personality of the Old English Squires, says that "the architectural follies of a Beckford were by-products of their individuality." But who was Beckford? He was the son of a rich Lord Mayor of London who outbid Walpole's Strawberry Hill and wrote a Persian tale in French. He merely went "Back to the Land" (and that is the way the land then went, in the age of Grand Tours, landscape-gardening, busts of Cato and expense for fun) as almost every rich Englishman, in any age, is inclined to do. Had he flourished under Edward VII he would probably have had a shoot to which the Ripons and Walsinghams would have been delighted to come—though being Beckford he would probably not have shot himself, but merely inquired casually about the bag.

"Farewell, Rewards and Fairies," wrote Bishop Corbet in the seventeenth century, lamenting the abbeys, the "bare ruined choirs where late the sweet birds sang." *The Fine Old English Gentleman* was about the same period; Sir Roger de Coverley was presented as a survival; Washington Irving, as a sympathetic American, described squires, old halls, old-fashioned Christmas, stage-coaches, and even snow and roast beef as things passing and irreplaceable.

But for myself—and I think for our author, who couldn't have existed or compiled this book if he didn't really think this way—the stress in the sentence "Plus ça change, plus c'est la même chose" is laid rather on the second than on the first part. Our fighting men are risking, and sometimes losing, their lives for a variety of reasons: honour and the pledged word against lies, kindness against cruelty, justice against injustice. But in their minds there is also the thought of the small island which our "spokesman" (to use the fashionable word) Shakespeare loved and represented. We have all deplored, in peace-time, "the march of industrialism," ribbon-development, the pitiless commercial destruction of ancient things; but we know, as they know, that we still possess far more than we have lost, that the big towns, seen from an aeroplane, are few and far between, and that the spirit of our nation, even though it sometimes has to be expressed in terms of charabancs and litter, remains unchanged.

Long after this war has been won there will still be prose-writers to celebrate our landscape and our friendly, domestic, country life—and to regret the passing of the age before them. They will probably refer to "the dear old days of 1941." That seems unbelievable to-day; but what would Dean Swift have said about the dear old days of "good Queen Anne"? The same may be said of pictures; a day may come when Mr. Ernest Bevin may be a Quaint Ancestor of "Ye Olde Tyme."

CONTENTS

I. THE MANOR

II. THE VILLAGE

III. FARM OR FACTORY

IV. LANDSCAPE

V. THE FIELD

VI. THE ROAD

VII. RELICS AND RITUALS

ALPHABETICAL LIST OF AUTHORS

ACKNOWLEDGMENT

THE Editor gratefully acknowledges his obligation to the following authors, their agents and publishers, for permission to include copyright and contemporary material in this book, namely: Jonathan Cape Ltd., for selections from *The Poacher* by H. E. Bates, *The Mind's Eye* by Edmund Blunden, Francis Kilvert's *Diary*, *Wolf Solent* by J. C. Powys, *Gone to Earth* and *Precious Bane* by Mary Webb; Chatto & Windus Ltd., for *Our Mr. Dormer* by R. H. Mottram (with the consent of A. P. Watt and Son), and "Walking Tours" from *Virginibus Puerisque* by R. L. Stevenson; Constable & Co. Ltd., and the Trustees of the Meredith Estate, for *Diana of the Crossways* by George Meredith; J. M. Dent and Sons Ltd., for *The South Country* by Edward Thomas; Cyril Bruyn Andrews, Esq. and Eyre & Spottiswoode (Publishers) Ltd. for The Hon. John Byng's *Torrington Diaries*; Faber and Faber Ltd., for *Memoirs of a Fox-hunting Man* by Siegfried Sassoon, and *Farmer's Glory* by A. G. Street; William Heinemann Ltd., for *The Freelands* by John Galsworthy, *English Journey* by J. B. Priestley (with the consent of A. D. Peters Esq.), and *Portrait of a Village* by Francis Brett Young; John Lane (The Bodley Head) Ltd., for *Corduroy* by Adrian Bell; Macmillan & Co. Ltd., and the Trustees of the Hardy Estate, for *Tess of the D'Urbervilles*, *The Mayor of Casterbridge*, and *Under the Greenwood Tree* by Thomas Hardy; C. D. Medley Esq., for *Esther Waters* by George Moore; Methuen & Co. Ltd., for *Anna of the Five Towns* by Arnold Bennett (with the consent of J. B. Pinker & Son Ltd.), *Hills and the Sea*, by Hilaire Belloc, and *A Shepherd's Life* by W. H. Hudson; Pearn, Pollinger & Higham Ltd., for *England, my England* by D. H. Lawrence; J. B. Pinker & Son Ltd., for *Rogue Herries* by Sir Hugh Walpole; Putnam & Co. Ltd., for *The Old Stag* by Henry Williamson; The Society of Authors, for a selection "reprinted from *The Hawbucks* by John Masefield, by permission of the author"; and H. G. Wells Esq., for *Mr. Polly*.

The Publishers would also like to make their acknowledgment to the owners of the various pictures included in the illustrations, and to Messrs. W. T. Spencer, of New Oxford Street, London, for the loan of prints from their invaluable collection. Most of the remaining subjects are taken from books, prints and drawings in their own possession.

2 A Meet of the Essex Hunt, 1831
After D. Wolstenholme, Junior

The Manor

IT has become fashionable to lay many evil offspring at the door of dictators. To one, however, a good deed in a naughty world, may be ascribed the birth of the English manor. Julius Cæsar invaded Britain: the Roman villa took root in our soil and during the four-hundred-year occupation the Manor's prototype developed. Wealthy settlers in large country houses farmed their estates by the work of slaves or dependants, and left the management of the villa to a villicus or bailiff. The villa house, built on the corridor plan round a square court, served as country house and farmstead combined: its features may be seen in such sites as Chedworth, Gloucestershire. After the inroads of Angles, Saxons, Jutes and Frisians the same type of communal organisation for defence and agriculture was maintained, this time by settlements in villages under local chiefs. When the Norman conqueror came his concern was only to carry out the idea of lordship to its fullest extent: every man must hold his land from some master. In the Great Survey of 1086 every estate in the country was written down with its owner, overlord, its assessment for taxation and its stock. The manor became the unit for social organisation. The lord of the manor had to fight for his feudal superior, but otherwise was a man whose interests lay in administering justice, offering protection and fulfilling his obligations to those who worked his land. His tenants, free or villein, as condition of their holding land, paid rent in tithe or service on the home farm. The manor was ideally a mutual benefit society and the nucleus of a stable civilisation. The lord depended on his villeins for their services as much as a villein depended on his lord for security. Until about 1300 the system proved acceptable.

In manor houses the architecture remained functional. The Norman plan still obtained in Scotland even in John Aubrey's time, "viz. a great open hall, a kitchen and buttery, a parlour, over which a chamber for my lord and lady, all the rest lye in common, viz. the men-servants in the hall (the women in a common room) or oriele, the folk at the side-tables. The hearth was commonly in the middle." Large establishments would include a bakehouse, brewhouse, malthouse, dairy, larder, salser and washhouse, while screens across the lower end of the hall allowed the erection of a minstrel gallery above it. In the court were quarters for the servants and also the stables, pigsty, goose-house and hen-houses: beyond again were the large barns, the granary and hay-house, a dovecote and a small house to hold the carts. Thus it need not be wondered at that management of a large manor required the services of a bailiff, reeve, shepherd, ploughman, swineherd, oxherd, wagoner, dairymaid, woodward, hayward and pindar. To these might be added, if the establishment would support them, a miller, baker, weaver, brewer, leather-worker and perhaps parchment-maker. At its most elaborate the manorial farm was a self-sufficing organisation and aimed at economic independence.

Adequate control of such an establishment demanded the presence of its lord. Unfortunately, even as Chaucer records of his gentil knight:

> "Ful worthy was he in his lordes werre
> And therto had he riden (no man ferre),
> As wel in Cristendom as hethenesse. . ."

so also the lord's business took him sometimes elsewhere. When John Paston was away from his estate in Norfolk, Margery Paston wrote to him of the difficulties she encountered in daily management. "Sir, as for your tenants of Marlingford, they withhold their cattle and themselves both from the court, and come not within the lordship, nor make none attournment, except Thomas Davy and John Water, which absenting of the tenants is to them a great hurt and loss, for lack of seeding of their lands with their winter corn; beseeching you for God's sake to remember some remedy for them." Sir John was likewise indispensable to the poor, for as autumn closes in they come pleading: "Moreover, Sir, liketh it your mastership to understand that winter and cold weather draweth nigh and I have few clothes but of your gift." When he is not in France, however, this lord is either busied with duties at court and a lawsuit in London, or else wastes his time reading, Lydgate or Chaucer, while land, wood and even household stuff has to be sold to pay the way of his estate. To his mother the occupation of preserving Paston and Mauteby and Drayton and Gresham proved hardly less exhausting than the passionate struggle to acquire lands, as old Sir John Fastolf had done with such pride after the victory of Agincourt in 1415.

Even half a century previous to the Black Death the manorial system had shewn signs of change. Markets were developing where a peasant might sell his surplus products: the villein was being allowed to pay a few pence instead of the day service owed to his lord. He was thus freer to work his own small farm as it needed. Similarly the lord could obtain for money payment what labour he required in season. The depopulation subsequent to the Black Death, however, caused an acute shortage of labour, and faced with lands rapidly going out of cultivation the lord turned to a new system of farming. He either enclosed his demesne land for sheep pasturage and so dispensed with much labour: or he let out his lands and stock on short lease to tenant farmers. In both cases the lord of a manor became more of a mere landlord and less of a working farmer. His place was sometimes usurped by the substantial freeholder, Chaucer's Franklin,

> "An householdere, and that a greet was he,
> Seint Julian he was in his contree."

Peasants who could not pay money rents were induced to add their strips to these freeholdings or sheepfarms, and themselves soon became landless labourers. While the woollen industry shewed rising profits, sheep-farming increased its hold and not infrequently whole manors would be appropriated to that purpose. "For look in what parts of the realm doth grow the finest, and therefore dearest wool, there noblemen and gentlemen; yea and certain abbots, holy men no doubt, not contenting themselves with the yearly revenues and profits, that were wont to grow to their forefathers and predecessors of their lands, nor being content that they live in rest and pleasure nothing profiting, yea much noying the weal public: leave no ground for tillage, they enclose all into pastures: they throw down houses: they pluck down towns, and leave nothing standing, but only the church to be made a sheep-house": so in 1516 asserted Sir Thomas More. The community of the manorial village was giving place to a commercial undertaking. When Henry VIII commandeered the manors attached to monasteries, he gave them to nobles and city men, whose interest lay only in moneymaking. By Elizabeth's time land had become a business proposition, attractive to wealthy townsmen who had no hesitation in maintaining cheap mass labour. The possession of landed estates denoted a social distinction but involved ever fewer of the manorial obligations towards a labouring tenantry. A border case of the new order of landed gentlemen is supplied by Shakespeare, who, according as he prospered, purchased estates in his home county, acquired a coat of arms and in his will was thus able to leave to his daughter Susanna Hall "all my barns, stables, orchards, gardens, lands, tenements and hereditaments whatsoever, situate, lying and being or to be had, received, perceived or taken, within the towns, hamlets, villages, fields and grounds of Stratford upon Avon, Old Stratford, Bushopton and Welcombe, or in any of them in the said county of Warr." Leland as early as 1540 had remarked in his *Itinerary* upon the increasing display of landed gentlemen: "The olde house of Cheyneis is so translatid by my Lorde Russel that litle or nothing of it yn a maner remaynith ontranslatid: and a great deale of the house is even newly set up made of brike and timber: and fair logginges be new erectid in the garden. The house is within diverse places richely paintid with antique works of white and blak. And there be about the house 2. parkes, as I remember."

The essayists and character writers who preceded the novelist proper, were quick to seize upon the figure of any social misfit as an object for satire. The more objectionable Upstart Countrey Knight received his deserts in John Earle's *Microcosmography*, 1628. "His father was a man of good stocke, though but a Tanner, or Usurer; hee purchast the Land, and his son the Title. He is garded with more Gold lace than all the Gentlemen o' the Country, yet his body makes his clothes stil out of fashion. A Hauke he esteemes the true burthen of Nobility, and is exceeding ambitious to seeme delighted in the sport, and have his fist Glov'd with his Jesses. A Justice of the peace hee is to domineere in his Parish, and doe his neighbour wrong with more right. Hee will bee drunke with his Hunters for company, and staine his Gentility with droppings of Ale. In summe, he's but a clod of his own earth; or his Land is the Dunghill, and he the Cocke that crowes over it." In his introduction to a survey of Wiltshire John Aubrey later laid to the charge of Henry VIII "that by selling of the church-lands, is the ballance of the Government quite altered, and put in the hands of the Common people." Even Sir Thomas Overbury introduced his Country Gentleman as "a thing, out of whose

3 A Medieval Manor-house in Decline: Stanton Harcourt, Oxfordshire, in 1796

After Joseph Farington, R.A.

4 A Tea-party in an Eighteenth-century Mansion, *ca.* 1720

From a painting of the Earl of Strafford and Family, by Gawen Hamilton

5 A Sporting Squire of the Regency with his Family, *ca.* 1820

From a painting of the Weston Family, by Ben Marshall

corruption the generation of a justice of the peace is produced." The hospitality of the manor house, consisting in Chaucer's age of baked meat, fish, game, white bread and ale, had likewise lost some of its earlier dignity. "At meals you shall have a scattered troop of dishes led in by some black-puddings, and in the rear some demolished pasties which are not yet fallen to the servingmen. Between meals there is bread and beer for all comers, and for a stranger a napkin and cold meat in the buttery may be obtained." Wye Saltonstall continues: "All the rooms smell of dogs and hawks and the walls bear arms, though it be but a musket and two corslets." Tradition dies hard.

From about the middle of the seventeenth century, the squirearchy controlled Parliament. Enclosure Acts were passed and squires became absolute masters of their land. Manor houses built to the Elizabethan design were of a more elaborate and durable construction in accordance with the profitable trade ventures of their owners. Estates were extolled for their decorative appearance, their deer parks and woodland rides as often as for their agricultural worth. "I should speak of the gardens, fountains and groves that adorne it," remarks John Evelyn of Wotton mansion, "were they not as generally knowne to be amongst the most natural, and the most magnificent England afforded, and which, indeed, gave one of the first examples of that elegancy since so much in vogue, and followed in the managing of their waters, and other ornaments of that nature. Let me add, the contiguity of five or six Mannors, the patronage of the livings about it, and, what is none of the least advantages, a good neighbourhood." After 1688 and their increased power following the Interregnum, the landed gentry gradually merged with the commercial interests into an indistinguishable society of upper class gentlemen. Although some manors were maintained in the old style, an Act of 1744 made lord of the manor an adventitious title. It was decreed that all men who bought one estate of land should receive the title of Esquire, those who bought two estates Knight and more than two Baron.

The most colourful gallery of squirehood is produced by the eighteenth century. Side by side with Samuel Butler's "Clown of rank and degree (whose) homely education has rendered him a native only of his own soil and a foreigner to all other places, the custom of the best man in his own territories has made him the worst everywhere else," stands Lady Mary Wortley Montagu's sketch, 1718, of "the honest English squire, who verily believes the Greek wines less delicious than March beer; and the becafiguas of Italy are not so well tasted as a rump of beef; and that in short, there is no perfect enjoyment in this life out of Old England." There was also developing the eighteenth-century type special, the cultured country gentleman. According to Macaulay "he generally receives a liberal education, passes from a distinguished school to a distinguished college, and has ample opportunity to become an excellent scholar. He has generally seen something of foreign countries. A considerable part of his life has generally been passed in the Capital; and the refinements of the Capital follow him into the country. . . . In the buildings good sense and taste combine to produce a happy union of the comfortable and the graceful. The pictures, the musical instruments, the library would in any other country be considered as proving the owner to be an eminently polished and accomplished man." For a fair picture of the squire one must mingle fiction with history. The Earl of Shaftesbury introduced into his autobiography the type nonpareil; a certain squire Hastings, the pattern for all hale, hospitable, sporting, unambitious country gentlemen. Slightly idealised he becomes Sir Roger de Coverley. On the other hand Tony Lumpkin's father, who "for winding the straight horn or beating a thicket for a hare, or a wench, never had his fellow," who brought in from the plough Diggory and Roger to make a shew at the side table, and lived in "an old rumbling mansion that looks for all the world like an inn," whose best visitors his wife declared were "old Mrs. Oddfish, the curate's wife, and little Cripplegate, the lame dancing master," finds warrant in Macaulay's description in Chapter III of the *History of England*, of the country squire at the end of the seventeenth century. "His chief pleasures were commonly derived from field sports and from an unrefined sensuality," says Macaulay; "it would be well for all the publicans within ten miles round of him" when he came of age, vowed Tony Lumpkin. Defoe was of the opinion that the English gentry were, by their wealth and resources, qualified to be the most completely happy of any people in the world: yet while forgetting nothing to improve their estate, they neglected entirely the heir. He was deplored as an object untaught and unpolished, with his land duly cultivated but not his brains. Moreover, in spite of their estates the early eighteenth-century gentry lived above themselves. Defoe demonstrates in *The Compleat English Gentleman* that there was no excuse for this falling into debt. The quotation also illustrates the lingering self-sufficiency of a manorial estate: "His first advantage is that he pays no rent, that his park having some meadow grounds within the pale, few parks are without it, affords him grass and hay for his coach horses and saddle horses, which goes also a great way in the expense of the family; besides that, he has venison perhaps in his park, sufficient for his own table at least, and rabbits in his own warren adjoining, pigeons from a dove house in the yard, fish from his own ponds or in some small river adjoining and within his own royalty, and milk with all the needful addenda to his kitchen, which a small dairy of four or five cows yields to him."

The selections from Addison, Fielding, Smollett and Austen which follow portray the squire in living detail and in his domains, while a letter by Walpole from his sham Gothic castle reveals that the foibles of the living could be at least as fanciful as the creations of fiction. With the turn of the century new direction was given to the tenor of the novel by the spate of enclosures and the reappearance of the parvenu landlord in the wake of industrial prosperity. Money again was the accepted solvent of all social differences: sixteenth-century social history was cast into a new mould. The middle-class merchants were able to buy squiredoms and obtain a hold on Parliament: they extolled private profit and regarded economic activity as involving no social obligations whatever. More and more parishes were enclosed, this time for cultivation, since the markets opened by the swollen population of manufacturing towns offered a quick profit for corn products. Cobbett, whose reforming zeal involved a return to the past, bitterly contrasts the old squire with the new, but turns a blind eye to the faults of the old, who might as well be a Western as an Allworthy. The theme is caught up in Peacock's satire, enriched by the addition of the bibulous, Epicurean Rev. Dr. Folliot, and employed again by Dickens in rousing caricature. During this period of prosperity for the landowner, noble houses flourished, painted in attractive miniature by George Eliot and Trollope, while their owners, as justices of the peace, controlled the wages, dwellings and morals of their cottage tenantry, hardly less effectively but far more irresponsibly than any lord of the manor might have done. Galsworthy shews the other side of this economic bondage in *The Freelands*. The graciousness of their surroundings changes little, although Eliot and George Moore remark the decline of some country estates, but imperceptibly the squire coarsens or becomes effete: or else, like the owner of Ullathorne Court he attempts a throwback to Jane Austen's society, while the novelist averts his gaze from the industrial chaos around him. The eighteenth century, when political power, prosperity and real estate were synonymous, was the squire's heyday. In Ireland, where there are but two classes of any importance—the peasant and the landlord, he still hangs on in his Georgian mansion, eccentric and splendid: for as George Moore has said, Ireland was never subjected to a nineteenth century. Of his political power one reads in *Caleb Williams*: "it was not a question of this or that candidate, seeing that any gentleman, who was a true friend to his country, would rather lose his election than do a thing which, if once established into a practice, would deprive them for ever of the power of managing any election." Local government was in their hands and through county constituencies or pocket boroughs squires thronged the House of Commons. By the end of the nineteenth century, however, industrial interests had almost completely usurped the place of agriculture, imported foods were supplanting home products and estate management was on the way to becoming a pastime rather than an investment. Mary Webb draws Squire Reddin close to the soil, but now only in spiritual fibre; Sassoon admits his squire's relationship to the land, but translates it in the superficial terms of a golfer. Many estates have become little more than the week-end retreats of stockbrokers, whose earlier game preserves and poacher-pounding so infuriated Cobbett; more often they have come under the auctioneer's hammer, as in May, 1940, came Harlestone Hall, Northamptonshire, the accepted original of Austen's *Mansfield Park*. Squire now is a term heard chiefly at horse and flower shows, in old hunting circles or as an anachronism gracing the descendants of an ancient family.

In isolated districts no doubt the English squire lives on, maintaining something of former style, as rare a bird as that eccentric naturalist Squire Waterton of Walton Hall. Waterton exaggerates a type of English landowner, cultured, curious, venturesome and a little cranky, to whom the modern world extends no welcome: his kind could conceive nothing better the whole world round than

> "Thus to live one's own sole king
> Upon one's own sole ground."

From among them were bred Grenvilles, Walpoles and Pitts in their due season: the architectural follies of a Beckford were by-products of their individuality. Waterton explored South American jungles barefoot, recited Vergil from the top of an elm tree, turned Walton Hall into a bird sanctuary, and added sun-bathing platforms to his pigsties. The appeal of such characters outlasts their value to society. The English, like Mr. Hardcastle, are temperamentally addicted to "everything that's old: old friends, old times, old manners, old books, old wines," and above all to the good old days. They take to their hearts any survival like Waterton, who won fame as an oddity and lived the life of the old breed, until his death in 1865. Then his house was sold, his park dismantled and a neighbouring soap-boiler took over the lands of Walton Hall.

The Squire at Church

My Friend Sir Roger being a good Church-man, has beautified the Inside of his Church with several Texts of his own chusing: He has likewise given a handsome Pulpit-Cloth and railed in the Communion-Table at his own Expence. He has often told me, that at his coming to his Estate he found his Parishioners very irregular; and that in order to make them kneel and join in the Responses, he gave every one of them a Hassock and a Common-prayer Book: and at the same Time employed an itinerant Singing-Master, who goes about the Country for that Purpose, to instruct them rightly in the Tunes of the Psalms; upon which they now very much value themselves, and indeed out-do most of the Country Churches that I have ever heard.

As Sir Roger is Landlord to the whole Congregation, he keeps them in very good Order, and will suffer no Body to sleep in it besides himself; for if by chance he has been surprised into a short Nap at Sermon, upon recovering out of it he stands up and looks about him, and if he sees any Body else nodding, either wakes them himself, or sends his Servants to them. Several other of the old Knight's Particularities break out upon these Occasions: Sometimes he will be lengthening out a Verse in the Singing-Psalms, half a minute after the rest of the Congregation have done with it; sometimes, when he is pleased with the Matter of his Devotion, he pronounces *Amen* three or four times to the same Prayer; and sometimes stands up when every Body else is upon their knees, to count the Congregation, or see if any of his Tenants are missing.

As soon as the Sermon is finished, no Body presumes to stir till Sir Roger is gone out of the Church. The Knight walks down from his Seat in the Chancel between a double Row of his Tenants, that stand bowing to him on each Side; and every now and then enquires how such an one's Wife, or Mother, or Son, or Father do whom he does not see at Church; which is understood as a secret Reprimand to the Person that is absent.

The Chaplain has often told me, that upon a Catechizing-day, when Sir Roger has been pleased with a Boy that answers well, he has ordered a Bible to be given him next Day for his Encouragement; and sometimes accompanies it with a Flitch of Bacon to his mother. Sir Roger has likewise added five Pounds a year to the Clerk's Place; and that he may encourage the young Fellows to make themselves perfect in the Church-Service, has promised upon the Death of the present Incumbent, who is very old, to bestow it according to Merit.

The fair Understanding between Sir Roger and his Chaplain, and their mutual Concurrence in doing Good, is the more remarkable, because the very next Village is famous for the Differences and Contentions that rise between the Parson and the 'Squire, who live in a perpetual State of War. The Parson is always preaching at the 'Squire, and the 'Squire to be revenged on the Parson never comes to Church. The 'Squire has made all his Tenants Atheists and Tithe-Stealers; while the Parson instructs them every *Sunday* in the Dignity of his Order, and insinuates to them in almost every Sermon, that he is a better Man than his Patron. In short, Matters are come to such an Extremity, that the 'Squire has not said his Prayers either in publick or private this half Year; and that the Parson threatens him, if he does not mend his Manners, to pray for him in the Face of the whole Congregation.

JOSEPH ADDISON *The Spectator*, 1711

The Gothic Castle at Strawberry Hill

You perceive that I am got into a new camp, and have left my tub at Windsor. It is a little plaything-house that I got out of Mrs. Chenevix's shop, and is the prettiest bauble you ever saw. It is set in enamelled meadows, with filigree hedges:

> " A small Euphrates through the piece is roll'd,
> And little finches wave their wings in gold."

Two delightful roads, that you would call dusty, supply me continually with coaches and chaises; barges as solemn as Barons of the Exchequer move under my window; Richmond Hill and Ham walks bound my prospect; but, thank God! the Thames is between me and the Duchess of Queensberry. Dowagers as plenty as flounders inhabit all around, and Pope's ghost is just now skimming under my window by a most poetical moonlight. I have about land enough to keep such a farm as Noah's when he set up in the ark with a pair of each kind; but my cottage is rather cleaner than I believe his was after they had been cooped up together forty days. The Chenevixes had tricked it out for themselves; up two pair of stairs is what they call Mr. Chenevix's library, furnished with three maps, one shelf, a bust of Sir Isaac Newton, and a lame telescope without any glasses. Lord John Sackville *predecessed* me here, and instituted certain games called *cricketalia*, which have been celebrated this very evening in honor of him in a neighbouring meadow.

The lawn before the house is situated on the top of a small hill, from whence to the left you see the town and church of Twickenham encircling a turn of the river, that looks exactly like a seaport in miniature. The opposite shore is a most delicious meadow, bounded by Richmond Hill, which loses itself in the noble woods of the park to the end of the prospect on the right, where is another turn of the river, and the suburbs of Kingston as luckily placed as Twickenham is on the left; and a natural terrace on the brow of my hill, with meadows of my own down to the river, commands both extremities. Is not this a tolerable prospect?

Now you shall walk into the house. The bow-window below leads into a little parlor hung with a stone-color Gothic paper and Jackson's Venetian prints.

From hence, under two gloomy arches, you come to the hall

and staircase, which it is impossible to describe to you, as it is the most particular and chief beauty of the castle. Imagine the walls covered with (I call it paper, but it is really paper painted in perspective to represent) Gothic fretwork: the lightest Gothic balustrade to the staircase, adorned with antelopes (our supporters) bearing shields; lean windows fattened with rich saints in painted glass, and a vestibule open with three arches on the landing-place, and niches full of trophies of old coats-of-mail, Indian shields made of rhinoceros's hides, broad-swords, quivers, long-bows, arrows, and spears,—all *supposed* to be taken by Sir Terry Robsart in the holy wars.

I must tell you, by the way, that the castle, when finished, will have two and thirty windows enriched with painted glass.

I have described so much that you will begin to think that all the accounts I used to give you of the diminutiveness of our habitation were fabulous; but it is really incredible how small most of the rooms are. The only two good chambers I shall have are not yet built: they will be an eating-room and a library, each twenty by thirty, and the latter fifteen feet high. For the rest of the house, I could send it you in this letter as easily as the drawing, only that I should have nowhere to live till the return of the post. The Chinese summer-house, which you may distinguish in the distant landscape, belongs to my Lord Radnor. We pique ourselves upon nothing but simplicity, and have no carvings, gildings, paintings, inlayings or tawdry businesses.

HORACE WALPOLE *Letters*, 1747

A Noble Prospect

THE Gothic style of building could produce nothing nobler than Mr. Allworthy's house. There was an air of grandeur in it that struck you with awe, and rivalled the beauties of the best Grecian architecture; and it was as commodious within as venerable without.

It stood on the south-east side of a hill, but nearer the bottom than the top of it, so as to be sheltered from the north-east by a grove of old oaks, which rose above it in a gradual ascent of near half a mile, and yet high enough to enjoy a most charming prospect of the valley beneath.

In the midst of the grove was a fine lawn, sloping down towards the house; near the summit of which rose a plentiful

6 Horace Walpole in his Library at Strawberry Hill
From a drawing by J. H. Müntz, 1756

7 An Eighteenth-century Mansion in its Park: Horton Hall, Northamptonshire, in 1837

From a drawing by G. S. Shepherd

8 A Gothic Revival Palace in 1823: Eaton Hall, Cheshire (since replaced)

After W. Westall, R.A.

spring, gushing out of a rock covered with firs, and forming a constant cascade of about thirty feet, not carried down a regular flight of steps, but tumbling in a natural fall over the broken and mossy stones till it came to the bottom of the rock; then running off in a pebbly channel, that with many lesser falls winded along, till it fell into a lake at the foot of the hill, about a quarter of a mile below the house, on the south side, and which was seen from every room in the front. Out of this lake, which filled the centre of a beautiful plain, embellished with groups of beeches and elms, and fed with sheep, issued a river, that for several miles was seen to meander through an amazing variety of meadows and woods, till it emptied itself into the sea: with a large arm of which, and an island beyond it, the prospect was closed.

On the right of this valley opened another of less extent, adorned with several villages, and terminated by one of the towers of an old ruined abbey, grown over with ivy, and part of the front, which remained still entire.

The left-hand scene presented the view of a very fine park, composed of very unequal ground, and agreeably varied with all the diversity that hills, lawns, wood, and water, laid out with admirable taste, but owing less to art than to nature, could give. Beyond this, the country gradually rose into a ridge of wild mountains, the tops of which were above the clouds.

HENRY FIELDING *Tom Jones*, 1749

A Squire's Idyll

WHAT kind of taste and organs must those people have, who really prefer the adulterated enjoyments of the town to the genuine pleasures of a country retreat?

At Brambleton-hall, I have elbow-room within doors, and breathe a clear, elastic, salutary air: I enjoy refreshing sleep, which is never disturbed by horrid noise, nor interrupted, but in a morning, by the sweet twitter of the martlet at my window. I drink the virgin lymph, pure and crystalline as it gushes from the rock, or the sparkling beverage, home-brewed from malt of my own making; or I indulge with cider, which my own orchard affords, or with claret of the best growth, imported for my own use by a correspondent on whose integrity I can depend; my bread is sweet and nourishing, made from my own wheat, ground in my own mill, and baked in my own oven;

my table is, in a great measure, furnished from my own ground; my five-year old mutton, fed on the fragrant herbage of the mountains, that might vie with venison in juice and flavour; my delicious veal, fattened with nothing but the mother's milk, that fills the dish with gravy; my poultry from the barn-door, that never knew confinement but when they were at roost; my rabbits panting from the warren; my game fresh from the moors; my trout and salmon struggling from the stream; oysters from their native banks; and herrings, with other sea-fish, I can eat in four hours after they are taken. My salads, roots, and pot-herbs, my own garden yields in plenty and perfection, the produce of the natural soil, prepared by moderate cultivation. The same soil affords all the different fruits which England may call her own, so that my dessert is every day fresh gathered from the tree; my dairy flows with nectareous tides of milk and cream, from whence we derive abundance of excellent butter, curds, and cheese; and the refuse fattens my pigs that are destined for hams and bacon. I go to bed betimes, and rise with the sun: I make shift to pass the hours without weariness or regret, and am not destitute of amusements within doors, when the weather will not permit me to go abroad: I read, and chat, and play at billiards, cards, or backgammon. Without doors, I superintend my farm, and execute plans of improvement, the effects of which I enjoy with unspeakable delight. Nor do I take less pleasure in seeing my tenants thrive under my auspices, and the poor live comfortably by the employment which I provide. You know I have one or two sensible friends, to whom I can open all my heart; a blessing which, perhaps, I might have sought in vain among the crowded scenes of life. There are a few others of more humble parts, whom I esteem for their integrity; and their conversation I find inoffensive, though not very entertaining. Finally, I live in the midst of honest men, and trusty dependents, who, I flatter myself, have a disinterested attachment to my person.

TOBIAS SMOLLETT — *Humphrey Clinker*, 1771

A Yorkshire Squire

Two days ago, we went across the country to visit Squire Burdock, who married a first cousin of my father, an heiress, who brought him an estate of a thousand a year. This gentleman is a declared opponent of the ministry in parliament; and, having an opulent fortune, piques himself on living in the country, and maintaining old English hospitality. By the bye, this is a phrase very much used by the English themselves, both in words and writing; but I never heard of it out of the island, except by way of irony and sarcasm.

The house, though large, is neither elegant nor comfortable. It looks like a great inn, crowded with travellers, who dine at the landlord's ordinary, where there is a great profusion of victuals and drink; but mine host seems to be misplaced; and I would rather dine of filberts with a hermit, than feed on venison with a hog. The footmen might be aptly compared to the waiters of a tavern, if they were more serviceable and less rapacious; but they are generally insolent and inattentive, and so greedy, that I think I can dine better, and for less expense, at the Star and Garter, in Pall-Mall, than at our cousin's castle in Yorkshire. The squire is not only accommodated with a wife, but he is also blessed with an only son, about two-and-twenty, just returned from Italy, a complete fiddler, and *dilettante;* and he slips no opportunity of manifesting the most perfect contempt for his own father.

Our Yorkshire cousin has been a mighty fox-hunter "before the Lord"; but now he is too fat and unwieldy to leap ditches and five-bar gates; nevertheless, he still keeps a pack of hounds, which are well exercised, and his huntsman every night entertains him with the adventures of the day's chase, which he recites in a tone and terms that are extremely curious and significant. In the mean time, his broad brawn is scratched by one of his grooms. This fellow, it seems, having no inclination to curry any beast out of the stable, was at great pains to scollop his nails in such a manner, that the blood followed at every stroke. He was in hopes that he would be dismissed from this disagreeable office, but the event turned out contrary to his expectations. His master declared he was the best scratcher in the family; and now he will not suffer any other servant to draw a nail on his carcass.

TOBIAS SMOLLETT *Humphrey Clinker*, 1771

An Abbey Manor Restored

As they drew near the end of their journey, her impatience for a sight of the abbey, for some time suspended by his conversation on subjects very different, returned in full force, and every bend in the road was expected, with solemn awe, to afford a glimpse of its massy walls of grey stone, rising amidst a grove of ancient oaks, with the last beams of the sun playing in beautiful splendour on its high Gothic windows. But so low did the building stand, that she found herself passing through the great gates of the lodge, into the very grounds of Northanger, without having discerned even an antique chimney.

An abbey! Yes, it was delightful to be really in an abbey! But she doubted, as she looked round the room, whether anything within her observation would have given her the consciousness. The furniture was in all the profusion and elegance of modern taste. The fire-place, where she had expected the ample width and ponderous carvings of former times, was contracted to a Rumford, with slabs of plain, though handsome, marble, and ornaments over it of the prettiest English china. The windows, to which she looked with peculiar dependence, from having heard the General talk of his preserving them in their Gothic form with reverential care, were yet less what her fancy had portrayed. To be sure the pointed arch was preserved, the form of them was Gothic, they might be even casements, but every pane was so large, so clear, so light! To an imagination which had hoped for the smallest divisions and the heaviest stone work, for painted glass, dirt, and cobwebs, the difference was very distressing.

She was struck, however, beyond her expectation, by the grandeur of the abbey, as she saw it for the first time from the lawn. The whole building enclosed a large court; and two sides of the quadrangle, rich in Gothic ornaments, stood forward for admiration. The remainder was shut off by knolls of old trees, or luxuriant plantations, and the steep woody hills rising behind to give it shelter were beautiful even in the leafless month of March. Catherine had seen nothing to compare with it; and her feelings of delight were so strong, that without waiting for any better authority, she boldly burst forth in wonder and praise. The General listened with assenting gratitude, and it seemed as if his own estimation of Northanger had waited unfixed till that hour.

The kitchen garden was to be next admired, and he led the way to it across a small portion of the park.

The number of acres contained in this garden was such as Catherine could not listen to without dismay, being more than double the extent of all Mr. Allen's, as well as her father's, including churchyard and orchard. The walls seemed countless in number, endless in length; a village of hot-houses seemed to arise among them, and a whole parish to be at work within the enclosure.

It was some relief that they were to return to the rooms in common use, by passing through a few of less importance, looking into the court, which, with occasional passages, not wholly unintricate, connected the different sides; and she was further soothed in her progress by being told that she was treading what had once been a cloister, having traces of cells pointed out, and observing several doors that were neither opened nor explained to her.

From the dining-room they proceeded by quick communication to the kitchen—the ancient kitchen of the convent, rich in the massy walls and smoke of former days, and in the stoves and hot closets of the present. The General's improving hand had not loitered here: every modern invention to facilitate the labour of the cooks had been adopted within this their spacious theatre; and, when the genius of others had failed, his own had often produced the perfection wanted. His endowments of this spot alone might at any time have placed him high among the benefactors of the convent.

With the walls of the kitchen ended all the antiquity of the Abbey; the fourth side of the quadrangle having, on account of its decaying state, been removed by the General's father, and the present erected in its place. All that was venerable ceased here. The new building was not only new, but declared itself to be so; intended only for offices, and enclosed behind by stable-yards, no uniformity of architecture had been thought necessary. Catherine could have raved at the hand which had swept away what must have been beyond the value of all the rest, for the purposes of mere domestic economy; and would willingly have been spared the mortification of a walk through scenes so fallen, had the General allowed it: but if he had a vanity, it was in the arrangement of his offices; and as he was convinced, that, to a mind like Miss Morland's, a view of the accommodations and comforts by which the labours of her inferiors were softened, must always be gratifying, he should make no apology for leading her on.

JANE AUSTEN *Northanger Abbey*, 1798

The Mansion House Garden

ALBURY is a little village consisting of a few houses, with a large house or two near it. At the end of the village we came to a park, which is the residence of Mr. Drummond. Having heard a great deal of this park, and of the gardens, I wished very much to see them. My way to Dorking lay through Shire, and it went along on the outside of the park. I *guessed*, as the Yankees say, that there must be a way through the park to Shire; and I fell upon the scheme of going into the park as far as Mr. Drummond's house, and then asking his leave to go out at the other end of it.

They say that these gardens were laid out for one of the Howards, in the reign of Charles the Second, by Mr. Evelyn, who wrote the *Sylva*. The mansion-house, which is by no means magnificent, stands on a little flat by the side of the parish church, having a steep, but not lofty, hill rising up on the south side of it. It looks right across the gardens, which lie on the slope of a hill which runs along at about a quarter of a mile distant from the front of the house. The gardens, of course, lie facing the south. At the back of them, under the hill, is a high wall; and there is also a wall at each end, running from north to south. Between the house and the gardens there is a very beautiful run of water, with a sort of little wild narrow sedgy meadow. The gardens are separated from this by a hedge, running along from east to west. From this hedge there go up the hill, at rightangles, several other hedges, which divide the land here into distinct gardens, or orchards. Along at the top of these there goes a yew hedge, or, rather, a row of small yew trees, the trunks of which are bare for about eight or ten feet high, and the tops of which form one solid head of about ten feet high, while the bottom branches come out on each side of the row about eight feet horizontally. This hedge, or row, is a quarter of a mile long. There is a nice hard sand-road under this species of umbrella; and, summer and winter, here is a most delightful walk! Behind this row of yews there is a space, or garden (a quarter of a mile long you will observe) about thirty or forty feet wide, as nearly as I can recollect. At the back of this garden, and facing the yew-tree row, is a wall probably ten feet high, which forms the breastwork of a *terrace;* and it is this terrace which is the most beautiful thing that I ever saw in the gardening way. It is a quarter of a mile long, and, I believe, between thirty and forty feet wide; of the finest green sward, and as level as a die.

The wall, along at the back of this terrace, stands close against the hill, which you see with the trees and underwood upon it rising above the wall. So that here is the finest spot for fruit trees that can possibly be imagined. At both ends of this garden the trees in the park are lofty, and there are a pretty many of them. The hills on the south side of the mansion-house are covered with lofty trees, chiefly beeches and chestnuts: so that a warmer, a more sheltered, spot than this, it seems to be impossible to imagine. Observe, too, how judicious it was to plant the row of yew trees at the distance, which I have described from the wall which forms the breastwork of the terrace: that wall, as well as the wall at the back of the terrace, are covered with fruit trees, and the yew-tree row is just high enough to defend the former from winds, without injuring it by its shade. In the middle of the wall, at the back of the terrace, there is a recess about thirty feet in front and twenty feet deep, and here is a *basin*, into which rises a spring coming out of the hill. The overflowings of this basin go under the terrace and down across the garden into the rivulet below. So that here is water at the top, across the middle, and along at the bottom of this garden. Take it altogether, this, certainly, is the prettiest garden that I ever beheld.

WILLIAM COBBETT *Rural Rides*, 1830

Old v. New Modes

HAVING done my business at Hartswood to-day about eleven o'clock, I went to a sale at a farm, which the farmer is quitting. Here I had a view of what has long been going on all over the country. The farm, which belongs to *Christ's Hospital*, has been held by a man of the name of Charington, in whose family the lease has been, I hear, a great number of years. The house is hidden by trees. It stands in the Weald of Surrey, close by the *River Mole*, which is here a mere rivulet, though just below this house the rivulet supplies the very prettiest flour-mill I ever saw in my life.

Everything about this farm-house was formerly the scene of *plain manners* and *plentiful living*. Oak clothes-chests, oak bedsteads, oak chests of drawers, and oak tables to eat on, long, strong, and well supplied with joint stools. Some of the things were many hundreds of years old. But all appeared to be in a state of decay and nearly of *disuse*. There appeared to have been hardly any family in that house, where formerly there were, in all probability, from ten to fifteen men, boys, and maids: and, which was the worst of all, there was a *parlour*. Aye, and a *carpet* and *bell-pull* too! One end of the front of this once plain and substantial house had been moulded into a "*parlour*"; and there was the mahogany table, and the fine chairs, and the fine glass, and all as bare-faced upstart as any stock-jobber in the kingdom can boast of. And there were the decanters, the glasses, the "dinner-set" of crockery ware, and all just in the true stock-jobber style. And I dare say it has been '*Squire* Charington and the *Miss* Charington's; and not plain Master Charington, and his son Hodge, and his daughter Betty Charington, all of whom this accursed system has, in all likelihood, transmuted into a species of mock gentlefolks, while it has ground the labourers down into real slaves. Why do not farmers now *feed* and *lodge* their work-people, as they did formerly? Because they cannot keep them *upon* so *little* as they give them in wages. This is the real cause of the change.

The land produces, on an average, what it always produced, but there is a new distribution of the produce. This 'Squire Charington's father used, I dare say, to sit at the head of the oak table along with his men, say grace to them, and cut up the meat and the pudding. He might take a cup of *strong beer* to himself, when they had none; but that was pretty nearly all the difference in their manner of living. So that *all* lived well. But the '*Squire* had many *wine-decanters* and *wine-glasses* and "*a dinner set*," and a "*breakfast set*," and "*dessert knives*"; and these evidently imply carryings on and a consumption that must of necessity have greatly robbed the long oak table if it had remained fully tenanted. That long table could not share in the work of the decanters and the dinner set. Therefore it became almost untenanted; the labourers retreated to hovels, called cottages; and instead of board and lodging, they got money; so little of it as to enable the employer to drink wine; but, then, that he might not reduce them to *quite starvation*, they were enabled to come to him, in the *king's name*, and demand food as *paupers*.

I could not quit this farm-house without reflecting on the thousands of scores of bacon and thousands of bushels of bread that had been eaten from the long oak table which, I said to myself, is now perhaps going at last to the bottom of a bridge that some stock-jobber will stick up over an artificial river in his cockney garden. "*By——it shan't*," said I, almost in a real passion: and so I requested a friend to buy it for me; and if he do so, I will take it to Kensington, or to Fleet Street, and keep it for the good it has done in the world.

When the old farm-houses are down (and down they must come in time), what a miserable thing the country will be!

WILLIAM COBBETT *Rural Rides*, 1830

The Upstart Squire

EBENEZER MAC CROTCHET, ESQUIRE, was the London-born offspring of a worthy native of the "north countrie," who had walked up to London on a commercial adventure, with all his surplus capital, not very neatly tied up, in a not very clean handkerchief, suspended over his shoulder from the end of a hooked stick extracted from the first hedge on his pilgrimage; and who (after having worked himself a step or two up the ladder of life), had won the virgin heart of the only daughter of a highly respectable merchant of Duke's Place, with whom he inherited the honest fruits of a long series of ingenuous dealings.

Mr. Mac Crotchet had derived from his mother the instinct, and from his father the rational principle, of enriching himself at the expense of the rest of mankind, by all the recognised modes of accumulation on the windy side of the law. After passing many years in the alley, watching the turn of the market, and playing many games almost as desperate as that of the oldiser of Lucullus, the fear of losing what he had so righteously gained predominated over the sacred thirst of paper-money; his caution got the better of his instinct, or rather transferred it from the department of acquisition to that of conservation.

He was desirous to obliterate alike the Hebrew and Caledonian vestiges in his name, and signed himself E. M. Crotchet, which by degrees induced the majority of his neighbours to think that his name was Edward Matthew. The more effectually to sink the Mac, he christened his villa Crotchet Castle, and determined to hand down to posterity the honours of Crotchet of Crotchet. He found it essential to his dignity to furnish himself with a coat of arms, which, after the proper ceremonies (payment being the principal), he obtained, videlicet: Crest, a crotchet rampant, in A sharp: Arms, three empty bladders turgescent, to show how opinions are formed; three bags of gold, pendent, to show why they are maintained; three naked swords, tranchant, to show how they are administered; and three barber's blocks, gaspant, to show how they are swallowed.

He was not without a plausible pretence for styling his villa a castle, for, in its immediate vicinity, and within his own enclosed domain, were the manifest traces, on the brow of the hill, of a Roman station, or *castellum*, which was still called the castle by the country people. The primitive mounds and trenches, merely overgrown with greensward, with a few patches of juniper and box on the vallum, and a solitary ancient beech surmounting the place of the prætorium, presented nearly the same depths, heights, slopes, and forms, which the Roman soldiers had originally given them. From this *castellum* Mr. Crotchet christened his villa. With his rustic neighbours he was of course immediately and necessarily a squire: Squire Crotchet of the castle; and he seemed to himself to settle down as naturally into an English country gentleman, as if his parentage had been as innocent of both Scotland and Jerusalem, as his education was of Rome and Athens.

But as, though you expel nature with a pitchfork, she will yet always come back; he could not become, like a true-born English squire, part and parcel of the barley-giving earth; he could not find in game-bagging, poacher-shooting, trespasser-pounding, footpath-stopping, common-enclosing, rack-renting, and all the other liberal pursuits and pastimes which make a country gentleman an ornament to the world and a blessing to the poor; he could not find in these valuable and amiable occupations, and in a corresponding range of ideas, nearly commensurate with that of the great King Nebuchadnezzar, when he was turned out to grass; he could not find in this great variety of useful action, and vast field of comprehensive thought, modes of filling up his time that accorded with his Caledonian instinct.

THOMAS PEACOCK *Crotchet Castle*, 1831

A Thorough-bred Englishman

THIS gentleman had various endearing appellations among his intimate friends. By some he was called "a country gentleman of the true school," by some "a fine old country gentleman," by some "a sporting gentleman," by some "a thorough-bred Englishman," by some "a genuine John Bull"; but they all agreed in one respect, and that was, that it was a pity there were not more like him, and that because there were not, the country was going to rack and ruin every day. He was in the commission of the peace, and could write his name almost legibly; but his greatest qualifications were, that he was more severe with poachers, was a better shot, a harder rider, had better horses, kept better dogs, could eat more solid food, drink more strong wine, go to bed every night more drunk and get up every morning more sober, than any man in the county. In knowledge of horseflesh he was almost equal to a farrier, in stable learning he surpassed his own head groom, and in gluttony not a pig on his estate was a match for him. He had no seat in Parliament himself, but he was extremely patriotic, and usually drove his voters up to the poll with his own hands. He was warmly attached to church and state, and never appointed to the living in his gift any but a three-bottle man and a first-rate fox-hunter. He mistrusted the honesty of all poor people who could read and write, and had a secret jealousy of his own wife (a young lady whom he had married for what his friends called "the good old English reason," that her father's property adjoined his own) for possessing those accomplishments in a greater degree than himself.

CHARLES DICKENS *Barnaby Rudge*, 1840

"Thornfield Hall"—Norton Conyers, Ripon

TRAVERSING the long and matted gallery, I descended the slippery steps of oak; then I gained the hall: I halted there a minute: I looked at some pictures on the walls (one I remember represented a grim man in a cuirass, and one a lady with powdered hair and a pearl necklace), at a bronze lamp pendent from the ceiling, at a great clock whose case was of oak curiously carved, and ebony black with time and rubbing. Everything appeared very stately and imposing to me: but then I was so little accustomed to grandeur. The hall-door, which was half of glass, stood open; I stepped over the threshold. It was a fine autumn morning; the early sun shone serenely on the embrowned groves and still green fields: advancing on to the lawn, I looked up and surveyed the front of the mansion. It was three stories high, of proportions not vast, though considerable: a gentleman's manor-house, not a nobleman's seat: battlements round the top gave it a picturesque look. Its grey front stood out well from the background of a rookery, whose cawing tenants were now on the wing: they flew over the lawn and grounds to alight in a great meadow, from which these were separated by a sunk fence, and where an array of mighty old thorn trees, strong, knotty, and broad as oaks, at once explained the etymology of the mansion's designation. Farther off were hills: not so lofty as those round Lowood, nor so craggy, nor so like barriers of separation from the living world; but yet quiet and lonely hills enough, and seeming to embrace Thornfield with a seclusion I had not expected to find existent so near the stirring locality of Millcote. A little hamlet whose roofs were blent with trees, straggled up the side of one of these hills; the church of the district stood nearer Thornfield: its old tower-top looked over a knoll between the house and gates.

CHARLOTTE BRONTË *Jane Eyre*, 1847

"*Cheverel Manor*"—*Arbury Hall, Warwickshire*

AND a charming picture Cheverel Manor would have made that evening, if some English Watteau had been there to paint it: the castellated house of grey-tinted stone, with the flickering sunbeams sending dashes of golden light across the many-shaped panes in the mullioned windows, and a great beech leaning athwart one of the flanking towers, and breaking, with its dark flattened boughs, the too formal symmetry of the front; the broad gravel-walk winding on the right, by a row of tall pines, alongside the pool—on the left branching out among swelling grassy mounds, surmounted by clumps of trees, where the red trunk of the Scotch fir glows in the descending sunlight against the bright green of limes and acacias; the great pool, where a pair of swans are swimming lazily with one leg tucked under a wing, and where the open water-lilies lie calmly accepting the kisses of the fluttering light-sparkles; the lawn, with its smooth emerald greenness, sloping down to the rougher and browner herbage of the park, from which it is invisibly fenced by a little stream that winds away from the pool, and disappears under a wooden bridge in the distant pleasure-ground; and on this lawn our two ladies, whose part in the landscape the painter, standing at a favourable point of view in the park, would represent with a few little dabs of red and white and blue.

GEORGE ELIOT *Mr. Gilfil's Love Story*, 1857

The Squire of Ullathorne

WILFRED THORNE, ESQ., of Ullathorne, was the squire of St. Ewold's; or rather the squire of Ullathorne; for the domain of the modern landlord was of wider notoriety than the fame of the ancient saint. He was a fair specimen of what that race has come to in our days, which a century ago was, as we are told, fairly represented by Squire Western. If that representation be a true one, few classes of men can have made faster strides in improvement. Mr. Thorne, however, was a man possessed of quite a sufficient number of foibles to lay him open to much ridicule. He was still a bachelor, being about fifty, and was not a little proud of his person. When living at home at Ullathorne there was not much room for such pride, and there, therefore, he always looked like a gentleman, and like that which he certainly was, the first man in his parish. But during the month or six weeks which he annually spent in London, he tried so hard to look like a great man there also, which he certainly was not, that he was put down as a fool by many at his club. He was a man of considerable literary attainment in a certain way and on certain subjects. His favourite authors were Montaigne and Burton, and he knew more perhaps than any other man in his own county, and the next to it, of the English essayists of the last two centuries. He possessed complete sets of the *Idler*, the *Spectator*, the *Tatler*, the *Guardian*, and the *Rambler*; and would discourse by hours together on the superiority of such publications to anything which has since been produced in our *Edinburghs* and *Quarterlies*. He was a great proficient in all questions of genealogy, and knew enough of almost every gentleman's family in England to say of what blood and lineage were descended all those who had any claim to be considered as possessors of any such luxuries. For blood and lineage he himself had a most profound respect. He counted back his own ancestors to some period long antecedent to the Conquest; and could tell you, if you would listen to him, how it had come to pass that they, like Cedric the Saxon, had been permitted to hold their own among the Norman barons. It was not, according to his showing, on account of any weak complaisance on the part of his family towards their Norman neighbours. Some Ealfried of Ullathorne once fortified his own castle, and held out, not only that, but the then existing cathedral of Barchester also, against one Geoffrey De Burgh, in the time of King John; and Mr. Thorne possessed the whole history of the siege written on vellum, and illuminated in a most costly manner. It little signified that no one could read the writing, as, had that been possible, no one could have understood the language. Mr. Thorne, could, however, give you all the particulars in good English, and had no objection to do so.

While we are on the subject of the Thornes, one word must be said of the house they lived in. It was not a large house, nor a fine house, nor perhaps to modern ideas a very commodious house; but by those who love the peculiar colour and peculiar ornaments of genuine Tudor architecture it was considered a perfect gem. We beg to own ourselves among the number, and therefore take this opportunity to express our surprise that so little is known by English men and women of the beauties of English architecture. The ruins of the Colosseum, the Campanile at Florence, St. Mark's, Cologne, the Bourse and Notre Dame, are with our tourists as familiar as household words; but they know nothing of the glories of Wiltshire, Dorsetshire, and Somersetshire. Nay, we much question whether many noted travellers, men who have pitched their tents perhaps under Mount Sinai, are not still ignorant that there are glories in Wiltshire, Dorsetshire, and Somersetshire. We beg that they will go and see.

Mr. Thorne's house was called Ullathorne Court, and was properly so called: for the house itself formed two sides of a quadrangle, which was completed on the other two sides by a wall about twenty feet high. This wall was built of cut stone, rudely cut indeed, and now much worn, but of a beautiful rich tawny yellow colour, the effect of that stonecrop of minute growth, which it had taken three centuries to produce. The top of this wall was ornamented by huge round stone balls of the same colour as the wall itself. Entrance into the court was had through a pair of iron gates, so massive that no one could comfortably open or close them, consequently they were rarely disturbed. From the gateway two paths led obliquely across the court; that to the left reaching the hall-door, which was in the corner made by the angle of the house, and that to the right leading to the back entrance, which was at the further end of the longer portion of the building.

The hall was hung round with family female insipidities by Lely, and unprepossessing male Thornes in red coats by Kneller; each Thorne having been let into a panel in the wainscoting, in the proper manner. At the further end of the room was a huge fire-place with an antiquated grate, that would hold about a hundredweight of coal, that had been stuck on to the hearth, by Mr. Thorne's father. This hearth had, of course, been intended for the consumption of wood fagots, and the iron dogs for the purpose were still standing, though half buried in the masonry of the grate.

At the end of the hall opposite to the fireplace a door led into the drawing-room, which was of equal size, and lighted with precisely similar windows. But yet the aspect of the room was very different. It was papered, and the ceiling, which in the hall showed the old rafters, was whitened and finished with a modern cornice. Miss Thorne's drawing-room, or, as she always called it, withdrawing-room, was a beautiful apartment. The windows opened on to the full extent of the lovely trim garden; immediately before the windows were plots of flowers in stiff, stately, stubborn little beds, each bed surrounded by a stone coping of its own; beyond, there was a low parapet wall, on which stood urns and images, fawns, nymphs, satyrs, and a whole tribe of Pan's followers; and then again, beyond that, a beautiful lawn sloped away to a sunk fence which divided the garden from the park. Mr. Thorne's study was at the end of the drawing-room, and beyond that were the kitchen and the offices. Doors opened into both Miss Thorne's withdrawing-room and Mr. Thorne's sanctum from the passage above alluded to; which, as it came to the latter room, widened itself so as to make space for the huge black oak stairs, which led to the upper regions.

Such was the interior of Ullathorne Court, but it is the outside that is so lovely. Let the tourist get admission at least into the garden, and fling himself on that soft sward just opposite to the exterior angle of the house. He will there get the double frontage, and enjoy that which is so lovely—the expanse of architectural beauty without the formal dullness of one long line.

The colour of Ullathorne is remarkable. It is all of that delicious tawny hue which no stone can give unless it has on it the vegetable richness of centuries. Strike the wall with your hand, and you will think that the stone has on it no covering, but rub it carefully, and you will find that the colour comes off on your finger. No colourist that ever yet worked from a palette has been able to come up to this rich colouring of years crowding themselves on years.

ANTHONY TROLLOPE *Barchester Towers*, 1857

The Hall Turned Farmstead

EVIDENTLY that gate is never opened: for the long grass and the great hemlocks grow close against it; and if it were opened, it is so rusty that the force necessary to turn it on its hinges would be likely to pull down the square stone-built pillars, to the detriment of the two stone lionesses which grin with a doubtful carnivorous affability above a coat of arms, surmounting each of the pillars. It would be easy enough, by the aid of the nicks in the stone pillars, to climb over the brick wall with its smooth stone coping; but by putting our eyes close to the rusty bars of the gate, we can see the house well enough, and all but the very corners of the grassy enclosure.

It is a very fine old place, of red brick, softened by a pale, powdery lichen, which has dispersed itself with happy irregularity, so as to bring the red brick into terms of friendly companionship with the limestone ornaments surrounding the three gables, the windows, and the door-place. But the windows are patched with wooden panes, and the door, I think, is like the gate—it is never opened. How it would groan and grate against the stone floor if it were! For it is a solid, heavy, handsome door, and must once have been in the habit of shutting with a sonorous bang behind a liveried lackey, who had just seen his master and mistress off the grounds in a carriage and pair.

But at present one might fancy the house in the early stage of a chancery suit, and that the fruit from that grand double row of walnut-trees on the right hand of the enclosure would fall and rot among the grass, if it were not that we heard the booming bark of dogs echoing from great buildings at the back. And now the half-weaned calves that have been sheltering themselves in a gorse-built hovel against the left-hand wall come out and set up a silly answer to that terrible bark, doubtless supposing that it has reference to buckets of milk.

Yes, the house must be inhabited, and we will see by whom, for imagination is a licensed trespasser: it has no fear of dogs, but may climb over walls and peep in at windows with impunity. Put your face to one of the glass panes in the right-hand window: what do you see? A large, open fireplace, with rusty dogs in it, and a bare, boarded floor; at the far end, fleeces of wool stacked up; in the middle of the floor, some empty corn-bags. That is the furniture of the dining-room. And what through the left-hand window? Several clothes-horses, a pillion, a spinning wheel, and an old box wide open and stuffed full of coloured rags. At the edge of this box there lies a great wooden doll, which, so far as mutilation is concerned, bears a strong resemblance to the finest Greek sculpture, and especially in the total loss of its nose. Near it there is a little chair, and the butt-end of a boy's leather long-lashed whip.

The history of the house is plain now. It was once the residence of a country squire, whose family, probably dwindling down to mere spinsterhood, got merged in the more territorial name of Donnithorne. It was once the Hall; and is now the Hall Farm. Like the life in some coast-town that was once a watering-place, and is now a port, where the genteel streets are silent and grass-grown, and the docks and warehouses busy and resonant, the life at the Hall has changed its focus, and no longer radiates from the parlour, but from the kitchen and the farmyard.

GEORGE ELIOT *Adam Bede*, 1859

The Decline of "Woodview"—Buckingham House, Shoreham

ESTHER's heart beat as she recognised the tower of the church between the trees, and the undulating line of downs behind the trees awakened terrible recollections. She knew the white gate was somewhere in this plantation, but could not remember its exact position. The gate had fallen from its hinge, and the lodge where the blind gatekeeper used to play the flute was closed; the park paling was falling, and the great holly hedge worn away by wandering sheep and cattle; and an elm in falling had broken through the garden wall.

She remembered the horses going to the downs, horses coming from the downs—stabling and the sound of hoofs everywhere. But now silence. She could see that many a roof had fallen, and that ruins of outhouses filled the yard. She remembered the kitchen windows, bright in the setting sun, and the white-capped servants moving about the great white table. But now the shutters were up, nowhere a light; the knocker had disappeared from the door, and she asked herself how she was to get in. She made her way through the shrubbery, tripping over fallen branches and trunks of trees; rooks rose out of the evergreens with a great clatter, her heart stood still, and she hardly dared to tear herself through the mass of underwood. At last she gained the lawn, and, still very frightened, sought for the bell. The socket plate hung loose on the wire, and only a faint tinkle came through the solitude of the empty house.

At last footsteps and a light; the chained door was opened a little, and a voice asked: "Who is it?" Esther explained; and then the door was opened, and she stood face to face with her old mistress, Mrs. Barfield.

At the end of the coombe, under the shaws, stood the old red-tiled farmhouse in which Mrs. Barfield had been born. Beyond it, downlands rolled on and on behind the square, dogmatic tower of the village church. Her husband lay beneath the chancel; her father, mother, all her relations, lay in the churchyard, and she would go there in a few years. Upon this downland all her life had been passed, all her life except the few months she had spent by her daughter's bedside in Egypt. She came from that coombe, from that farmhouse beneath the shaws, and only crossed the down.

And this barren landscape meant as much to Esther as to her mistress. The women paused and went towards the garden; and removing some pieces of the broken gate they entered a miniature wilderness. The espalier apple-trees had disappeared beneath climbing weeds, and long briars had shot out from the bushes, leaving few traces of the former walks—a damp, dismal place that the birds seemed to have abandoned. Of the greenhouse only some broken glass and a black broken chimney remained. A great elm had carried away a large portion of the southern wall, and under the dripping trees an aged peacock screamed for his lost mate.

George Moore *Esther Waters*, 1894

Gentry

Becket was almost a show place. It stood in its park and pastures two miles from the little town of Transham and the

Morton Plough Works. The white house, timbered with dark beams in true Worcestershire fashion, and added-to from time to time, had preserved, thanks to a fine architect, an old-fashioned air of spacious presidency above its gardens and lawns. On the long artificial lake, with innumerable rushy nooks and water-lilies and coverture of leaves floating flat and bright in the sun, the half-tame wild duck and shy water-hens had remote little worlds, and flew and splashed when all Becket was abed, quite as if the human spirit, with its monkey-tricks and its little divine flame, had not yet been born.

This very heart of English country that the old Moretons in their paternal way had so religiously farmed, making out of its lush grass and waving corn a simple and by no means selfish or ungenerous subsistence, was now entirely lawns, park, coverts, and private golf course. They were of a breed that was already gone, the simplest of all country gentlemen, dating back to the Conquest, without one solitary conspicuous ancestor, save the one who had been physician to a king and perished without issue—marrying from generation to generation exactly their own equals; living simple, pious, parochial lives; never in trade, never making money, having a tradition and a practice of gentility more punctilious than the so-called aristocracy; constitutionally paternal and maternal to their dependants, constitutionally so convinced that those dependants, and all indeed who were not "gentry," were of different clay, that they were entirely simple and entirely without arrogance, carrying with them even now a sort of early atmosphere of archery and home-made cordials, lavender and love of clergy, together with frequent use of the word "nice," a peculiar regularity of feature, and a complexion that was rather parchmenty. High Church people and Tories, naturally, to a man and woman, by sheer inbred absence of ideas, and sheer inbred conviction that nothing else was nice; but withal very considerate of others, really plucky in bearing their own ills; not greedy, and not wasteful.

JOHN GALSWORTHY *The Freelands*, 1915

The Squire at Undern Hall

UNDERN HALL, with its many small-paned windows, faced the north sullenly. It was a place of which the influence and magic wore not good. Even in May, when the lilacs frothed into purple, paved the lawn with shadows, steeped the air with scent; when soft leaves lipped each other consolingly; when blackbirds sang, fell in their effortless way from the green height to the green depth, and sang again—still, something that haunted the place set the heart fluttering.

It was only at midsummer that the windows were coloured by dawn and sunset; then they had a sanguinary aspect, staring into the delicate skyey dramas like blind, bloodshot eyes. Secretly, under the heavy rhododendron leaves and in the furtive sunlight beneath the yew-trees, gnats danced. Their faint motions made the garden stiller; their smallness made it oppressive; their momentary life made it infinitely old. Then Undern Pool was full of leaf shadows like multitudinous lolling tongues, and the smell of the mud tainted the air—half sickly, half sweet. The clipped bushes and the twisted chimneys made inky shadows like steeples on the grass, and great trees of roses, beautiful in desolation, dripped with red and white and elbowed the guelder roses and the elders set with white patens. Cherries fell in the orchard with the same rich monotony, the same fatality, as drops of blood. They lay under the fungus-riven trees till the hens ate them, pecking gingerly and enjoyably at their lustrous beauty as the world does at a poet's heart. In the kitchen-garden also the hens took their ease, banqueting sparsely beneath the straggling black boughs of a red-currant grove. In the sandstone walls of this garden hornets built undisturbed, and the thyme and lavender borders had grown into forests and obliterated the path. The cattle drowsed in the meadows, birds in the heavy trees; the golden day-lilies drooped like the daughters of pleasure; the very principle of life seemed to slumber. It was then, when the scent of the elder blossom, decaying fruit, mud and hot yew brooded there, that the place attained one of its most individual moods—narcotic, aphrodisiac.

In winter the yews and firs were like waving funeral plumes and mantled, headless goddesses; then the giant beeches would lash themselves to frenzy, and, stooping, would scourge the ice on Undern Pool and the cracked walls of the house, like beings drunken with the passion of cruelty. This was the second mood of Undern—brutality.

Reddin of Undern cared as little for the graciousness of life as he did for its pitiful rhapsodies, its purple-mantled tragedies. He had no time for such trivialities. Fox-hunting, horse-breeding, and kennel lore were his vocation. He rode straight, lived hard, exercised such creative faculties as he had on his work, and found it very good. Three times a year he stated in the Undern pew at Wolfbatch that he intended to continue leading a godly, righteous and sober life. At these times, with amber lights from the windows playing over his well-shaped head, his rather heavy face looked, as the Miss Clombers from Wolfbatch Hall said, "so chivalrous, so uplifted." The Miss Clombers purred when they talked, like cats with a mouse. The younger still hunted, painfully compressing an overfed body into a riding habit of some forgotten cut, and riding with so grim a mouth and such a bloodthirsty expression that she might have had a blood-feud with all foxes. Perhaps, when she rode down the anxious red-brown streak, she thought she was riding down a cruel fate that had somehow left her life vacant of joy. Perhaps, when the little creature was torn piece-meal, she imagined herself tearing so the frail unconquerable powers of love and beauty. Anyway, she never missed a meet, and she and her sister never ceased their long silent battle for Reddin, who remained as unconscious of them as if they were his aunts. He was, of course, beneath them, very much beneath them—hardly more than a farmer, but still—a man.

MARY WEBB *Gone to Earth*, 1917

The End of a Tradition

OVER at Amblehurst, about four miles away, there is a hazard less nine-hole course round Squire Maundle's sheep-nibbled park. The park faces south-west, sloping to a friendly little river—the Neaze—which at that point, so I have been told, though I never trouble to verify it—divides the counties of Kent and Sussex. On the other side of the river is the village. Squire Maundle's clanging stable clock shares with the belfry of the village school the privilege of indicating the Amblehurst hours. My progress up and down the park from one undersized green to another is accompanied by the temperate clamour of sheep-bells (and in springtime by the loud litanies of baa-ing lambs and anxious ewes). The windows of Squire Maundle's eighteenth-century mansion overlook my zigzag saunterings with the air of a county family dowager who has not yet made up her mind to leave cards on those new people at the Priory. As a rule I have the links to myself, but once in a while "young" Squire Maundle (so-called because his eighty-seven-year-old father is still above ground) appears on the sky-line in his deer-stalker hat, with a surly black retriever at his heels and we play an amicable round.

Without wishing to ridicule him, for he was always kind and courteous, I may say that both his features and his tone of voice have something in common with the sheep who lift their mild munching faces to regard him while he plays an approach shot in his cautious, angular, and automatic style. He is one of those shrewdly timorous men who are usually made a butt of by their more confident associates. Falstaff would have borrowed fifty pounds off him, though he has the reputation of being close with his money. His vocabulary is as limited as his habit of mind, and he speaks with an old-fashioned word-clipping conciseness. His lips are pursed up as if in a perpetual whistle. The links—on which he knows every tussock and molehill intimately—are always "in awful good condition" and "That's a hot 'un!" he exclaims when I make a long drive, or "That's for Sussex!" (a reference to the remote possibility that my ball may have gone over the river). But the best instance I can give of his characteristic mode of expressing himself is one which occurred when I once questioned him about a group of little grey stones among the laurel bushes outside his stable-yard. After whistling to his retriever he replied, "House-dogs bury in the shrubbery: shooting-dogs bury in the park" . . .

SIEGFRIED SASSOON *Memoirs of a Fox-hunting Man*, 1928

9 A Jacobean Mansion in Half-timber: Meer Hall, Worcestershire

10 A Sixteenth-century Yeoman's House in Decay: Kempston, Bedfordshire

From a drawing by Francis Stevens (1815)

11 Sunday Service in a Village Church

A satirical drawing by F. Wright (1790)

The Village

CHAUCER gave the village and the villager their place in English literature. Until the emergence of the novel there was neither scope nor suitable medium for a picture of village life complete in its local environment and historical background, but nearly four hundred years before Fielding the *Canterbury Tales* provided a composite sketch of the village community. As a narrator and master of character Chaucer may stand for the archetype of English novelists.

Figures typical of all manorial villages were the ploughman, the miller, the yeoman: at opposite ends of the scale stood the poor widow and the franklin. By the tales they tell and their introduction in the prologue Chaucer admits his reader to the centre of village affairs. The *Nonne Preestes* tale begins:

> "A povre widwe, somdel stape in age,
> Was whylom dwelling in a narwe cotage,
> Three large sowes hadde she, and namo,
> Three kyn, and eek a sheep that highte Malle,
> Ful sooty was hir bour, and eek hir halle,
> In which she eet ful many a sclendre meel.
> Hir bord was served most with whyt and blak,
> Milk and broun breed, in which she fond no lak,
> Seynd bacoun, and somtyme an ey or tweye,
> For she was as it were a maner deye."

This widow supported herself and her two daughters by careful husbandry of her stock and by her work as a "maner deye" or manorial dairywoman. Her condition was just humbler than that of the ploughman, brother to the poor parson ;

> "A trewe swinker and a good was he,
> Living in pees and parfit charitee.
> He wolde thresshe, and ther-to dyke and delve
> For Cristes sake for every povre wight
> Withouten hyre, if it lay in his might.
> His tythes payed he full faire and wel
> Both of his propre swink and his catel."

A man of more substance and less scruple, unsurpassed in wrestling or jesting, the miller won Chaucer's humorous tolerance despite his cunning.

> "Wel coude he stelen corn, and tollen thryes;
> And yet he had a thomb of gold, pardee."

In the Reeve's tale, however, a certain miller of Trumpington, near Cambridge, was paid his deserts with characteristic ribaldry. The squire's servant, the yeoman, was a capable forester and dressed the part, while the franklin or freehold farmer found a good table his chief attraction and kept one always standing ready loaded with meat and drink. Although he was "Epicurus' own son," he had for all that acted as county auditor and sheriff, had presided at the sessions and took rank next to a baron. A less popular official, the reeve, who managed the manor farm accounts, curried his lord's favour and held any misdealing of theirs over the villagers' heads:

> "Wel wiste he by the droghte and by the reyn,
> The yelding of his seed, and of his greyn
> His lordes sheep, his neet, his dayerye,
> His swyn, his hors, his stoor, and his pultrye,
> Was hoolly in this reves governing,
> And by his covenant yaf the rekening."

Reading between the lines of the Reeve's character one may catch an echo of the grievances felt by the mediæval commons.

Behind the apparent permanence of these English villagers, impervious, it seems, to social change, we find in the *Vision of Piers the Plowman* evidence of the discontent and misery of the lower classes, whose ranks had been thinned by the famines of 1314–21, devastated by the Black Death in 1348–50, and whose duties on the Manor farm, now doubly arduous, had not secured a proportionate increase in wages. The rate of 1d. a day for haymaking, 2d. for reaping customary in 1346 served but a poor fraction of the needs of the times. The wolf was rarely kept from the door for long together: in the ploughman's words:

> "And yet I sey, by my soule I have no salt bacoun,
> Ne no kokeney, bi Cryst coloppes for to maken.
> Ac I have percil and porettes and many kole plantes,
> And eke a cow and a kalf and a cart-mare
> To drawe afelde my donge the while the drought lasteth
> And bi this lyflode we mot lyve til lammasse tyme."

Eventually, when Wat Tyler forced the issue in the Peasants' Revolt of 1381, hasty assurances of redress were made by the king, and no less promptly repudiated. In the opening years of the struggle Langland, viewing in imagination his plain full of folk from the Malvern Hills, appealed equally to all classes to observe their bonds of duty. Kings, nobles, clergy and workers must model their life on the Gospels. A labourer, who with better wages demanded better food, was rebuked as a seeker after idle luxury:

"Laboreres that have no land to lyve on but her handes
Deyned nought to dyne aday nyght-olde wortes;
May no peny-ale hem paye ne no pece of bakoun,
But if it be fresch flesch other fische fryed other bake,
And that chaud or plus chaud for chillyng of her mawe;
And but if he be heighlich huyred ellis will he chyde,
And that he was werkman wrought waille the tyme."

We may wonder what Langland would have to say of Chaucer's franklin: but as a reactionary reformer he might answer that a man must not seek to go out of his class.

Although *Piers Plowman* preceded the *Canterbury Tales*, Langland does not usurp Chaucer's claim to be forerunner of the novel: his method is allegory and his matter moral prophecy. Many, however, of his concourse of craftsmen, ploughmen, preachers, cooks, inn-keepers, pilgrims, beggars, hermits and minstrels have a rich individuality and contribute to the village microcosm. There were tricks in other trades than milling:

"My wife was a webbe and wollen cloth made;
She spak to spynnesteres to spynnen it oute,
Ac the pounde that she payed by poised a quarteroun more
Than myne owne auncere who-so weyghed treuthe . . .
Rose the regratere was hir righte name,
She hath holden hokkerye al hire lyf-tyme."

Among Rose's trades was brewing: no Dutch interior could have been more vivid than Langland's picture of the noisy, rascally, nondescript company at the mediæval ale-house.

Over a century after Piers and his pilgrims fared forth to plough, Thomas Tusser returned to the theme in a rough English Georgic at first entitled *A Hundreth Points of Good Husbandrie*. A farmer born of good lineage at Rivenhall in

Essex, Tusser composed an agricultural calendar and interspersed it with frequent miniatures of East Anglian country life. His verses on the good huswive's day, on diet, on husbandly furniture are the gleanings of practical experience: his advice tires only the academic:

> "Good Ploughmen looke wekely of custome and right
> for rostmeat on Sundaies and Thursdaies at night:
> Thus doing and helping such custome and guise,
> they call thee good huswife, they love thee likewise."

Unmarried ploughmen might live in, but for harvest extra help was hired: again Tusser shews how to get the best out of his men:

> "Grant harvest lord, more, by a penny or two,
> to call on his fellows the better to do:
> Give gloves to thy reapers, a largess to cry,
> and daily to loiterers have a good eye."

The independent cultivator himself expected to employ his waking hours on the land and required his wife and children to do their share. There is none of the decorative pastoral treatment of his domestics, whether "Foul privies are now to be cleansed and fyed" or the boar needs shifting for ill air; the bidding is:

> "And diligent Cisley, my dairy good wench,
> make cleanly his cabin, for measling and stench."

Those village small-holders, who were now released from manorial service, saw in Tusser's practice their chance to prosper by following his advice.

There were, however, three ways of viewing country conditions: either with due balance of good and evil, undissembling and undismayed, or with always the worst in view, indignant but largely impotent, or else as the country never has been and never will be, through the idyllic vision of the jaded imagination. The last was the literary habit of Theocritus at the court of Ptolemy Philadelphus, of Vergil at the wish of an emperor who required fresh settlers on the land, and of Claudius Claudianus, who, in an age sated with Roman imperialism, voiced his spiritual nostalgia:

> "Felix, qui patriis aevum transegit in agris . . . "

As sixteenth-century England developed centres of civilization increasingly urban, trade and the woollen industry and court life all accelerating the process, escapism reared its ostrich head. Influenced by classical traditions Wyatt and Surrey idealised the countryside: the simple life came into fashion again. Here, for example, is Thomas Overbury, knight of Warwickshire, on Tusser's dairy wench, re-christened *A Fair and Happy Milkmaid*: "In milking a cow, and straining the teats through her fingers, it seems that so sweet a milk-press makes the milk the whiter or sweeter. . . . The golden ears of corn fall and kiss her feet when she reaps them. Her breath is her own, which scents all the year long of June, like a new-made haycock. She bestows her year's wages at next fair: and in choosing her garments counts no bravery in the world like decency." Her first cousin is to be found in Spenser's *Shepheard's Calendar*, a shepherd boy who tuned his pipe and plained to Pan, while his flock fed in the sunshine. Both are fitted only to inhabit the world charmed into existence in the *Winter's Tale*, a world where shepherds' chief concern is the sheep-shearing feast and where pedlars, vending golden quoifs and stomachers, sing philosophically:

"Jog on, jog on the footpath way,
And merrily hent the stile-a:
A merry heart goes all the way,
Your sad tires in a mile-a."

Remote indeed from East Anglia is this elusive Arcady.

Although Overbury's landed gentleman and franklin are nearer to earth, the ideal of country contentment and a quiet mind largely informs his contemporary's sketches of character. John Stephen's shepherd of 1615 remains akin to the Corin, who in *As You Like It* declared: "Sir, I am true labourer; I earn that I eat, get that I wear, owe no man hate, envy no man's happiness, glad of other men's good, content with my harm; and the greatest of my pride is to see my ewes graze and my lambs suck." From this it is but a step to the Utopian countryman: "He proves quietness to be best contentment and that there is no quietness like a certain rest. His flock affords him his whole raiment, outside and linings, cloth and leather: and instead of much costly linen, his little garden yields hemp enough to make his lockram shirts. . . . His daily life is a delightful work, whatsoever the work be; whether to mend his garments, cure a diseased sheep, instruct his dog or change pastures: and these be pleasant actions because voluntary, patient and not interrupted. The worst temptation of his idleness teaches him no further mischief than to love entirely some nut-brown milk-maid, or hunt the squirrel or make his cosset wanton."

Before the real villager recedes from view altogether a rector of Bishopton in Wiltshire recasts our *Plaine Country Fellow* in recognisable terms. John Earle's *Microcosmography*, 1628, depicts the manners living as they rise. Covering a wide field of human nature, the character writers of this century opened the way for the more developed treatment of Addison's *De Coverley* papers and gave promise of the coming novel. Earle had observation, humour and understanding. The interests of his peasant are limited, his tastes coarse, but his reality indisputable. He is "one that manures his ground well, but lets himself lie fallow and untilled. His hand guides the Plough, and the Plough his thoughts, and his ditch and Land-marke is the very mound of his meditations. . . . His habitation is some poore thatched Roofe, distinguished from his Barne by the loopholes that let out Smoak, which the rain had long since washed thorow, but for the double seeling of Bacon on the inside. . . . His religion is part of his Copy-hold, which hee takes from his Landlord, and referres it wholly to his discretion. His compliment with his Neighbour is a good thumpe on the backe: and his salutation, commonly some blunt curse. . . . He is a niggard all the weeke except only Market-day, where if his Corne sell well, hee thinks hee may be drunk with a good conscience." Wye Saltonstall in his *Picturæ Loquentes*, 1631, adds witness of the workaday gait and daily fare of this revised Colin Cloute: "When he hangs between the plough stilts, you have his true posture, where he's seldom an upright man, for he leans most to one side. . . . The smell of earth makes him hungry, for he brings home an invincible stomach, and nothing holds him back but a barley pudding. . . . His meals are not lasting because violent; for he eats hard for the time, and when he finds himself satisfied, puts up his knife with a 'God be praised.' " Thereafter his steps tend towards the ale-house, a recurrent motif in the literature of village life, and with Saltonstall he may be left there to drown his cares in Lethe: "A country ale-house is the centre of the town's good fellowship, or some humble roofed cottage licensed to sell ale. The inward hanging is a painted cloth, with a row of ballads painted on it. It smells only of smoke and new wort, and yet the usual guests there think it a rare perfume. They drink no healths here to mistresses, but their only compliment is, 'Here is to thee neighbour Jobson.' They pay here by the poll, for they think that many purses make light shots as many hands make light work. Their only game here is Noddy, and that but for a pot of ale for pastime. . . . They often make bargains here, but before they go out can hardly stand to them. . . . To strangers 'tis known by the advancement of a maypole, and is the only guest-house to pedlars' pilgrimages."

The preceding quotations will indicate the range of interest in village affairs before the novel. In the earlier novels of the eighteenth century the attention so far paid to character continued, but characters were now seen in their place in the community. *Tom Jones* revealed whole layers of society and its conflicting types. Later novelists, filling in a more precise and limited background, re-discovered the importance of the village as a unit of English country life. Here was material manageable in size, rich in local interest, compact, diversified, and yet in its way complete. With Jane Austen experience and selection tended to isolate the leisured way of life, to present the country only as seen from behind the palings of the great park, but her followers hastened to correct this view. *Our Village* stiffened with a dash of *Rural Rides* prepares the way for the uncompromising revelation of country conditions in *Sybil* or *Alton Locke*. While Mary Mitford colours her retrospection with sentiment, Cobbett stands dour champion of the agricultural labourer, his food, his cottage and his rights; Kingsley and Disraeli impart to a just indictment the vigour of the political reformer. Again, in another field, Crabbe's *Parish Register* depicts the squalor and dreariness of lower-class life in the small town of the eighteenth century "as Truth will paint it and as bards will not." From a cross-section of each half century of literature living examples can be collated to form a humanised history of the village tradition.

The accelerated transfer of population to industrial centres gave to the village that appeal which belongs to the place where one is no longer living. It is the Englishman's foible to account the simple life more satisfactory than the sophisticated, to accredit to the past virtues denied to the present, but rarely to act upon his credo. The villages of Hardy and Mary Webb belonged to a disappearing England and are invested with the allure of the irrecoverable and irreplaceable. Dorset and Shropshire chanced to become backwaters in the main flood of industrial development, but even there the irrepressible newfound methods of infiltration. In *Tess of the D'Urbervilles* each Lady Day sees fewer craftsmen, maidservants, families of sons settling down to situations in the country. Whereas a romantic atmosphere pervades the majority of reactionary novels, their portrayal of individual countrymen is not thus invalidated and a measure of the truth can be applied from other sources. Galsworthy was at pains to view the village both from the weekender's and the native's standpoint; Blunden sees beneath its post-war surface the essential integrity of country life; a typical composite portrait by Francis Brett Young allows the visitor gradually to become aware of the difference between the village seen from outside and known from within.

It is through the moulding of tradition to modern needs that the village will endure, absorbing the new and adapting its ageless features to the appearance of change. Many remoter hamlets, such as Appletreewick, Skyreholme, Beckermonds, Yockenthwaite in Wharfedale, seem shaped in their permanent form and likely to preserve it. The needs that created Wetwang and Huggate, Fridaythorpe and Nunburnholme were mainly those whereby their inhabitants still follow the same occupations. After the eighteenth century, it is true, some of the best features of village life, the independent craftsman and the old social institutions, were superannuated: but even though there remain few manorial villages on the farm-plan of Laxton, Nottinghamshire, or with the feudal architecture of Lowther, Westmorland, Chaucer's villagers maintain their communities in many counties of England. Whether hand-plough or tractor turn it, their interests belong to the soil. The aim of the following selections is to make articulate the Englishman's notion of a way of life which is inviolable and fundamental to his race.

Local Dialect

In my return to my western progress, I pass'd some little part of Somersetshire, as thro' Evil, or Yeovil, upon the river Ivil, in going to which we go down a long steep hill, which they call Babylon-Hill; but from what original I could find none of the country people to inform me.

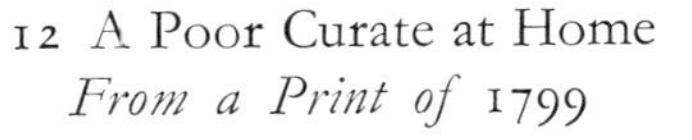

12 A Poor Curate at Home
From a Print of 1799

13 An Eighteenth-century Farmer at Home
From a painting of Garrick and Mrs. Cibber in "The Farmer's Return," by John Zoffany, R.A.

14 A Half-timber Village in the Peace of the nineteenth century: Hadzor, Worcestershire

15 A Village Church before the Age of Restorations: Tiffield, Northamptonshire

From a drawing by H. Trotter, 1799

This Yeovil is a market town of good resort, and some clothing is carry'd on, in, and near it, but not much, its main manufacture at this time is making of gloves.

It cannot pass my observation here, that when we are come this length from London, the dialect of the English tongue, or the country way of expressing themselves is not easily understood, it is so strangely altered; it is true, that it is so in many parts of England besides, but in none in so gross a degree as in this part. This way of boorish country speech, as in Ireland, it is call'd the brogue upon the tongue; so here 'tis call'd *jouring*, and 'tis certain, that tho' the tongue be all meer natural English, yet those that are but a little acquainted with them, cannot understand one half of what they say: It is not possible to explain this fully by writing, because the difference is not so much in the orthography of words, as in the tone, and diction; their abridging the speech, *cham* for *I am*, *chil* for *I will*, *don* for *put on*, and *doff* for *put off*, and the like. And I cannot omit a short story here on this subject; coming to a relation's house, who was a school-master at Martock in Somersetshire, I went into his school to beg the boys a play day, as is usual in such cases; I should have said to beg the master a play day, but that by the way; coming into the school, I observ'd one of the lowest scholars was reading his lesson to the usher, which lesson it seems was a chapter in the Bible, so I sat down by the master, till the boy had read out his chapter: I observ'd the boy read a little oddly in the tone of the country, which made me the more attentive, because on enquiry, I found that the words were the same, and the orthography the same as in all our Bibles. I observ'd also the boy read it out with his eyes still on the book, and his head like a meer boy, moving from side to side, as the lines reach'd cross the columns of the book; his lesson was in the Cant. 5, 3, of which the words are these,

"I have put off my coat, how shall I put it on, I have washed my feet, how shall I defile them?"

The boy read thus, with his eyes, as I say, full on the text.

"Chav a doffed my cooat, how shall I don't, chav a washed my veet, how shall I moil 'em?"

How the dexterous dunce could form his mouth to express so readily the words (which stood right printed in the book) in his country jargon, I could not but admire.

DANIEL DE FOE *A Tour through England*, 1724

The Curate

THE time between this event and dinner I passed in observing a game at cards between two farmers, an exciseman, and a young fellow in a rusty gown and cassock, who, as I afterwards understood, was curate of a neighbouring parish. It was easy to perceive that the match was not equal, and that the two farmers, who were partners, had to do with a couple of sharpers, who stripped them of all their cash in a very short time. But what surprised me very much, was to hear this clergyman reply to one of the countrymen, who seemed to suspect foul play, in these words, "D—n me, friend, d'ye question my honour?" I did not at all wonder to find a cheat in canonicals, this being a character frequent in my own country, but I was scandalised at the indecency of his behaviour, which appeared in the oaths he swore, and the songs which he sang. At last, to make amends, in some sort, for the damage he had done to the unwary boors, he pulled out a fiddle from the lining of his gown, and, promising to treat them at dinner, began to play most melodiously, singing in concert all the while. This good-humour of the parson inspired the company with so much glee, that the farmers soon forgot their losses, and all present went to dancing in the yard.

While we were agreeably amused in this manner, our musician, spying a horseman riding towards the inn, stopped all of a sudden, crying out, "Gad so! gentlemen I beg your pardon, there's our dog of a doctor coming into the inn." He immediately concealed his instrument, and ran towards the gate, where he took hold of the vicar's bridle, and helped him off, inquiring very cordially into the state of his health.

This rosy son of the church, who might be about the age of fifty, having alighted and intrusted the curate with his horse, stalked, with great solemnity, into the kitchen, where, sitting down by the fire, he called for a bottle of ale and a pipe, scarce deigning an answer to the submissive questions of those who inquired about the welfare of his family. While he indulged himself in this state, amidst a profound silence, the curate, approaching him with great reverence, asked if he would not be pleased to honour us with his company at dinner? To which interrogation he answered in the negative, saying, he had been to visit Squire Bumpkin, who had drunk himself into a high fever at the last assizes, and that he had, on leaving his own house, told Betty he should dine at home. Accordingly, when he had made an end of his bottle and pipe, he rose, and moved with prelatical dignity to the door, where his journeyman stood ready with his nag. He had no sooner mounted, than the facetious curate, coming into the kitchen, held forth in this manner: "There the old rascal goes, and the d—l go with him. You see how the world wags, gentlemen. By Gad, this rogue of a vicar does not deserve to live, and yet he has two livings worth 400l, per annum, while poor I am fain to do all his drudgery, and ride twenty miles every Sunday to preach—for what? Why, truly, for 20l a year. I scorn to boast of my own qualifications, but—comparisons are odious. I should be glad to know how this swag-bellied doctor deserves to be more at ease than me. He can loll in his elbow-chair at home, indulge himself in the best of victuals and wine, and enjoy the conversation of Betty, his housekeeper. You understand me, gentlemen. Betty is the doctor's poor kinswoman, and a pretty girl she is; but no matter for that; ay, and a dutiful girl to her parents, whom she visits regularly every year, though I must own I could never learn in what country they live. My service t'ye gentlemen."

By this time, dinner being ready, I waked my companion, and we ate all together with great cheerfulness. When our meal was ended, and every man's share of the reckoning adjusted, the curate went out on pretence of some necessary occasion, and, mounting his horse, left the two farmers to satisfy the host in the best manner they could. We were no sooner informed of this piece of finesse, than the exciseman, who had been silent hitherto, began to open with a malicious grin: "Ay, ay, this is an old trick of Shuffle; I could not help smiling when he talked of treating. You must know this is a very curious fellow. He picked up some scraps of learning while he served young Lord Trifle at the university. No man knows his talents better than I, for I was valet-de-chambre to Squire Tattle, an intimate companion of Shuffle's lord. He got himself into a scrape by pawning some of his lordship's clothes, on which account he was turned away; but, as he was acquainted with some particular circumstances of my lord's conduct, he did not care to exasperate him too much, and so made interest for his receiving orders, and afterwards recommended him to the curacy which he now enjoys. However, the fellow cannot be too much admired for his dexterity in making a comfortable livelihood, in spite of such a small allowance. You hear he plays a good stick, and is really diverting company. These qualifications make him agreeable wherever he goes; and, as for playing at cards, there is not a man within three counties a match for him. The truth is, he is a d—able cheat, and can shift a card with such address that it is impossible to discover him.

TOBIAS SMOLLETT *Roderick Random*, 1748

Country Minister

THE place of our retreat was in a little neighbourhood, consisting of farmers, who tilled their own grounds, and were equal strangers to opulence and poverty. As they had almost all the conveniences of life within themselves, they seldom visited towns or cities in search of superfluity. Remote from the polite, they still retained the primeval simplicity of manners; and, frugal by habit, they scarce knew that temperance was a virtue. They wrought with cheerfulness on days of labour; but observed festivals as intervals of idleness and pleasure. They kept up the Christmas carol, sent true-love-knots on Valentine morning, eat pancakes on Shrovetide, showed their wit on the first of April, and religiously cracked nuts on Michaelmas eve. Being apprised of our approach, the whole neighbourhood came out to meet their minister, dressed in their fine clothes, and preceded by a pipe and tabor. A feast was also provided for our reception, at which we sat cheerfully down; and what the conversation wanted in wit was made up in laughter.

Our little habitation was situated at the foot of a sloping hill, sheltered with a beautiful underwood behind, and a prattling river before; on one side a meadow, on the other a green. My farm consisted of about twenty acres of excellent land, having given an hundred pound for my predecessor's good-will. Nothing could exceed the neatness of my little enclosures, the elms and the hedgerows appearing with inexpressible beauty. My house consisted of but one story, and was covered with thatch, which gave it an air of great snugness; the walls, on the inside, were nicely whitewashed, and my daughters undertook to adorn them with pictures of their own designing. Though the same room served us for parlour and kitchen, that only made it the warmer. Besides, as it was kept with the utmost neatness, the dishes, plates, and coppers being well scoured, and all disposed in bright rows on the shelves, the eye was agreeably relieved, and did not want richer furniture. There were three other apartments; one for my wife and me, another for our two daughters within our own, and the third, with two beds, for the rest of the children.

The little republic to which I gave laws, was regulated in the following manner: by sunrise we all assembled in our common apartment, the fire being previously kindled by the servant. After we had saluted each other with proper ceremony—for I always thought fit to keep up some mechanical forms of good breeding, without which freedom ever destroys friendship—we all bent in gratitude to that Being who gave us another day. This duty being performed, my son and I went to pursue our usual industry abroad, while my wife and daughters employed themselves in providing breakfast, which was always ready at a certain time. I allowed half an hour for this meal, and an hour for dinner; which time was taken up in innocent mirth between my wife and daughters, and in philosophical arguments between my son and me.

As we rose with the sun, so we never pursued our labours after it was gone down, but returned home to the expecting family, where smiling looks, a neat hearth, and pleasant fire, were prepared for our reception. Nor were we without guests: sometimes farmer Flamborough, our talkative neighbour, and often the blind piper, would pay us a visit, and taste our gooseberry wine, for the making of which we had lost neither the receipt nor the reputation. These harmless people had several ways of being good company; while one played, the other would sing some soothing ballad,—Johnny Armstrong's Last Goodnight, or the Cruelty of Barbara Allen. The night was concluded in the manner we began the morning, my youngest boys being appointed to read the lessons of the day; and he that read loudest, distinctest, and best, was to have a halfpenny on Sunday to put in the poor's box.

At a small distance from the house, my predecessor had made a seat, overshadowed by a hedge of hawthorn and honeysuckle. Here, when the weather was fine and our labour soon finished, we usually sat together, to enjoy an extensive landscape in the calm of the evening. Here, too, we drank tea, which now was become an occasional banquet; and, as we had it but seldom, it diffused a new joy, the preparations for it being made with no small share of bustle and ceremony. On these occasions, our two little ones always read for us, and they were regularly served after we had done. Sometimes, to give a variety to our amusements, the girls sang to the guitar; and while they thus formed a little concert, my wife and I would stroll down the sloping field, that was embellished with bluebells and centaury, talk of our children with rapture, and enjoy the breeze that wafted both health and harmony.

In this manner we began to find that every situation in life may bring its own peculiar pleasures: every morning waked us to a repetition of toil; but the evening repaid it with vacant hilarity.

OLIVER GOLDSMITH *The Vicar of Wakefield*, 1766

A Hampshire Village

AT the foot of the hill, one stage or step from the uplands, lies the village, which consists of one single straggling street, three-quarters of a mile in length, in a sheltered vale, and running parallel with the Hanger.

The cart-way of the village divides, in a remarkable manner, two very incongruous soils. To the south-west is a rank clay, that requires the labour of years to render it mellow; while the gardens to the north-east, and small enclosures behind, consist of a warm, forward, crumbling mould, called *black malm*, which seems highly saturated with vegetable and animal manure; and these may perhaps have been the original site of the town; while the wood and coverts might extend down to the opposite bank.

At each end of the village, which runs from south-east to north-west, arises a small rivulet: that at the north-west end frequently fails; but the other is a fine perennial spring little influenced by drought or wet seasons, called Well-head. Our wells, at an average, run to about sixty-three feet, and when sunk to that depth seldom fail; but produce a fine limpid water, soft to the taste, and much commended by those who drink the pure element, but which does not lather well with soap.

To the north-west, north and east of the village, is a range of fair enclosures, consisting of what is called a *white malm*, a sort of rotten or rubble stone, which, when turned up to the frost and rain, moulders to pieces, and becomes manure to itself.

In the centre of the village, and near the church, is a square piece of ground surrounded by houses, and vulgarly called the Plestor. In the midst of this spot stood, in old times, a vast oak, with a short squat body, and huge horizontal arms extending almost to the extremity of the area. This venerable tree, surrounded with stone steps, and seats above them, was the delight of old and young, and a place of much resort in summer evenings; where the former sat in grave debate, while the latter frolicked and danced before them.

The village of Selborne, and large hamlet of Oakhanger, with the single farms, and many scattered houses along the verge of the forest, contain upwards of six hundred and seventy inhabitants. We abound with poor; many of whom are sober and industrious, and live comfortably in good stone or brick cottages, which are glazed, and have chambers above stairs: mud buildings we have none. Besides the employment from husbandry, the men work in hop gardens, of which we have many; and fell and bark timber. In the spring and summer the women weed the corn; and enjoy a second harvest in September by hop-picking. Formerly, in the dead months they availed themselves greatly by spinning wool, for making *barragons*, a genteel corded stuff, much in vogue at that time for summer wear; and chiefly manufactured at Alton, a neighbouring town, by some of the people called Quakers; but from circumstances this trade is at an end. The inhabitants enjoy a good share of health and longevity: and the parish swarms with children.

GILBERT WHITE *The Natural History of Selborne*, 1789

The Old Style

UPPERCROSS was a moderate-sized village, which a few years back had been completely in the old English style, containing only two houses superior in appearance to those of the yeomen and labourers: the mansion of the 'squire, with its high walls, great gates, and old trees, substantial and unmodernised, and the compact, tight parsonage, enclosed in its own neat garden, with a vine and a pear-tree trained round its casements; but upon the marriage of the young 'squire, it had received the improvement of a farmhouse, elevated into a cottage, for his residence; and Uppercross Cottage, with its veranda, French windows, and other prettinesses, was quite as likely to catch the traveller's eye as the more consistent and considerable aspect and premises of the Great House, about a quarter of a mile farther on.

JANE AUSTEN *Persuasion*, 1816

Living Conditions

Yesterday morning (Sunday, the 25th) I walked out to the village of Knighton, two miles on the Bosworth road, where I breakfasted, and then walked back. This morning I walked out to Hailstone, nearly three miles on the Lutterworth road, and got my breakfast there. You have nothing to do but to walk through these villages to see the cause of the increase of the gaols. Standing on the hill at Knighton, you see the three ancient and lofty and beautiful spires rising up at Leicester; you see the river winding down through a broad bed of the most beautiful meadows that man ever set his eyes on; you see the bright verdure covering all the land, even to the tops of the hills, with here and there a little wood, as if made by God to give variety to the beauty of the scene, for the river brings the coal in abundance, for fuel, and the earth gives the brick and the tile in abundance. But go down into the villages; invited by the spires, rising up amongst the trees in the dells, at scarcely ever more than a mile or two apart; invited by these spires, go down into these villages, view the large, and once the most beautiful, churches; see the parson's house, large, and in the midst of pleasure-gardens; and then look at the miserable sheds in which the labourers reside! Look at these hovels, made of mud and of straw; bits of glass, or of old off-cast windows, without frames or hinges frequently, but merely stuck in the mud wall. Enter them, and look at the bits of chairs or stools; the wretched boards tacked together to serve for a table; the floor of pebble, broken brick, or of the bare ground; look at the thing called a bed; and survey the rags on the backs of the wretched inhabitants; and then wonder if you can that the gaols and dungeons and treadmills increase, and that a standing army and barracks are become the favourite establishments of England!

At the village of Hailstone, I got into the purlieu, as they call it in Hampshire, of a person well known in the Wen; namely, the Reverend Beresford, rector of that fat affair, St. Andrew's, Holborn! In walking through the village, and surveying its deplorable dwellings, so much worse than the cowsheds of the cottagers on the skirts of the forests in Hampshire, my attention was attracted by the surprising contrast between them and the house of their religious teacher. I met a labouring man. Country people *know everything*. If you have ever made a *faux-pas* of any sort of description; if you have anything about you of which you do not want all the world to know, never retire to a village, keep in some great town; but the Wen, for your life, for there the next-door neighbour will not know even your name; and the vicinage will judge of you solely by the quantity of money that you have to spend. This labourer seemed not to be in a very great hurry. He was digging in his garden; and I, looking over a low hedge, *pitched him up* for a gossip, commencing by asking him whether that was the parson's house. Having answered in the affirmative, and I having asked the parson's name, he proceeded thus: "His name is Beresford; but though he lives there, he has not this living now, he has got the living of St. Andrew's Holborn; and they say it is worth a great many thousands a year. He could not, they say, keep this living and have that too, because they were so far apart. And so this living was given to Mr. Brown, who is the rector of Hobey, about seven miles off." "Well," said I "but *how comes Beresford to live here now*, if the living be given to another man?" "Why, sir," said he, "this Beresford married a daughter of Brown; and so, you know (smiling and looking very archly), Brown comes and takes the payment for the tithes, and pays a curate that lives in that house there in the field; and Beresford lives at that fine house still, just as he used to do." I asked him what the living was worth, and he answered twelve hundred pounds a year. It is a rectory, I find, and of course the parson has great tithes as well as small.

WILLIAM COBBETT *Rural Rides*, 1830

The Village Oracle

I USED to meet him every spring, when we lived at our old house, whose park-like paddock, with its finely clumped oaks and elms, and its richly-timbered hedgerows, edging into wild, rude, and solemn fir-plantations, dark, and rough, and hoary, formed for so many years my constant and favourite walk. Here, especially under the great horse-chestnut, and where the bank rose high and naked above the lane, crowned only with a tuft of golden broom; here the sweetest and prettiest of wild flowers, whose very name hath a charm, grew like a carpet under one's feet, enamelling the young green grass with their white and purple blossoms, and loading the air with their delicious fragrance; here I used to come almost every morning, during the violet-tide; and here almost every morning I was sure to meet Isaac Bint.

I think that he fixed himself the more firmly in my memory by his singular discrepancy with the beauty and cheerfulness of the scenery and the season. Isaac is a tall, lean, gloomy personage, with whom the clock of life seems to stand still. He has looked sixty-five for these last twenty years, although his dark hair and beard, and firm manly stride, almost contradict the evidence of his sunken cheeks and deeply-lined forehead. The stride is awful: he hath the stalk of a ghost. His whole air and demeanour savour of one that comes from underground. His appearance is "of the earth, earthy." His clothes, hands, and face, are of the colour of the mould in which he delves. The little round traps which hang behind him over one shoulder, as well as the strings of dead moles which embellish the other, are encrusted with dirt like a tombstone; and the staff which he plunges into the little hillocks, by which he traces the course of his small quarry, returns a hollow sound, as if tapping on the lid of a coffin. Images of the churchyard come, one does not know how, with his presence. Indeed he does officiate as assistant to the sexton in his capacity of grave digger, chosen, as it should seem, from a natural fitness; a fine sense of congruity in good Joseph Reed, the functionary in question, who felt, without knowing why, that, of all men in the parish, Isaac Bint was best fitted to that solemn office.

His remarkable gift of silence adds much to the impression produced by his remarkable figure. I don't think that I ever heard him speak three words in my life. An approach of that bony hand to that earthy leather cap was the greatest effort of courtesy that my daily salutations could extort from him. For this silence, Isaac has reasons good. He hath a reputation to support. His words are too precious to be wasted. Our mole-catcher, ragged as he looks, is the wise man of the village, the oracle of the village-inn, foresees the weather, charms away agues, tells fortunes by the stars, and writes notes upon the almanack—turning and twisting about the predictions after a fashion so ingenious, that it's a moot point which is oftenest wrong—Isaac Bint, or Francis Moore.

Our mole-catcher is, as might be conjectured, an old bachelor. He lives on the edge of a pretty bit of scenery, called the Penge, in a snug cottage of two rooms, of his own building, surrounded by a garden cribbed from the waste, well fenced with quickset, and well stocked with fruit-trees, herbs, and flowers. One large apple-tree extends over the roof—a pretty bit of colour when in blossom, contrasted with the thatch of the little dwelling, and relieved by the dark wood behind. Although the owner be solitary, his demesne is sufficiently populous. A long row of bee-hives extends along the warmest side of the garden—for Isaac's honey is celebrated far and near; a pig occupies a commodious stye at one corner; and large flocks of ducks and geese (for which the Penge, whose glades are intersected by water, is famous) are generally waiting round a back gate leading to a spacious shed, far larger than Isaac's own cottage, which serves for their feeding and roosting-place. The great tameness of all these creatures—for the ducks and geese flutter round him the moment he approaches, and the very pig follows him like a dog—gives no equivocal testimony of the kindness of our mole-catcher's nature.

MARY MITFORD *Our Village*, 1832

Tradition

THE small town of Hazelby, in Dorsetshire, is a pretty little place, where every thing seems at a standstill. It was originally built in the shape of the letter T; a long, broad market-place (still so called, although the market be gone) serving for the perpendicular stem, traversed by a straight, narrow, horizontal street, to answer for the top line. Not one addition has occurred to interrupt this architectural regularity since, fifty years ago, a rich London tradesman built, at the west end of the horizontal street, a wide-fronted single house, with two low wings, iron pallisades before, and a fish-pond opposite, which still goes by the name of New Place, and is balanced, at the east end of the street, by an erection of nearly the same date, a large, square, dingy mansion enclosed with high walls, inhabited by three maiden sisters, and called, probably by way of nickname, the Nunnery. New Place being on the left of the road, and the Nunnery on the right, the T has now something the air of the Italic capital *T*, turned up at one end and down on the other. The latest improvements are the bow-window in the market-place, commanding the pavement both ways, which the late brewer, Andrews, threw out in his snug parlour some twenty years back, and where he used to sit smoking, with the sash up, in summer afternoons, enjoying himself, good man;

and the great room at the Swan, originally built by the speculative publican, Joseph Allwright, for an assembly-room.

In short, Hazelby is an insignificant place;—my readers will look for it in vain in the map of Dorsetshire;—it is omitted, poor dear town!—left out by the map-maker with as little remorse as a dropped letter!—and it is also an old-fashioned place. It has not even a cheap shop for female gear. Every thing in the one store which it boasts, kept by Martha Deane, linen-draper and haberdasher, is dear and good, as things were wont to be. You may actually get there thread made of flax, from the gouty, uneven, clumsy, shiny fabric, yclept white-brown, to the delicate commodity of Lisle, used for darning muslin. I think I was never more astonished than when, on asking, from the mere force of habit, for thread, I was presented, instead of the pretty lattice-wound balls or snowy reels of cotton, with which that demand is usually answered, with a whole drawerful of skeins, peeping from their blue papers—such skeins as in my youth a thrifty maiden would draw into the nicely stitched compartments of that silken repository, a housewife, or fold into a congeries of graduated thread-papers, "fine by degrees, and beautifully less." The very literature of Hazelby is doled out at the pastry-cook's, in a little one-windowed shop, kept by Matthew Wise. Tarts occupy one end of the counter, and reviews the other; whilst the shelves are parcelled out between books, and dolls, and gingerbread. It is a question, by which of his trades poor Matthew gains least; he is so shabby, so threadbare, and so starved.

MARY MITFORD *Our Village*, 1832

A Depressed Area

THE situation of the rural town of Marney was one of the most delightful easily to be imagined. In a spreading dale, contiguous to the margin of a clear and lively stream, surrounded by meadows and gardens, and backed by lofty hills, undulating and richly wooded, the traveller on the opposite heights of the dale would often stop to admire the merry prospect, that recalled to him the traditional epithet of his country.

Beautiful illusion. For behind that laughing landscape, penury and disease fed upon the vitals of a miserable population!

The contrast between the interior of the town and its external aspect, was as striking as it was full of pain. With the exception of the dull high street, which had the usual characteristics of a small agricultural market town, some sombre mansions, a dingy inn, and a petty bourse, Marney mainly consisted of a variety of narrow and crowded lanes formed by cottages built of rubble, or unhewn stones without cement, and from age, or badness of the material, looking as if they could scarcely hold together. The gaping chinks admitted every blast; the leaning chimneys had lost half their original height; the rotten rafters were evidently misplaced; while in many instances the thatch, yawning in some parts to admit the wind and wet, and in all utterly unfit for its original purpose of giving protection from the weather, looked more like the top of a dunghill than a cottage. Before the doors of these dwellings, and often surrounding them, ran open drains full of animal and vegetable refuse, decomposing into disease, or sometimes in their imperfect course filling foul pits or spreading into stagnant pools, while a concentrated solution of every species of dissolving filth was allowed to soak through and thoroughly impregnate the walls and ground adjoining.

These wretched tenements seldom consisted of more than two rooms, in one of which the whole family, however numerous, were obliged to sleep, without distinction of age, or sex, or suffering.

This town of Marney was a metropolis of agricultural labour, for the proprietors of the neighbourhood having for the last half century acted on the system of destroying the cottages of their estates, in order to become exempted from the maintenance of the population, the expelled people had flocked to Marney, where, during the war, a manufactory had afforded them some relief, though its wheels had long ceased to disturb the waters of the Mar.

Deprived of this resource, they had again gradually spread themselves over that land which had as it were rejected them; and obtained from its churlish breast a niggardly subsistence. Their re-entrance into the surrounding parishes was viewed with great suspicion; their renewed settlement opposed by every ingenious contrivance; those who availed themselves of their labour were careful that they should not become dwellers on the soil; and though, from the excessive competition, there were few districts in the kingdom where the rate of wages was more depressed; those who were fortunate enough to obtain the scant remuneration, had, in addition to their toil, to endure each morn and even a weary journey before they could reach the scene of their labour, or return to the squalid hovel which profaned the name of home. To that home, over which Malaria hovered, and round whose shivering hearth were clustered other guests besides the exhausted family of toil—Fever, in every form, pale Consumption, exhausting Synochus, and trembling Ague,—returned after cultivating the broad fields of merry England the bold British peasant, returned to encounter the worst of diseases with a frame the least qualified to oppose them; a frame that subdued by toil was never sustained by animal food; drenched by the tempest could not change its dripping rags; and was indebted for its scanty fuel to the windfalls of the woods.

BENJAMIN DISRAELI *Sybil*, 1845

A Yorkshire Interior

WUTHERING HEIGHTS is the name of Mr. Heathcliff's dwelling. "Wuthering" being a significant provincial adjective, descriptive of the atmospheric tumult to which its station is exposed in stormy weather. Pure, bracing ventilation they must have up there at all times, indeed. One may guess the power of the north wind blowing over the edge by the excessive slant of a few stunted firs at the end of the house, and by a range of gaunt thorns all stretching their limbs one way, as if craving alms of the sun. Happily, the architect had foresight to build it strong: the narrow windows are deeply set in the wall, and the corners defended with large, jutting stones.

Before passing the threshold, I paused to admire a quantity of grotesque carving lavished over the front, and especially about the principal door, above which, among the wilderness of crumbling griffins and shameless little boys, I detected the date "1500."

One step brought us into the family sitting-room, without any introductory lobby or passage: they call it here "the house" pre-eminently. It includes kitchen and parlour generally; but I believe at Wuthering Heights the kitchen is forced to retreat altogether into another quarter; at least I distinguished a clutter of tongues, and a clatter of culinary utensils, deep within; and I observed no signs of roasting, boiling, or baking, about the huge fireplace, nor any glitter of copper saucepans and tin cullenders on the walls. One end, indeed, reflected splendidly both light and heat from ranks of immense pewter dishes, interspersed with silver jugs and tankards, towering row after row on a vast oak dresser to the very roof. The latter had never been underdrawn; its entire anatomy lay bare to an inquiring eye, except where a frame of wood, laden with oatcakes and clusters of legs of beef, mutton, and ham, concealed it. Above the chimneys were sundry villainous old guns, and a couple of horse-pistols; and, by way of ornament, three gaudily-painted canisters disposed along its ledge. The floor was of smooth, white stone; the chairs high-backed, primitive structures, painted green: one or two heavy black ones lurking in the shade. In an arch under the dresser, reposed a huge, liver-coloured bitch pointer, surrounded by a swarm of squealing puppies; and other dogs haunted other recesses.

The apartment and furniture would have been nothing extraordinary as belonging to a homely, northern farmer, with a stubborn countenance, and stalwart limbs set out to advantage in knee-breeches and gaiters. Such an individual, seated in his armchair, his mug of ale frothing on the round table before him, is to be seen in any circuit of five or six miles among those hills, if you go at the right time after dinner.

EMILY BRONTË *Wuthering Heights*, 1847

The Church at Shepperton—Chilvers Coton, Warwick

I RECALL with a fond sadness Shepperton Church as it was in the old days, with its outer coat of rough stucco, its red-tiled roof, its heterogeneous windows patched with desultory bits of painted glass, and its little flight of steps with their wooden rail running up the outer wall, and leading to the school-children's gallery.

Then inside, what dear old quaintnesses! There was the chancel, guarded by two little cherubims looking uncomfortably squeezed between arch and wall, and adorned with the escutcheons of the Oldinport family, which showed me inexhaustible possibilities of meaning in their blood-red hands, their death's-heads and cross-bones, their leopard's paws, and Maltese crosses. There were inscriptions on the panels of the singing gallery, telling of benefactions to the poor of Shepperton, with an involuted elegance of capitals and final flourishes. which my alphabetic erudition traced with ever-new delight. No benches in those days; but huge roomy pews, round which devout church-goers sat during "lessons," trying to look anywhere else than into each other's eyes. No low partitions allowing you, with a dreary absence of contrast and mystery, to see everything at all moments; but tall dark panels, under whose shadow I sank with a sense of retirement through the Litany, only to feel with more intensity my burst into the conspicuousness of public life when I was made to stand up on the seat during the psalms or the singing.

And the singing was no mechanical affair of official routine; it had a drama. As the moment of psalmody approached, by some process to me as mysterious and untraceable as the opening of the flowers or the breaking-out of the stars, a slate appeared in front of the gallery, advertising in bold characters the psalm about to be sung, lest the sonorous announcement of the clerk should still leave the bucolic mind in doubt on that head. Then followed the migration of the clerk to the gallery where, in company with a bassoon, two key-bugles, a carpenter understood to have an amazing power of singing "counter," and two lesser musical stars, he formed the complement of a choir regarded in Shepperton as one of distinguished attraction, occasionally known to draw hearers from the next parish. The innovation of hymn books was as yet undreamed of; even the New Version was regarded with a sort of melancholy tolerance, as part of the common degeneracy in a time when prices had dwindled, and a cotton gown was no longer stout enough to last a lifetime; for the lyrical taste of the best heads in Shepperton had been formed on Sternhold and Hopkins. But the greatest triumphs of the Shepperton choir were reserved for the Sundays when the slate announced an *Anthem*, with a dignified abstinence from particularisation, both words and music lying far beyond the reach of the most ambitious amateur in the congregation—an anthem in which the key-bugles always ran away at a great pace, while the bassoon every now and then boomed a flying shot after them.

GEORGE ELIOT *Scenes of Clerical Life*, 1857

The Village Inn

HALF-AN-HOUR's walking brought me from this place to a small town or large village, with a church at the entrance and the usual yew tree in the churchyard. Seeing a kind of inn I entered it, and was shown by a lad-waiter into a large kitchen, in which were several people. I had told him in Welsh that I wanted some ale, and as he opened the door he cried with a loud voice, "Cumro!" as much as to say, Mind what you say before this chap, for he understands Cumraeg—that word was enough. The people, who were talking fast and eagerly as I made my appearance, instantly became silent and stared at me with most suspicious looks. I sat down, and when my ale was brought I took a hearty draught, and observing that the company were still watching me suspiciously and maintaining the same suspicious silence, I determined to comport myself in a manner which should to a certain extent afford them ground for suspicion. I therefore slowly and deliberately drew my note-book out of my waistcoat pocket, unclasped it, took my pencil from the loops at the side of the book, and forthwith began to dot down observations upon the room and company, now looking to the left, now to the right, now aloft, now alow, now skewing at an object, now leering at an individual, my eyes half closed and my mouth drawn considerably aside. Here follow some of my dottings:—

"A very comfortable kitchen with a chimney corner on the south side—immense grate and brilliant fire—large kettle hanging over it by a chain attached to a transverse iron bar—a settle on the left-hand side of the fire—seven fine large men near the fire—two upon the settle, two upon chairs, one in the chimney-corner smoking a pipe, and two standing up—table near the settle with glasses, amongst which is that of myself, who sit nearly in the middle of the room a little way on the right-hand side of the fire.

"The floor is of slate; a fine brindled greyhound lies before it on the hearth, and a shepherd's dog wanders about, occasionally going to the door and scratching as if anxious to get out. The company are dressed mostly in the same fashion, brown coats, broad-brimmed hats, and yellowish corduroy breeches with gaiters. One who looks like a labouring man has a white smock and a white hat, patched trowsers, and highlows covered with gravel—one has a blue coat.

"There is a clock on the right-hand side of the kitchen; a warming-pan hangs close by it on the projecting side of the chimney-corner. On the same side is a large rack containing many plates and dishes of Staffordshire ware. Let me not forget a pair of fire-irons which hang on the right-hand side of the chimney-corner!"

I made a great many more dottings, which I shall not insert here. During the whole time I was dotting the most marvellous silence prevailed in the room, broken only by the occasional scratching of the dog against the inside of the door, the ticking of the clock, and the ruttling of the smoker's pipe in the chimney-corner. After I had dotted to my heart's content I closed my book, put the pencil into the loops, then the book into my pocket, drank what remained of my ale, got up, and, after another look at the apartment and its furniture, and a leer at the company, departed from the house without ceremony, having paid for the ale when I received it. After walking some fifty yards down the street I turned half round and beheld, as I knew I should, the whole company at the door staring after me. I leered sideways at them for about half a minute, but they stood my leer stoutly. Suddenly I was inspired by a thought. Turning round I confronted them, and pulling my note-book out of my pocket, and seizing my pencil, I fell to dotting vigorously. That was too much for them. As if struck by a panic, my quondam friends turned round and bolted into the house; the rustic-looking man with the smock-frock and gravelled highlows nearly falling down in his eagerness to get in.

The name of the place where this adventure occurred was Cemmaes.

GEORGE BORROW *Wild Wales*, 1862

Down the Lane

MIXEN LANE was the Adullam of all the surrounding villages. It was the hiding place of those who were in distress, and in debt, and trouble of every kind. Farm-labourers and other peasants, who combined a little poaching with their farming, and a little brawling and bibbing with their poaching, found themselves sooner or later in Mixen Lane. Rural mechanics too idle to mechanize, rural servants too rebellious to serve, drifted or were forced into Mixen Lane.

The lane and its surrounding thicket of thatched cottages

16 Mayday outside a Village Inn
From an early Victorian print

17 The Taproom of a Village Inn
From an eighteenth-century print

18 An Inn on the outskirts of Bradford-on-Avon, Wiltshire, in 1806
After J. C. Nattes

19 A Half-timber Village of the Western Midlands
From an early nineteenth-century print

stretched out like a spit into the moist and misty lowland. Much that was sad, much that was low, some things that were baneful, could be seen in Mixen Lane. Vice ran freely in and out certain of the doors of the neighbourhood; recklessness dwelt under the roof with the crooked chimney; shame in some bow-windows; theft (in time of privation) in the thatched and mud-walled houses by the sallows. Even slaughter had not been altogether unknown here. In a block of cottages up an alley there might have been erected an altar to disease in years gone by.

Yet this mildewed leaf in the sturdy and flourishing Casterbridge plant lay close to the open country; not a hundred yards from a row of noble elms, and commanding a view across the moor of airy uplands and corn-fields, and mansions of the great. A brook divided the moor from the tenements, and to outward view there was no way across it—no way to the houses but round by the road. But under every householder's stairs there was kept a mysterious plank nine inches wide; which plank was a secret bridge.

If you, as one of those refugee householders, came in from business after dark—and this was the business time here—you stealthily crossed the moor, approached the border of the aforesaid brook, and whistled opposite the house to which you belonged. A shape thereupon made its appearance on the other side bearing the bridge on end against the sky; it was lowered; you crossed, and a hand helped you to land yourself, together with the pheasants and hares gathered from neighbouring manors. You sold them slily the next morning, and the day after you stood before the magistrates, with the eyes of all your sympathizing neighbours concentrated on your back. You disappeared for a time; then you were again found quietly living in Mixen Lane.

Yet amid so much that was bad, needy respectability also found a home. Under some of the roofs abode pure and virtuous souls whose presence there was due to the iron hand of necessity, and to that alone. Families from decayed villages—families of that once bulky, but now nearly extinct, section of village society called "liviers," or lifeholders—copy-holders and others, whose roof-trees had fallen for some reason or other, compelling them to quit the rural spot that had been their home for generations—came here, unless they chose to lie under a hedge by the wayside.

The inn called Peter's Finger was the church of Mixen Lane.

It was centrally situate, as such places should be, and bore about the same social relation to the Three Mariners as the latter bore to the King's Arms. At first sight the inn was so respectable as to be puzzling. The front door was kept shut, and the step was so clean that evidently but few persons entered over its sanded surface. But at the corner of the public-house was an alley, a mere slit, dividing it from the next building. Half-way up the alley was a narrow door, shiny and paintless from the rub of infinite hands and shoulders. This was the actual entrance to the inn.

The company at the Three Mariners were persons of quality in comparison with the company which gathered here; though it must be admitted that the lowest fringe of the Mariner's party touched the crest of Peter's at points. Waifs and strays of all sorts loitered about here. The landlady was a virtuous woman who years ago had been unjustly sent to gaol as an accessory to something or other after the fact. She underwent her twelvemonth, and had worn a martyr's countenance ever since, except at times of meeting the constable who apprehended her, when she winked her eye.

THOMAS HARDY *The Mayor of Casterbridge*, 1886

Change

"MY brother's Cow," wrote Gilbert White in his journal, "when there is no extraordinary call for cream, produces three pounds of butter each week. The footman churns the butter over night, and puts it in water. In the morning one of my nieces beats it and makes it up and prints it." When the excellent Edward Jesse in 1834 printed this fifty-year-old entry among his "Gleanings," he could not repress an exclamatory *tempora mutantur*. Since those days, our walks in our country places, our observations on village and farm aspects, are apt to resolve themselves into a sustained elegy, *tempora mutantur*. In many districts, we have perhaps ceased altogether to seek for bucolic effects, and the apparition of a milkmaid or a "smock-frocked boor" flail in hand would be something against nature. Change has worked with rapidity in the England that used to be so busy with harvests, corn-markets, the last load and the mill-wheel. Instead of going into the country for an adventure in primitive and pretty encounters, and a peep at an abundant round of skilful practical doings, from the wagon-shed to the wood-riding, we more and more assume the character of connoisseurs in beauty of scenery and of architecture. "A pleasing circumstance" (to quote White's note-book again), "mixed with some degree of regret."

There are those still, such as the author of the *Corduroy* trilogy, who in their genuine chronicles of the farmer's world during these years assure us that many corners of the country retain their simplicities, their personalities, their earth-secrets, and almost their Sunday congregations. They nearly persuade us that the country still has its peasantry. From their natural and experienced narrative we rise and take the road rejoicing that there are still countrymen, powerful or poverty-stricken, who could show Virgil a thing or two about hogs and horses, and keeping a farm like a garden. We shall be rewarded from time to time by meeting a shepherd and his dog, when the wethers' bells make the breeze musical; or by passing a few hours where the cowman placidly riding his bicycle to his allotment is followed by his faithful servant the sow; or by hearing long songs about emigration and Victoria, Great and Good from the black benches of the "Crooked Chimney" parlour. Will the little huntsman be induced to attempt "John Peel" this evening, a song which he has yet to learn is known to his countrymen generally?

The surfaces of the countryside inevitably display your *tempora mutantur* in a conspicuous violence, but beneath them remains, even in the less promising surroundings, a deal of country community and integrity. There is a village I know which, through the influences of the War, of education, of the motor in all its forms, of broadcasting, of social modifications, of business combinations and the rest, frequently appears to be—not the same village. Half the hop-oasts whose conical white-fingered cowls used to shine above the trees on a blue sky like sailing-ships on summer lagoons are gone or going; the streams which formerly were kept so full and clear for water supply, with their little hatches and tumbling bays, are scarcely now worth walking along; you hardly know your neighbours, who seem to live as much elsewhere as in the parish, for work or play; the baker's vans are superseded by hasty visiting cars, and so it is with the other roundsmen and their cheerful word with every cottage for miles. Such signs, some of many, seem like an epitaph; but when I find myself thinking that way, it is time to pay a call on Old Sid. He will be, this evening, in his kitchen, heated like a bakehouse (he was a baker for about thirty-five years); he will push his spectacles back to take a good, grandfather-clock look at his visitor, and then, as his hand-coloured pack of cards begins to circulate, he will speak of all he has done, and seen, and heard around the village since we last met. What with hop-picking, cow-keeping, apple-gathering, faggotting and fetching and carrying he has been as busy as a bee; and as his talk thrives, the scene of village community and of rural affairs awakens in the listener almost as fresh and copious as it ever did. He too laments; not so much for the fiddle-playing in the church for which his father was famous; not for this particular tree gone, or that old character extinct; but in a broad view for a relationship of various talents and masteries, and courteous differences, which composed a serene, just kind of life. The spirit of our village may be declining and doomed, but in such a man (who tells youth what it should do, and is seldom resented) it fights finely for survival.

EDMUND BLUNDEN *The Mind's Eye*, 1934

The Ideal and the Real

WHEN the earliest of the Monk's Norton cottages were built, Arden still was green, and a squirrel could cross two counties by leaping from bough to bough. Even now, though the glades of great trees have vanished, the depth of the soil is so great, its nature so fruitful, and the Atlantic air that ebbs and flows over the Severn basin is so bland, that these villages, set within orchards and gardens, still wear a woodland air. Their gentle shapes and hues do no violence to the surrounding greenness, adopting, indeed, in their dapplings of rusty lichen and clambering ivy and mossy thatch, a sort of protective colouring that makes them appear a natural part of it.

The irregular line of cottages, each different from its neighbour, which prolongs the main street of Monk's Norton to the gates of the Grange, occupies only one side of the road, the left as you go downhill. Though the road falls gradually, the bank on which they are built maintains its level, so that all of them—if the struggling fruit-trees of their front gardens would permit it, and if the buildings themselves did not huddle so closely to the soil—would look out, from this wild elevation, over billows of green fields and dark spinney, to a blue line of distant hills: the stark serrations of the Malverns and their more wooded northern prolongations, and, even more distant, the filmy shapes of the Clees. Between the road and the bank on which the cottages stand runs a ditch, clogged in summer with lush grasses and horse-mint, which holds in winter a permanent trickle of water and becomes, at last, a tributary of the Brandon Brook. It is so deep and so wide that here and there it is spanned for convenience by culverts and wooden bridges uniting the road and the path, which is no more than a strip of foot-trodden earth between turfy verges.

All these dwellings (or all save Ivy Cottage, the last in the row) are built with half-timber frames of black oak and roofed with straw-thatch. Some, in which the spaces between the framework are filled with plastered rubble, are whitewashed. Others, in which the filling is of brick, have the natural hue of the material from which the soft local bricks were once made, a tawny clay which, in its fine granular texture, and in the power which its granules possess of reflecting (one might almost say of retaining) warm light, resembles the Permian sandstone of which the church tower is built.

Except in one or two of the earliest examples—hovels dating from the end of the fifteenth century whose main skeleton consists of two gigantic curved timbers that spring from the earth in which their butts are imbedded and meet under the thatch overhead in an acute-angled Gothic arch, like the ribs of an inverted ship or an arch of whalebone—the Monk's Norton half-timber is usually of a simple design: nothing more than a rectangular trellis of filled framing with diagonal cross-pieces inserted only at the angles to counter the roof's outward strain. No inventive fancy has found vent in carving or patternwork. The timber is planned to fulfil a constructive function; and since most of it has now weathered three centuries the builders' ghosts have not very much to complain of.

In the seventeenth century, when they were new, the black and white cottages may not have fallen far below the standard of sanitation and comfort allotted to a brutish and ignorant peasantry. In the nineteenth, when urban conditions were even more degrading, and whole cities were improvised out of noisome and verminous back-to-backs, they might just have been tolerated. In the twentieth their romantic picturesqueness does not excuse them: they are a social disgrace. Not one of them has room for a bath or what is politely called "indoor sanitation." Their domestic water-supply must be drawn laboriously, bucket by bucket, from shallow wells, the purity of which is not above suspicion. Their thatched roofs, if they do not leak, become, in winter, half-sodden sponges of rotting straw exhaling odours of mildew, while the slate-slabbed floors which are laid upon clammy clay are always cold and darkened here and there by patches of damp which show where water is lying. The treads of the stairs and the floors of the rooms upstairs are worn into holes and warped to disclose crevasses with rat-gnawed edges. Ventilation they have in plenty, for no door fits and no window is watertight, though the chinks in the casements and frames are stuffed with brown paper; but the sanitary virtue of airiness (if perpetual draughts deserve that euphemism) is heavily overbalanced by the dungeon darkness to which their inmates are condemned not merely by the inadequate window-space of their small-paned lattices but by the shadow of the dripping thatch, the festoons of clambering greenery that envelop them, and the pallid pot-plants set to catch the sun on the sills. There are corners in those low-ceilinged living-rooms and in the dank lean-to sculleries that no direct light save that of lamp or candle has ever illuminated.

During the only season in which adventurous strangers exploring the countryside are likely to discover them, the black-and-white cottages "down the road" do not reveal their defects. It is natural and easy enough to find life idyllic when April enchants the mossy paths with clumps of polyanthus and gilly-flowers and pale-spiked daffodils, and the bare boughs of plum-trees, smooth and dusky as gun-metal, are sprayed with flurries of living snow: easier still in June, when lazy cuckoos are calling, when the apple-blow falls petal by petal on growing grass, and cider-fruit is settling amid clusters of pale green leaf. At this season, indeed, the very daylight seems loth to leave the sky; the air is so kind and the sense of lush growth and soft abandonment in every live thing so persuasive that the mere state of living becomes endowed with a peculiar, wistful sweetness; and where could one's days be more placidly spent, the stranger asks himself, than in these humble dwellings where life demands so little.

The people who inhabit these cottages are a long-lived race.

The ills which cripple and kill them, Dr. Hemming will tell you, are mainly those which are due to exposure and damp: rheumatic diseases of joints and nerves and muscles and bronchitic infections, recurring each winter until they come once too often. They are a prolific race (or have been till lately) with plenty of stalwart sons and buxom daughters, brought up, in a not very distant past, on a labourer's wage of less than a pound a week, who work on the land and "go into service" as soon as they are old enough to fend for themselves. They are poor folk. In not one of those cottages "down the road" is there a man who earns more than forty shillings a week. And even that is precarious, depending not merely on health but on the fortunes and sometimes the caprices of his employer. They are essentially a respectable race. Very few ever get into troubles more serious than the results of riding bicycles on footpaths or without a light, the offences that P.C. Homes has most often to deal with. They have a strict sense of duty. It is part of the young people's acknowledged debt to contribute to their parents' living as soon as they come to need it. Daughters-in-law are sometimes a little jealous; but tradition in this matter is usually stronger than Scripture, and few parents with sons in good jobs want as long as they live. They are a capable race. Though most of them would be described on a census-paper as "unskilled labourers," their labour is very different from that of the better-paid workers, themselves machines, who tend machines in factories. They are masters of many complicated and exquisite crafts—land-drainage, shepherding, forestry, hedge-laying, thatching, ploughing—and the repository of much knowledge, part traditional and part acquired by experience and acute observation, of the vagaries of nature. They know the peculiarities of the land on which they work: how one pasture is sour and another kind, how it lies to wind and to water. They are skilled in the habits and handling of stock, knowing which crosses succeed and which invite failure and what feeding, in given cases, gives good results and what leads to disaster. They are experts in weather, and can read the face of the sky with as little margin of error as a wireless weather-forecast. In the handling of the soil and the things that grow in it, their calloused fingers have a fine delicacy, like that of a surgeon's. And not only are they expert in these crafts; they are also (and reasonably) proud of the skill that can drive a straight furrow over uneven land, or insert a graft that will grow like a natural break in the bark of a plum or apple-tree, or shear an awkward sheep without drawing blood, or fell a tree to lie as it should, or geld a bullock. There is no such thing in Monk's Norton as an unskilled farm-labourer.

FRANCIS BRETT YOUNG *Portrait of a Village*, 1937

20 Rural Suffolk, in the early nineteenth century: the Glebe Farm

From a mezzotint by David Lucas, after John Constable, R.A.

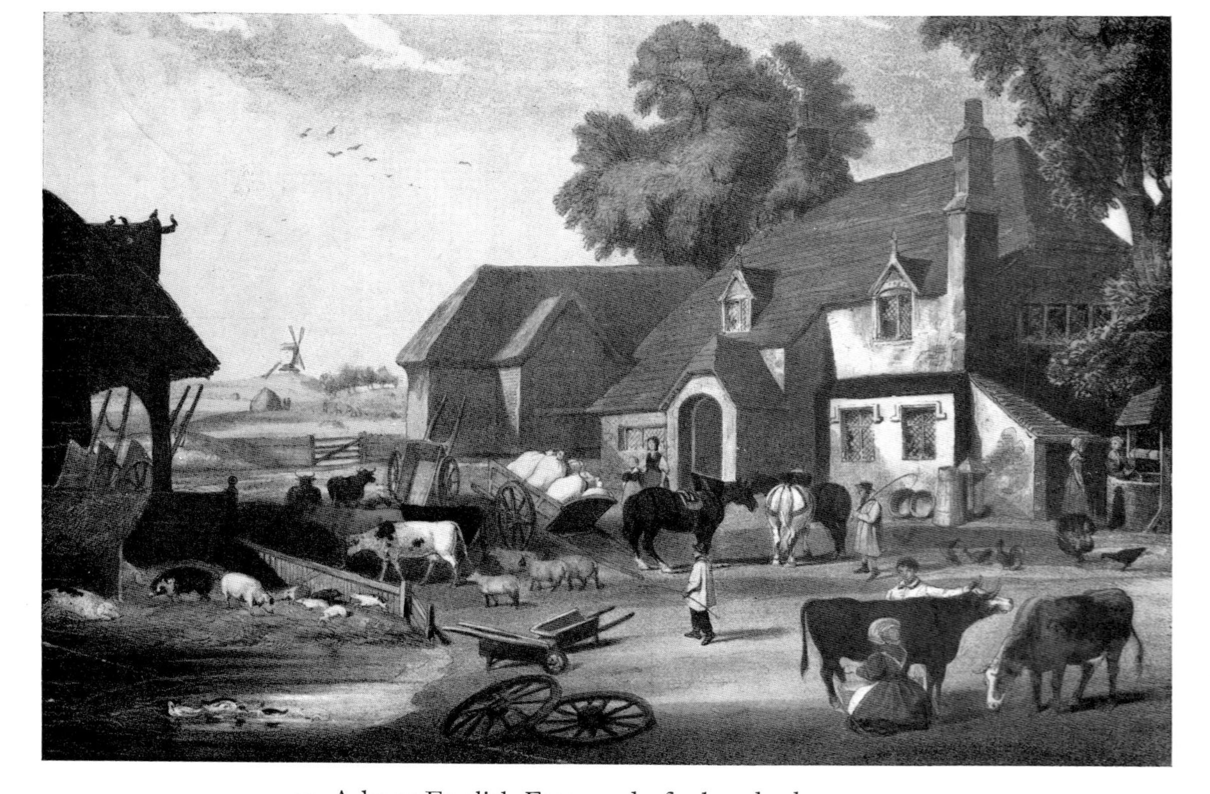

21 A busy English Farmyard of a hundred years ago

From a contemporary print

Farm or Factory

THE spirit of the factory was felt long before the machine age had evolved. The movement towards a factory method begins when production by a community for its common needs changes into the employment of mass labour by a speculator for an outside market and private profit.

Under the early manorial system village farming was organised primarily for home-production and home-consumption. The lord of the manor required from his tenants tribute of corn, honey, wool or butter and also service on his home farm, but in return villeins or cottars held their own acres of corn in the three open fields and enjoyed rights of grazing, turf- and wood-gathering on the heaths and commons. Until money and better roads made for easier exchange, very little buying or selling was done between villages. Although this localised farming, pursued for many years, was leading to exhaustion of the soil and an increased difficulty in persuading its land to support each community, not until after the Black Death was change really imperative. When a population of perhaps 2,000,000 had been reduced by half, these manorial farms could no longer be worked. The ensuing struggle between lord and peasant for hold on the land has already been noticed. After the abortive Peasants' Revolt of 1381 the villein soon became a landless labourer: in addition, by the first game law of 1389 he lost the right to kill hares, rabbits and partridges in woods and heaths.

With Langland's admonition to all classes to keep to the bond of duty forgotten, and with John Ball's sermon on the text "When Adam dalf and Eve span, Who was then the gentleman" unfulfilled, the times showed a general decline in communal undertaking and an increase in private enterprise. The yeoman farmer, whose aim was to raise cattle and crops for market and to accumulate individual wealth, was developing from the "stock and land" leaseholder. About 1400 the word "farm," which had meant the rent in money or kind produced by the land, came to denote the area of land required to support the occupier. The farm was a man's living rather than a contribution to village economy. For labourers the change was burdensome: their employer imposed their hours of work and their produce went to him. By a statute of 1405 work commenced at 5 a.m. or 7 a.m., and went on until 9 p.m. from mid-March to September, with half an hour for breakfast and one-and-a-half hours for dinner and nap. In the same year the other factor is shown at work in a letter by William to Sir John Paston: "Also I beseech you that ye will see a remedy for the common of Snailswell, for the bailiff of Snailswell and one of the farmers, was with my tutor and me, and shewed me that all the common should be taken away, but for Master Cotton and the Vicar of Fordham." The results of increasing enclosures were visited in two ways on the peasant: he was deprived of employment and his cost of living rose. In his *Utopia*, 1516, More observes "For one shepherd or herdsman is enough to eat up that ground with cattle, to the occupying whereof about husbandry many hands were requisite. And this is also the cause why victuals be now in many places dearer . . . by one means therefore or another, either by hook or by crook they must needs depart away, poor, silly, wretched souls, men, women, husbands, fatherless children, widows, woeful mothers with their young babes, and their whole household small in substance and much in number, as husbandry requireth many hands." Meanwhile the woollen industry grew apace.

Certainly the yeoman farmer had his troubles to bear, but he at any rate could guide his own fortune. When manorial estates were split up some business eyes had seen their opportunity, bought land and run their estate on the sole consideration of a quick return. One method that provoked Latimer's protest was rack-renting. "That which herebefore went for twenty or forty pounds by year—which is an honest portion to be had gratis by another man's sweat and labour—now is let for fifty or a hundred by year" on renewal of lease. On the other hand Tusser in 1557 testifies to the benefit to agriculture of "severall" over and above "champion" land, that is enclosed instead of open fields. The independent farmer could discourage weeds and blights from spreading, could ensure that his stock did not make contact with infected beasts, and could prevent herds overrunning his fields. The strip system was now proved wasteful:—

"In Norfolk, behold the despair
Of tillage, too much to be born,
By drovers from fair to fair,
And others destroying the corn."

The method of common pasturage also often gave rise to confusion:

"Some pester the common with jades and with geese,
With hog without ring and with sheep without fleece:
Some lose a day's labour with seeking their own,
Some meet with a booty they would not have known."

Tusser's example doubtless inspired many a Tudor farmer: now was his opportunity to rise by his own hard efforts to the dignity of "Master" in place of the freeman's appellation of "Goodman."

Meanwhile Ket's rising of 1549 and march to Norwich with demands for the peasants' rights had been crushed in the same way as the 1381 revolt: the landless peasants became a wandering tribe of squatters. After some years laws were passed to prevent the eviction of those who still worked on manorial estates, and it was even laid down that cottages were to be provided with four acres of land: the laws, however, were to be administered by the Quarter Sessions, controlled by the very squires who favoured appropriations! The general indifference of the upper classes to the "base mechanicals" can be seen in Sidney's *Arcadia* and in Spenser. The latter disposed of a giant who sat on a rock preaching communism, "All the world he would weigh equally," by making Sir Artegall cast him into the sea. In the next century the state found it convenient to assume that all labourers had a plot of land, fixed low wages accordingly and let the subsistence level slide. When the price of corn rose in 1572, and from 12s. 1d. a quarter reached eventually 38s. 2d., all who could secured land, even turning grass back to tilth. In vain was to be raised the voice of Gerard Winstanley, declaring that "the Earth must be freed from entanglements of Lords and Landlords to become a common Treasury for all" and denouncing conditions under which "a few covetous proud men should bag and barn up the Treasures of the Earth from others": his followers were dispersed by soldiers.

Henry Best in his *Rural Economy*, 1641, records that he hired free labourers in harvest as mowers at 10d., shearers at 8d., and haymakers at 4d. a day. By an act of 1563 workmen could not leave any parish for other employment without a certificate of lawful departure from a constable and two honest householders. Thus, already landless and underpaid, they were rendered immobile as well. In contrast to this restrictive treatment of the labouring class, the development of the soil's resources was expansive and enlightened. The seventeenth century, with a metropolitan market instead of a local exchange to cater for, produced many handbooks of husbandry: new ideas of fertilising were encouraged and discussed in Evelyn's *Terra*, Dutch cattle cake was introduced, the Bedford level was reclaimed and according to Dugdale's *History of Imbanking and Drayning* great tracts of land from Lincolnshire to Suffolk made productive for the first time. The upheaval of the Civil War, however, delayed the fruition of these experiments until the next century: then with such leaders as Coke of Holkham, Lord Townsend and Arthur Young, English Agriculture made a revolutionary stride: the country was again to be self-supporting in food. Once more enclosures were the order of the day, this time for tillage instead of pasture, and now rapidly devoured that half of the arable land which still remained open, as well as absorbing over 800,000 acres of common. When costs of draining and fencing proved too much for the small farmer, he was forced to sell out to a larger estate and his family helped to swell the ranks of dependent labourers.

> "Times are altered: trade's unfeeling train
> Usurp the land and dispossess the swain."

Agriculture had become a scientific industry: its methods required capital, cheap labour and large estates. Only a reversionary like Aubrey regretted the loss of "a lovely champain, as that about Sherston and Cotswold; very few enclosures, unless near houses: my grandfather Lyte did remember when all between Cromhall and Castle Comb was so, when Easton, Yalton and Comb did inter-common together."

By this time other signs were in the sky. John Leland, in his tour of Worcestershire, is perhaps the first to remark the spoliation of the countryside in the name of industrial progress. He "askyd a saltar how much wood he supposed yearly to be spent at the furnacis, and he answeryd that by estimation ther was spent a 6000 loads by yere. . . . They be forced to seeke wood as far as Worcester towne, and all the parties about

Bremisgrove, Alchirch and Alcester." That was in 1540, and aside Leland added: "The people that be about the fornacis be very ille colorid." In one of the earliest novels of everyday life, *Jack of Newberie*, 1597, Thomas Deloney reveals the grievances of woollen weavers. When England and France were at war, trade with the low countries came to a standstill and so "the Clothiers had most of their cloath lying on their hands, and that which they sold was at so low a rate that the money scantly paid for the wooll and workemanship. Whereupon they sought to ease themselves by abating the poore workemen's wages. And when that did not prevaile, they turnd away many of their people, Weavers, Shearmen, Spinsters and Carders, so that where there was a hundred Looms kept in one towne, there was scant fifty: and hee that kept twenty put downe tenne. . . . This bred great woe in most places in England." About the middle of the next century John Evelyn felt new concern for a nation "whose only protection (under God) are her wooden walls" when he considered "the prodigious waste which these voracious iron and glass works have formerly made but in one county alone, the county of Sussex, for 120 miles in length and thirty in breadth (for so wide and spacious was the ancient Andradswald, of old one entire wood, but of which there remains now little or no sign.)" With its effects thus foreshadowed the Industrial Revolution now darkened the land. The factory system, it has been argued, was already applied to agriculture: henceforward the issue of farm *v.* factory was thrown into sharper focus. With the increasing convergence of population into manufacturing towns, large new markets were opened for the farmer, competition grew keener and again the small man was squeezed out. Arthur Young, himself the advocate of enclosure, regretted its effect on the labourer: without pasturage, garden or living wage he was in a desperate position. "Go to an alehouse kitchen of an old enclosed country, and there you will see the origin of poverty and poor rates. For whom are they to be sober? For whom are they to save? (Such are their questions.) For the parish? If I am diligent shall I have leave to build a cottage? If I am sober, shall I have land for a cow? If I am frugal shall I have half an acre of potatoes? You offer no motives: you have nothing but a parish officer and a workhouse! Bring me another pot . . ." The more machinery there was employed, the less again were the labourer's subsidiary handicrafts able to command a local sale and ward off penury. So began the drift of the country worker to the town: and so the opportunity was given for the manufacturer to secure labour, dependent, cheap and unprotected by legislation. As Goldsmith wrote of another occasion:

> "Into the city sped—what waits him there?
> To see profusion that he must not share!
> To see ten thousand baneful arts combin'd
> To pamper luxury and thin mankind."

This is not the place to investigate the abuses of the industrial nineteenth century or to recount the struggles towards Unions and enfranchisement of the agricultural employee. To set down from the pages of the novel the living and working conditions of those on the land and in the factory, as seen by the eyes both of critic and sentimentalist, will enable the discerning to balance the account of progress. Here also the effect of industrial development and agricultural encroachment may be observed on the face of the land. The possibility of home industry and a landed peasantry may have vanished for ever, but it is at least instructive to contemplate the mode of its passing. Defoe and Cobbett, although separated by a century, give complementary pictures of a centralised industry. The general conditions that incensed the Luddites are dramatically recorded by Mrs. Gaskell and Charlotte Brontë. While Mary Mitford's nostalgic pastoral is fresh to the mind, it may be well to recall with Kingsley the actualities that provided agriculture with its Tolpuddle martyrs, or to join for a moment Hardy's stacking gang. The personal response to farm or factory work is further suggested by Galsworthy and by Street, who adopts a less idyllic attitude without disparaging Mary Webb. Apparently Cobbett liked Hull, but it hardly needs the mnemonic "From Hell, Hull and Halifax, Good Lord deliver us" to bring to mind many such infernal regions as the Swansea of Borrow's day or Bursley of our own. Two travellers with shrewd eyes for the vagaries of human existence and a robust habit of saying what they think, will serve to link the two centuries under survey: J. B. Priestley and John Byng both saw a countryside stricken by the hand of greed and power: their reactions supply a measure by which this changing England may be brought to rule.

22 The Industrialisation of a Yorkshire Dale: Todmorden, on the Calder, in 1845

After A. F. Tait

23 The Rural Peace of a Yorkshire Dale: Rosedale, with its Abbey, in 1843

After W. Richardson

24 Haymakers

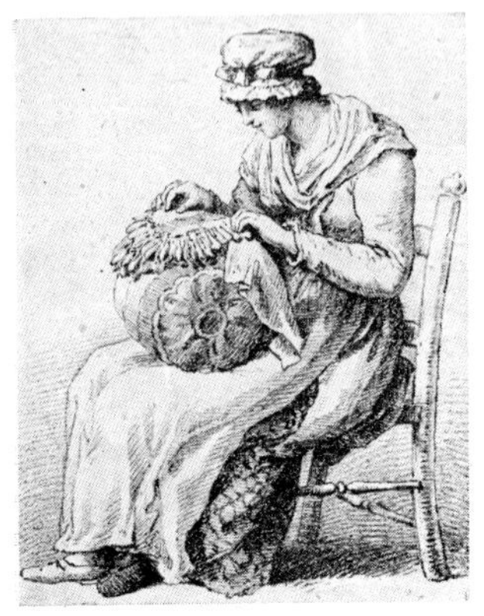

25 The Lace-maker

26 The Cottage Loom

27 The Cottagers' Evening Meal

Village Life in the Early Nineteenth Century
After W. H. Pyne

Norwich Weaving

When we come into Norfolk, we see a face of diligence spread over the whole country; the vast manufactures carry'd on (in chief) by the Norwich weavers, employs all the country round in spinning yarn for them; besides many thousand packs of yarn which they receive from other countries, even from as far as Yorkshire, and Westmoreland, of which I shall speak in its place.

This side of Norfolk is very populous, and throng'd with great and spacious market-towns, more and larger than any other part of England so far from London, except Devonshire, and the West-riding of Yorkshire.

An eminent weaver of Norwich, gave me a scheme of their trade on this occasion, by which, calculating from the number of looms at that time employ'd in the city of Norwich only, besides those employ'd in other towns in the same county, he made it appear very plain, that there were 120,000 people employ'd in the woollen and silk and wool manufactures of that city only, not that the people all lived in the city, tho' Norwich is a very large and populous city too: But I say, they were employ'd for spinning the yarn used for such goods as were all made in that city. This account is curious enough, and very exact, but it is too long for the compass of this work.

This shews the wonderful extent of the Norwich manufacture, or stuff-weaving trade, by which so many thousands of families are maintained. Their trade indeed felt a very sensible decay, and the cries of the poor began to be very loud, when the wearing of painted callicoes was grown to such an height in England, as was seen about two or three years ago; but an Act of Parliament having been obtained, tho' not without great struggle, in the years 1720 and 1721, for prohibiting the use and wearing of callico's, the stuff trade reviv'd incredibly; and as I pass'd this part of the country in the year 1723, the manufacturers assured me, that there was not in all the eastern and middle part of Norfolk, any hand, unemploy'd, if they would work; and that the very children after four or five years of age, could every one earn their own bread.

Norwich is the capital of all the county, and the center of all the trade and manufactures which I have just mention'd; an antient, large, rich, and populous city. If a stranger was only to ride thro' or view the city of Norwich for a day, he would have much more reason to think there was a town without inhabitants, than there is really to say so of Ipswich; but on the contrary, if he was to view the city, either on a Sabbath-day, or on any publick occasion, he would wonder where all the people could dwell, the multitude is so great; but the case is this; the inhabitants being all busie at their manufactures, dwell in their garretts at their looms, and in their combing-shops, so they call them, twisting-mills, and other work-houses; almost all the works they are employ'd in, being done within doors.

DANIEL DE FOE *A Tour Through England*, 1724

The Peasantry's Eclipse

THOSE who travell with fashionable haste, (or slowly for the first time,) will not discover the decrease of halls, farms, and cottages; but I well-acquainted with the county of Bedford can sigh over the decay of its yeomanry and cottages: so may I suppose of this county; and most wretchedly does Hamerton proclaim it.—To be convinced that such houses were, (in opposition to some who fancy otherwise,) let them observe the numbers of small, narrow enclosures, formerly, and severally, belonging to the cottages; of these, the hedges are, for the most part, stock'd up, tho' some banks or trees mark the line. Where any apple or walnut or plum trees remain, you may be certain there was an orchard; and a well, cover'd over, or choak'd up, leaves no doubt of a building having been near: of these, and such like remembrances, what numbers I could shew.—How should the poor exist, when the landlord that should protect, and support them, is gone off to reside in Marybone-Parish; whilst of his formerly squirelike place nothing remains but some decay'd garden walls.

How wisely did the fost'ring hand of ancestry provide for the poor, by an allotment of a cottage right of common in the open fields; the village green before their door; the orchard adjoining the house; and the long close behind it!—These two latter being seiz'd by the greedy farmer, and the two former being forced from them by the hand of power (upon some inadequate infamous bargain) has driven away the poor; has levell'd the cottage; has impoverish'd the country; and must, finally, ruin it. When the gentle perspiration, and the smaller ducts of the human body are stopt; with difficulty, and pain, will the larger vessells pant to the heart; and idly may the possessor brag of his bone and his courage.—

I, sometimes, perceive a large farm rebuilt; and a violent addition of barns, adequate to the increase of the farmers land, and rent: but where do you perceive a revival, or renewal of comfortable cottages, and to be kept by a proper portion of land alloted to them? For without that, it becomes a cruel fantasy to decorate without, what you must know to be miserable within; it is like the skinning over a sore, without properly probing the wound.—

HON. JOHN BYNG *A Tour into Lincolnshire*, 1791

Industrial Depopulation

AFTER Cheltenham we had to reach this pretty little town of Fairford, the regular turnpike road to which lay through Cirencester; but I had from a fine map, at Sir Thomas Winnington's, traced out a line for us along through a chain of villages, leaving Cirencester away to our right, and never coming nearer than seven or eight miles to it. We came through Dodeswell, Withington, Chedworth, Winston, and the two Colnes. At Dodeswell we came up a long and steep hill, which brought us out of the great vale of Gloucester and up upon the Cotswold Hills, which name is tautological, I believe; for I think that *wold* meant *high lands of great extent*.

How melancholy is the sight of these decayed and still decaying villages in the dells of the Cotswold, where the building materials being stone, the ruins do not totally disappear for ages! The village of Withington (mentioned above) has a church like a small cathedral, and the whole of the population is now only 603 persons, men, women and children! So that according to the Scotch fellows, this immense and fine church, which is as sound as it was 700 or 800 years ago, was built by and for a population containing, at most, only about 120 grown-up and able-bodied men! But here, in this once populous village, or I think town, you see *all* the indubitable marks of most melancholy decay. There are several lanes, crossing each other, which *must* have been *streets* formerly. There is a large open space where the principal streets meet. There are, against this open place, two large, old, roomy houses, with gateways into back parts of them, and with large stone *upping-*

blocks against the walls of them in the street. These were manifestly considerable *inns*, and in this open place markets or fairs or both, used to be held. I asked two men, who were threshing in a barn, how long it was since their public-house was put down or dropped. They told me about sixteen years. One of these men, who was about fifty years of age, could remember *three* public-houses, one of which was what was called an *inn!* The place stands by the side of a little brook, which here rises, or rather issues, from a high hill, and which, when it has winded down for some miles, and through several villages, begins to be called the River Colne, and continues on, under this name, through Fairford and along, I suppose, till it falls into the Thames. Withington is very prettily situated; it was, and not very long ago, a gay and happy place; but it now presents a picture of dilapidation and shabbiness scarcely to be equalled. Here are the yet visible remains of two gentlemen's houses. Great farmers have supplied their place as to inhabiting; and I dare say that some tax-eater, or some blaspheming Jew, or some still more base and wicked loan-mongering robber is now the owner of the land; aye, and all these people are his *slaves* as completely, and more to their wrong, than the blacks are the slaves of the planters in Jamaica, the farmers here acting, in fact, in a capacity corresponding with that of the negro drivers there.

A part, and perhaps a considerable part, of the decay and misery of this place is owing to the use of *machinery*, and to the *monopolising* in the manufacture of blankets, of which fabric the town of Witney was the centre, and from which town the wool used to be sent round to, and the yarn, or warp, come back from, all these Cotswold villages, and quite into a part of Wiltshire. Where manufacturing is mixed with agriculture, where the wife and daughters are at the needle, or the wheel, while the men and the boys are at plough, and where the manufacturing, of which one or two towns are the centres, is spread over the whole country round about, and particularly where it is, in very great part, performed by females at their *own homes*, and where the earnings come *in aid of the man's wages;* in such case the misery cannot be so great. This work is all now gone, and so the women and the girls are a "surplus *popalashon*, *mon*," and are, of course, to be dealt with by the "Emigration Committee" of the "Collective Wisdom!" There were, only a few years ago, above thirty blanket-manufacturers at Witney: twenty-five of these have been swallowed up by the five that now have all the manufacture in their hands! And all this has been done by that system of gambling and of fictitious money, which has conveyed property from the hands of the many into the hands of the few.

William Cobbett *Rural Rides*, 1830

Pastoral Methods

Amongst the country employments of England none is so delightful to see or to think of as haymaking. It comes in the pleasantest season, amidst a green, and flowery, and sunshine world; it has for scene the prettiest places—park, or lawn, or meadow, or upland pasture; and withal it has more of innocent merriment, more of the festivity of an out-of-door sport, and less of the drudgery and weariness of actual labour, than any other of the occupations of husbandry. One looks on it, pretty picture as it is, without the almost saddening sympathy produced by the slow and painful toil of the harvest-field, and, moreover, one looks on it much oftener. A very little interval of dressed garden shall divide a great country mansion from the demesne, where hay-cocks repose under noble groups of oaks and elms, or mingle their fragrance with the snowy wreaths of the acacia, or the honeyed tassels of the lime; and the fair and delicate lady who cannot tell wheat from barley, and the mincing fine gentleman who "affects an *ignorance* if he have it not," shall yet condescend not merely to know hay when they see it, but even to take some interest in the process of getting it up.

Last summer was, as most of my readers probably remember, one of no small trial to haymakers in general, the weather being what is gently and politely termed "unsettled," which in this pretty climate of ours, during "the leafy month of June," may commonly be construed into cloudy, stormy, drizzly, cold. In this instance the silky, courtly, flattering epithet, being translated, could hardly mean other than wet—fixed, determined, settled rain. Sheridan's wicked interpolation in Mr. Coleridge's tragedy, "drip, drip, drip, there's nothing here but dripping," seemed made expressly for the season. Cut or uncut, the grass was spoiling; the more the hay was made the clearer it appeared that it would never make to any purpose; the poor cattle shook their ears as if aware of an impending scarcity;

salt, the grand remedy for sopped hay, rose in the market; "farmers fretted, and gentlemen fumed."

So passed the "merry month of June." Towards the beginning of July, however, matters mended. Encouraged by the slow, gentle rising of the weather-glass, which the knowing in such matters affirm to be much more reliable than a sudden and violent jump of the quicksilver, we gave orders to cut the little mead without delay, and prepared for a day's haymaking in that favourite spot.

Our good neighbour the shoemaker, an in-door oracle, whose speculations on the atmosphere are not very remarkable for their correctness, prognosticated wet; whilst our other good neighbour, Farmer Bridgwater, an out-of-door practical personage, whose predictions—and it is saying much for them —are almost as sure to come true as the worthy cordwainer's to prove false, boldly asseverated that the day would prove fine, and made his preparations and mustered his troops (for Farmer Bridgwater is generalissimo in our hay-field) with a vigour and energy that would have become a higher occasion. He set six men on to mowing by a little after sunrise, and collected fourteen efficient haymakers by breakfast-time. Fourteen active haymakers for our poor three acres! not to count the idle assistants; we ourselves, with three dogs and two boys to mind them, advisers who came to find fault and look on, babies who came to be nursed, children who came to rock the babies, and other children who came to keep the rockers company and play with the dogs; to say nothing of this small rabble, we had fourteen able-bodied men and women in one hay-field, besides the six mowers who had got the grass down by noon, and finding the strong beer good and plentiful, magnanimously volunteered to stay and help to get in the crop. N.B.—This abundance of aid is by no means so extravagant as it seems, especially in catching weather. Beer, particularly in country affairs, will go twice as far as money, and, if discreetly administered (for we must not make even haymakers quite tipsy), really goes as near to supply the place of the sun as anything well can do. In our case the good double X was seconded by this bright luminary, and our operations prospered accordingly.

MARY MITFORD *Our Village*, 1832

A Factory Riot

It was now the middle of the month of February; by six o'clock therefore, dawn was just beginning to steal on night, to penetrate with a pale ray its brown obscurity, and give a demi-translucence to its opaque shadows. Pale enough that ray was on this particular morning; no colour tinged the east, no flush warmed it.

The mill-windows were alight, the bell still rung loud, and now the little children came running in, in too great a hurry, let us hope, to feel very much nipped by the inclement air; and, indeed, by contrast, perhaps the morning appeared rather favourable to them than otherwise; for they had often come to their work that winter through snow-storms, through heavy rain, through hard frost.

Mr. Moore stood at the entrance to watch them pass: he counted them as they went by; to those who came rather late he said a word of reprimand, which was a little more sharply repeated by Joe Scott when the lingerers reached the work-rooms. Neither master nor overlooker spoke savagely; they were not savage men either of them, though it appeared both were rigid, for they fined a delinquent who came considerably too late: Mr. Moore made him pay his penny down ere he entered, and informed him that the next repetition of the fault would cost him twopence.

Rules, no doubt, are necessary in such cases, and coarse and cruel masters will make coarse and cruel rules, which, at the time we treat of at least, they used sometimes to enforce tyrannically; but, though I describe imperfect characters (every character in this book will be found to be more or less imperfect, my pen refusing to draw anything in the model line), I have not undertaken to handle degraded or utterly infamous ones. Child-torturers, slave masters and drivers, I consign to the hands of jailers; the novelist may be excused from sullying his page with the record of his deeds.

Mr. Moore haunted his mill, his mill-yard, his dye-house, and his warehouse, till the sickly dawn strengthened into day. The sun even rose,—at least a white disk, clear, tintless, and almost chill-looking as ice,—peeped over the darkness of a hill, changed to silver the livid edge of the cloud above it, and looked solemnly down the whole length of the den, or narrow dale, to whose strait bounds we are at present limited. It was eight o'clock; the mill lights were all extinguished; the signal was given for breakfast; the children, released for half an hour from toil, betook themselves to the little tin cans which held their coffee, and to the small baskets which contained their allowance of bread. Let us hope they have enough to eat; it would be a pity were it otherwise.

Moore went out, chuckling drily. He advanced into the yard, one hand in his pocket, the other in his waistcoat, his cap brim over his eyes, shading in some measure their deep dancing ray of scorn. Twelve men waited in the yard, some in their shirt-sleeves, some in blue aprons: two figured conspicuously in the van of the party. One, a little dapper strutting man, with a turned-up nose: the other, a broad-shouldered fellow, distinguished no less by his demure face and cat-like, trustless eyes, than by a wooden leg and stout crutch: there was a kind of leer about his lips, he seemed laughing in his sleeve at some person or thing, his whole air was anything but that of a true man.

"Good morning, Mr. Barraclough," said Moore debonairly, for him.

"Peace be unto you!" was the answer: Mr. Barraclough entirely closing his naturally half-shut eyes as he delivered it.

"I'm obliged to you: peace is an excellent thing; there's nothing I more wish for myself; but that is not all you have to say to me, I suppose? I imagine peace is not your purpose?"

"Or iver you set up the pole o' your tent amang us, Mr. Moore, we lived i' peace and quietness; yea, I may say, in all loving-kindness. I am not myself an aged person as yet, but I can remember as far back as maybe some twenty year, when hand-labour were encouraged and respected, and no mischief-maker had ventured to introduce these here machines, which is so pernicious. Now, I am not a cloth-dresser myself, but by trade a tailor; howsiver, my heart is of a softish natur': I'm a very feeling man, and when I see my brethren oppressed, like my great namesake of old, I stand up for 'em; for which intent, I this day speak with you face to face, and advises you to part wi' your infernal machinery and tak' on more hands."

"What if I don't follow your advice, Mr. Barraclough?"

"The Looard pardon you! The Looard soften your heart, sir!"

"Are you in connection with the Wesleyans now, Mr. Barraclough?"

"Praise God! Bless His name! I'm a joined Methody!"

28, 29, 30 Yorkshire Factory Children and Workers of the Industrial Revolution (*ca.* 1814)

After G. Walker

31 Ironworks at Coalbrookdale, Shropshire, in 1805
After P. J. de Loutherbourg, R.A.

"Which in no respect prevents you from being at the same time a drunkard and a swindler. I saw you one night a week ago laid dead-drunk by the road-side, as I returned from Stilbro' market; and while you preach peace, you make it the business of your life to stir up dissension."

Barraclough was going to speak.

"Silence! You have had your say, and now I will have mine. As to being dictated to by you or any Jack, Jem or Jonathan on earth, I shall not suffer it for a moment. You desire me to quit the country: you request me to part with my machinery; in case I refuse, you threaten me. I *do* refuse—point-blank! Here I stay; and by this mill I stand; and into it will I convey the best machinery inventors can furnish. What will you do? The utmost you *can* do—and this you will never *dare* to do—is to burn down my mill, destroy its contents, and shoot me. What then? Suppose that building was a ruin and I was a corpse, what then? You lads behind these two scamps, would that stop invention or exhaust science?—Not for the fraction of a second of time! Another and better gig mill would rise on the ruins of this, and perhaps a more enterprising owner come in my place. Hear me!—I'll make my cloth as I please, and according to the best lights I have. In its manufacture I will employ what means I choose. Whoever, after hearing this, shall dare to interfere with me, may just take the consequences. An example shall prove I'm in earnest."

He whistled shrill and loud. Sugden, his staff and warrant, came on to the scene.

Moore turned sharply to Barraclough: "You were at Stilbro'," said he; "I have proof of that. You were on the moor, —you wore a mask,—you knocked down one of my men with your own hand,—you! a preacher of the Gospel! Sugden, arrest him!"

Moses was captured. There was a cry and a rush to rescue, but the right hand which all this while had lain hidden in Moore's breast, reappearing, held out a pistol.

"Both barrels are loaded," said he. "I'm quite determined! —keep off!"

Stepping backwards, facing the foe as he went, he guarded his prey to the counting-house. He ordered Joe Scott to pass in with Sugden and the prisoner, and to bolt the door inside.

* * * * *

A crash—smash—shiver—stopped their whispers. A simultaneously-hurled volley of stones had saluted the broad front of the mill, with all its windows; and now every pane of every lattice lay in shattered and pounded fragments. A yell followed this demonstration—a rioters' yell—a North-of-England—a Yorkshire—a West-Riding—a West-Riding-clothing-district-of-Yorkshire rioters' yell. You never heard that sound, perhaps, reader? So much the better for your ears—perhaps for your heart.

What was going on now? It seemed difficult to distinguish, but something terrible, a still-renewing tumult, was obvious: fierce attacks, desperate repulses; the mill-yard, the mill itself, was full of battle movement: there was scarcely any cessation now of the discharge of firearms; and there was struggling, rushing, trampling, and shouting between. The aim of the assailants seemed to be to enter the mill, that of the defendants to beat them off. They heard the rebel leader cry, "To the back, lads!" They heard a voice retort, "Come round, we will meet you!"

"To the counting-house!" was the order again.

"Welcome!—We shall have you there!" was the response. And accordingly, the fiercest blaze that had yet glowed, the loudest rattle that had yet been heard, burst from the counting-house front, when the mass of rioters rushed up to it.

Moore had expected this attack for days, perhaps weeks: he was prepared for it at every point. He had fortified and garrisoned his mill, which in itself was a strong building: he was a cool, brave man: he stood to the defence with unflinching firmness; those who were with him caught his spirit, and copied his demeanour. The rioters had never been so met before. At other mills they had attacked, they had found no resistance; an organised, resolute defence was what they never dreamed of encountering. When their leaders saw the steady fire kept up from the mill, witnessed the composure and determination of its owner, heard themselves coolly defied and invited on to death, and beheld their men falling wounded round them, they felt that nothing was to be done here. In haste, they mustered their forces, drew them away from the building: a roll was called over, in which the men answered to figures instead of names: they dispersed wide over the fields, leaving silence and ruin behind them. The attack, from its commencement to its termination, had not occupied an hour.

It was no cheering spectacle: these premises were now a mere blot of desolation on the fresh front of the dawn. All the copse up the Hollow was shady and dewy, the hill at its head was green; but just here in the centre of the sweet glen, Discord, broken loose in the night from control, had beaten the ground with his stamping hoofs, and left it waste and pulverised. The mill yawned all ruinous with unglazed frames; the yard was thickly bestrewn with stones and brickbats, and, close under the mill, with the glittering fragments of the shattered windows, muskets and other weapons lay here and there; more than one deep crimson stain was visible on the gravel; a human body lay quiet on its face near the gates; and five or six wounded men writhed and moaned in the bloody dust.

CHARLOTTE BRONTË *Shirley*, 1849

Agricultural Malcontents

I ARRIVED in the midst of a dreary, treeless country whose broad brown and grey fields were only broken by an occasional line of dark, doleful firs, at a knot of thatched hovels, all sinking and leaning every way but the right, the windows patched with paper, the doorways stopped with filth, which surrounded a beer-shop. That was my destination—unpromising enough for anyone but an agitator.

About eight o'clock the next morning I started forth with my guide, the shoemaker, over as desolate a country as man can well conceive. Not a house was to be seen for miles, except the knot of hovels which we had left, and here and there a great lump of farm-buildings, with its yard of yellow stacks. Beneath our feet the earth was iron, and the sky iron above our heads. Dark curdled clouds, "which had built up everywhere an under-roof of doleful grey," swept on before the bitter northern wind, which whistled through the low leafless hedges and rotting wattles, and crisped the dark sodden leaves of the scattered hollies, almost the only trees in sight.

We trudged on, over wide stubbles, with innumerable weeds; over wide fallows, in which the deserted ploughs stood frozen fast; then over clover and grass, burnt black with frost; then over a field of turnips, where we passed a large fold of hurdles, within which some hundred sheep stood, with their heads turned from the cutting blast. One wondered where the people lived, who cultivated so vast a tract of civilised, over-peopled, nineteenth-century England.

With such thoughts I walked across the open down, toward a circular camp, the earthwork, probably, of some old British town. Inside it, some thousand or so of labouring people were swarming restlessly round a single large block of stone, some relic of Druid times, on which a tall man stood, his dark figure thrown out in bold relief against the dreary sky. As we pushed through the crowd, I was struck with the wan, haggard look of all faces; their lacklustre eyes and drooping lips, stooping shoulders, heavy, dragging steps, gave them a crushed, dogged air, which was infinitely painful, and bespoke a grade of misery more habitual and degrading than that of the excitable and passionate artisan.

They glared with sullen curiosity at me and my Londoner's clothes, as, with no small feeling of self-importance, I pushed my way to the foot of the stone. The man who stood on it seemed to have been speaking some time.

"—The farmers make slaves on us. I can't hear no difference between a Christian and a nigger, except they flogs the niggers and starves the Christians; and I don't know which I'd choose. I served Farmer —— seven year, off and on, and arter harvest he tells me he's no more work for me, nor my boy nether, acause he's getting too big for him, so he gets a little 'un instead, and we does nothing; and my boy lies about, getting into bad ways, like hundreds more; and then we goes to board, and they bids us go and look for work; and we goes up next part to London. I couldn't get none; they'd enough to do, they said, to employ their own; and we begs our way home, and goes into the Union; and they turns us out again in two or three days, and promises us work again, and gives us two days' gravel-picking, and then says they has no more for us; and we was sore pinched, and laid a-bed all day; then next board day we goes to 'em and they gives us one day more—and that threw us off another week, and then next board-day we goes into the Union again for three days, and gets sent out again: and so I've been starving one-half of the time, and they putting us off and on o' purpose like that; and I'll bear it no longer, and that's what I says."

He came down, and a tall, powerful, well-fed man, evidently in his Sunday smock-frock and clean yellow leggings, got up and began:—

"I hav'n't no complaint to make about myself. I've a good master, and the parson's a right kind 'un, and that's more than all can say, and the squire's a real gentleman; and my master, he don't need to lower his wages. I gets my ten shillings a week all the year round, and harvesting, and a pig, and a 'lotment—and that's just why I come here. If I can get it, why can't you?

"'Cause our masters baint like yourn."

"No, by George, there baint no money round here like that, I can tell you."

"And why ain't they?" continued the speaker. "There's the shame on it. There's my master can grow five quarters where yourn only grows three; and so he can live and pay like a man; and so he say he don't care for free trade. You know, as well as I, that there's not half o' the land round here grows what it ought. They ain't no money to make it grow more, and besides, they won't employ no hands to keep it clean. I come across more weeds in one field here, than I've seen for nine year on our farm. Why arn't some of you a-getting they weeds up? It 'ud pay 'em to farm better—and they knows that, but they're too lazy; if they can just get a living off the land, they don't care; and they'd sooner save money out of your wages, than save it by growing more corn—it's easier for 'em, it is. There's the work to be done, and they won't let you do it. There's you crying out for work, and work crying out for you—and neither of you can get to the other. I say that's a shame, I do. I say a poor man's a slave. He daren't leave his parish—nobody won't employ him, as can employ his own folk. And if he stays in his own parish, it's just a chance whether he gets a good master or a bad 'un. He can't choose, and that's a shame, it is. Why should he go starving because his master don't care to do the best by the land? If they can't till the land, I say let them get out of it and let them work it as can. And I think as we ought all to sign a petition to government, to tell 'em all about it; though I don't see as how they could help us, unless they'd make a law to force the squires to put in nobody to a farm as hasn't money to work it fairly."

"I says," said the next speaker, a poor fellow whose sentences were continually broken by a hacking cough, "just what he said. If they can't till the land, let them do it as can. But they won't; they won't let us have a scrap on it, though we'd pay 'em more for it nor ever they'd make for themselves. But they says it 'ud make us too independent, if we had an acre or so o' land; and so it 'ud for they. And so I says as he did—they want to make slaves on us altogether, just to get the flesh and bones off us at their own price. Look at this here down.—If I had an acre on it, to make a garden on, I'd live well with my wages, off and on. Why, if this here was in garden, it 'ud be worth twenty, forty times o' that it be now. And last spring I lays out o' work from Christmas till barley-sowing, and I goes to the farmer and axes for a bit o' land to dig and plant a few potatoes—and he says, 'You be d——d! If you're minding your garden after hours, you'll not be fit to do a proper day's work for me in hours—and I shall want you by and by, when the weather breaks'—for it was frost most bitter, it was. 'And if you gets potatoes, you'll be getting a pig—and then you'll want straw, and meal to fat 'un—and then I'll not trust you in my barn, I can tell ye'; and so there it was. And if I'd had only one half-acre of this here very down as we stands on, as isn't worth five shillings a year—and I'd a given ten shillings for it—my belly wouldn't a been empty now."

"Gentlemen!" cried my guide, the shoemaker, in a somewhat conceited and dictatorial tone, as he skipped up by the speaker's side, and gently shouldered him down, "you just take my advice, and sign a round robin to the squires—you tell 'em as you're willing to till the land for 'em, if they'll let you. There's draining and digging enough to be done as 'ud keep ye all in work, arn't there?"

"Ay, ay; there's lots o' work to be done, if so be we could get at it. Everybody knows that."

"Well, you tell 'em that. Tell 'em here's hundreds, and hundreds of ye starving, and willing to work; and then tell 'em, if they won't find ye work, they shall find ye meat. There's lots o' victuals in their larders now; haven't you as good a right to it as their jackanapes o' footmen? The squires is at the bottom of it all. What do you stupid fellows go grumbling at the farmers for? Don't they squires tax the land twenty or thirty shillings an acre; and what do they do for that? The best of 'em, if he gets five thousand a year out o' the land, don't give back five hundred in charity, or schools, or poor-rates—and what's that to speak of? And the main of 'em—curse 'em!—they drains the money out o' the land, and takes it up to London, or into foreign parts, to spend on fine clothes and fine dinners; or throws it away at elections, to make folks beastly drunk, and sell their souls for money—and we gets no good on it. I'll tell you what it's come to, my men—that we can't afford no more landlords. We can't afford 'em, and that's the truth of it."

The crowd growled a dubious assent.

A tall, fierce man, with a forbidding squint, sprung jauntily on the stone, and setting his arms akimbo, broke out:—

"Here be I, Blinkey, and I has as good a right to speak as ere a one. You're all blarned fools, you are. You sticks like pigs in a gate, hollering and squeeking, and never helping yourselves. Why can't you do like me? I never does no work—darned if I'll work to please the farmers. The rich folks robs me, and I robs them, and that's fair and equal. You only turn poachers—you only go stealing turmits, and fire-ud, and all as you can find—and then you'll not need to work. Arn't it yourn? The game's no one's, is it now?—you know that. And if you takes turmits or corn they're yourn—you helped to grow 'em. And if you're put to prison, I tell ye, it's a darned deal warmer, and better victuals too, than ever a one of you gets at home, let alone the Union. Oh, you blockheads!—to stand here shivering with empty bellies.—You just go down to the farm and burn they stacks over the old rascal's head; and then they that let you starve now, will be forced to keep you then. If you can't get your share of the poor-rates, try the county-rates, my bucks—you can get fat on them at the Queen's expense—and that's more than you'll do in ever a Union as I hear on. Who'll come down and pull the farm about the folks' ears? Warn't it he as turned five on yer off last week? and ain't he more corn there than 'ud feed you all round this day, and won't sell it, just because he's waiting till folks are starved enough, and prices rise? Curse the old villain!—who'll help to disappoint him o' that? Come along!"

CHARLES KINGSLEY *Alton Locke*, 1850

Trade Effects

FOR several miles before they reached Milton, they saw a deep lead-coloured cloud hanging over the horizon in the direction in which it lay. It was all the darker from contrast with the pale grey-blue of the wintry sky. Nearer to the town, the air had a faint taste and smell of smoke; perhaps, after all, more a loss of the fragrance of grass and herbage than any positive taste or smell. Quickly they were whirled over long, straight, hopeless streets of regularly-built houses, all small and of brick. Here and there a great oblong many-windowed factory stood up, like a hen among her chickens, puffing out black "unparliamentary" smoke and sufficiently accounting for the cloud which Margaret had taken to foretell rain. As they drove through the larger and wider streets, from the station to the hotel, they had to stop constantly; great loaded lorries blocked up the not over-wide thoroughfares. Margaret had now and then been into the city in her drives with her aunt. But there the heavy lumbering vehicles seemed various in their purposes and intent; here every van, every wagon and truck, bore cotton, either in the raw shape in bags, or the woven shape in bales of calico.

"New Street," said Mr. Hale. "This, I believe, is the principal street in Milton. Bell has often spoken to me about it. It was the opening of this street from a lane into a great thoroughfare, which has caused his property to rise so much in value."

"Seventy years ago," said Mr. Thornton "what was it? And now what is it not? Raw, crude materials came together; men of the same level, as regarded education and station, took suddenly the different positions of masters and men, owing to the mother-wit, as regarded opportunities and probabilities, which distinguished some, and made them far-seeing as to what great future lay concealed in that rude model of Sir Richard Arkwright's. The rapid development of what might be called a new trade, gave those early masters enormous power of wealth and command. I don't mean merely over the workmen; I mean over purchasers—over the whole world's market. Why, I may give you, as an instance, an advertisement inserted not fifty years ago in a Milton paper, that so-and-so (one of the half-dozen calico-printers of the time) would close his warehouse at noon each day; therefore, that all purchasers must come before that hour. Fancy a man dictating in this manner the time when he would sell and when he would not sell. Now, I believe, if a good customer chose to come at midnight, I should get up, and stand hat in hand to receive his orders."

Margaret's lip curled, but somehow she was compelled to listen; she could no longer abstract herself in her own thoughts.

"I only name such things to show what almost unlimited power the manufacturers had about the beginning of this century. The men were rendered dizzy by it. Because a man was successful in his ventures, there was no reason that in all other things his mind should be well balanced. On the contrary, his sense of justice, and his simplicity, were often utterly smothered under the glut of wealth that came down upon him; and they tell strange tales of the wild extravagance of living indulged in on gala-days by those early cotton-lords. There can be no doubt, too, of the tyranny they exercised over their work-people. You know the proverb, Mr. Hale, 'Set a beggar on horseback, and he'll ride to the devil'—well, some of these early manufacturers did ride to the devil in a magnificent style—crushing human bone and flesh under their horses' hoofs without remorse. But by and by came a reaction; there were more factories, more masters; more men were wanted. The power of masters and men became more evenly balanced; and now the battle is pretty fairly waged between us. We will hardly submit to the decision of an umpire, much less to the interference of a meddler with only a smattering of the knowledge of the real facts of the case, even though that meddler be called the High Court of Parliament."

ELIZABETH GASKELL *North and South*, 1855

The Path of Industry

IT was about two o'clock of a dull and gloomy afternoon when I started from Abertawy or Swansea, intending to stop at Neath, some eight miles distant. As I passed again through the suburbs I was struck with their length and the evidences of enterprise which they exhibited—enterprise, however, evidently chiefly connected with iron and coal, for almost every object looked awfully grimy. Crossing a bridge I proceeded to the east up a broad and spacious valley, the eastern side of which was formed by russet-coloured hills, through a vista of which I could descry a range of tall blue mountains. As I proceeded I sometimes passed pleasant groves and hedgerows, sometimes huge works; in this valley there was a singular mixture of nature and art, of the voices of birds and the clanking of chains, of the mists of heaven and the smoke of furnaces.

I reached Llan——, a small village halfway between Swansea and Neath, and without stopping continued my course, walking very fast. I had surmounted a hill, and had nearly descended that side of it which looked towards the east, having on my left, that is to the north, a wooded height, when an extraordinary scene presented itself to my eyes. Somewhat to the south rose immense stacks of chimneys surrounded by grimy diabolical-looking buildings, in the neighbourhood of which were huge heaps of cinders and black rubbish. From the chimneys, notwithstanding it was Sunday, smoke was proceeding in volumes, choking the atmosphere all around. From this pandemonium, at the distance of about a quarter of a mile to the south-west, upon a green meadow, stood, looking darkly grey, a ruin of vast size with window holes, towers, spires, and arches. Between it and the accursed pandemonium, lay a horrid filthy place, part of which was swamp and part pool: the pool black as soot, and the swamp of a disgusting leaden colour. Across this place of filth stretched a tramway leading seemingly from the abominable mansions to the ruin. So strange a scene I had never beheld in nature. Had it been on canvas, with the addition of a number of diabolical figures, proceeding along the tramway, it might have stood for Sabbath in Hell—devils proceeding to afternoon worship, and would have formed a picture worthy of the powerful but insane painter, Jerome Bos.

After standing for a considerable time staring at the strange spectacle I proceeded. Presently meeting a lad, I asked him what was the name of the ruin.

"The Abbey," he replied.

"Neath Abbey?" said I.

"Yes!"

George Borrow *Wild Wales*, 1862

Field Labour

It is the threshing of the last wheat-rick at Flintcomb-Ash Farm. The dawn of the March morning is singularly inexpressive, and there is nothing to show where the eastern horizon lies. Against the twilight rises the trapezoidal top of the stack, which has stood forlornly here through the washing and bleaching of the wintry weather.

When Izz Huett and Tess arrived at the scene of operations only a rustling denoted that others had preceded them; to which, as the light increased, there were presently added the silhouettes of two men on the summit. They were busily "unhaling" the rick, that is, stripping off the thatch before beginning to throw down the sheaves; and while this was in progress Izz and Tess, with other women-workers, in their whitey-brown pinners, stood waiting and shivering, Farmer

Groby having insisted upon their being on the spot thus early to get the job over if possible by the end of the day. Close under the eaves of the stack, and as yet barely visible, was the red tyrant that the women had come to serve—a timber-framed construction, with straps and wheels appertaining—the threshing-machine which, whilst it was going, kept up a despotic demand upon the endurance of their muscles and nerves.

A little way off there was another indistinct figure; this one black, with a sustained hiss that spoke of strength very much in reserve. The long chimney running up beside an ash-tree, and the warmth which radiated from the spot, explained without the necessity of much daylight that here was the engine which was to act as the *primum mobile* of this little world.

The rick was unhaled by full daylight; the men then took their places, the women mounted and the work began. Farmer Groby—or, as they called him, "he"—had arrived ere this, and by his orders Tess was placed on the platform of the machine, close to the man who fed it, her business being to untie every sheaf of corn handed on to her by Izz Huett, who stood next, but on the rick; so that the feeder could seize it and spread it over the revolving drum, which whisked out every grain in one moment.

They were soon in full progress, after a preparatory hitch or two, which rejoiced the hearts of those who hated machinery. The work sped on till breakfast-time, when the thresher was stopped for half an hour; and on starting again after the meal the whole supplementary strength of the farm was thrown into the labour of constructing the straw-rick, which began to grow beside the stack of corn. A hasty lunch was eaten as they stood, without leaving their positions, and then another couple of hours brought them near to dinner-time; the inexorable wheels continuing to spin, and the penetrating hum of the thresher to thrill to the very marrow all who were near the revolving wire-cage.

The old men on the rising straw-rick talked of the past days when they had been accustomed to thresh with flails on the oaken barn-floor; when everything, even to winnowing, was effected by hand-labour, which, to their thinking, though slow, produced better results. Those, too, on the corn-rick talked a little; but the perspiring ones at the machine, including Tess, could not lighten their duties by the exchange of many words. It was the ceaselessness of the work which tired her so severely, and began to make her wish that she had never come to Flintcomb-Ash.

THOMAS HARDY *Tess of the D'Urbervilles*, 1891

One Aspect of the Struggle

BURSLEY, the ancient home of the potter, has an antiquity of a thousand years. It lies towards the north end of an extensive valley, which must have been one of the fairest spots in Alfred's England, but which is now defaced by the activities of a quarter of a million of people. Five contiguous towns—Turnhill, Bursley, Hanbridge, Knype, and Longshaw—united by a single winding thoroughfare some eight miles in length, have inundated the valley like a succession of great lakes. Of these five Bursley is the mother, but Hanbridge is the largest. They are mean and forbidding of aspect—sombre, hard-featured, uncouth; and the vapourous poison of their ovens and chimneys has soiled and shrivelled the surrounding country till there is no village lane within a league but what offers a gaunt and ludicrous travesty of rural charms. Nothing could be more prosaic than the huddled, red-brown streets; nothing more seemingly remote from romance. Yet be it said that romance is even here—the romance which, for those who have an eye to perceive it, ever dwells amid the seats of industrial manufacture, softening the coarseness, transfiguring the squalor, of these mighty alchemic operations. Look down into the valley from this terrace-height, embrace the whole smoke-girt amphitheatre in a glance, and it may be that you will suddenly comprehend the secret and superb significance of the vast Doing which goes forward below. Because they seldom think, the townsmen take shame when indicted for having disfigured half a county in order to live. They have not understood that this disfigurement is merely an episode in the unending warfare of man and nature, and calls for no contrition. Here, indeed, is Nature repaid for some of her notorious cruelties. She imperiously bids man sustain and reproduce himself, and this is one of the places where in the very act of obedience he wounds and maltreats her. Out beyond the municipal confines, where the subsidiary industries of coal and iron prosper amid a wreck of verdure, the struggle is grim, appalling, heroic—so ruthless is his havoc of her, so indomitable her ceaseless recuperation. On the one side is a wresting from Nature's own bowels of the means to waste her; on the other, an undismayed, enduring fortitude. The grass grows; though it is not green, it grows. In the very heart of the valley, hedged about with furnaces, a farm still stands, and at harvest-time the sooty sheaves are gathered in.

ARNOLD BENNETT *Anna of the Five Towns*, 1902

Another View

WHEN Edmund Moreton, about 1780, took the infection disseminated by the development of machinery, and left the farming of his acres to make money, that thing was done which they were all now talking about trying to undo, with their cries of: "Back to the land! Back to peace and sanity in the shade of the elms! Back to the simple and patriarchal state of feeling which old documents disclose. Back to a time before these little squashed heads and bodies and features jutted every which way; before there were long squashed streets of grey houses; long squashed chimneys emitting smoke-blight; long squashed rows of graves; and long squashed columns of the daily papers. Back to well-fed countrymen who could not read, with Common rights, and a kindly feeling for old 'Moretons,' who had a kindly feeling for them!" Back to all that? A dream! Sirs! A dream! There was nothing for it now, but—progress! Progress! On with the dance! Let engines rip, and the little, squash-headed fellows with them! Commerce, literature, religion, science, politics, all taking a hand; what a glorious chance had money, ugliness, and ill will!

Such were the reflections of Felix. And this green parcel of his native land, from which the half of his blood came, and that the dearest half, had a potency over his spirit that he might well be ashamed of in days when the true Briton was a town-bred creature with a foot of fancy in all four corners of the globe. There was ever to him a special flavour about the elm-girt fields, the flowery coppices, of this country of the old Moretons, a special fascination in its full, white-clouded skies, its grass-edged roads, its pied and creamy cattle, and the blue-green loom of the Malvern Hills. If God walked anywhere for him, if was surely here. Sentiment! Without sentiment, without that love, each for his own corner, "the Land" was lost indeed. To fortify men in love for their motherland, to see that insecurity, grinding poverty, interference, petty tyranny, could no longer undermine that love—this was to be, surely must be, done! Monotony? Was that cry true? What work now performed by humble men was less monotonous than work on the land? What work was even a tenth part so varied? Never quite the same from day to day: Now weeding, now hay, now roots, how hedging; now corn, with sowing, reaping, threshing, stacking, thatching; the care of beasts, and their companionship; shearing, wool-dipping, wood-gathering, apple-picking, cider-making; fashioning and tarring gates; whitewashing walls; carting; trenching—never, never two days quite the same! Monotony! The poor devils in factories, in shops, in mines; poor devils driving buses, punching tickets, cleaning roads; baking; cooking; sewing; typing! Stokers; machine-tenders; bricklayers; dockers; clerks! Ah! that great company from towns might well cry out: Monotony!

JOHN GALSWORTHY *The Freelands*, 1915

Transition

IN about a quarter of an hour Wolf found himself in the centre of the village of King's Barton.

All the cottages he saw here had protective cornices, carved above windows and doors, chiselled and moulded with as much elaboration as if they were ornamenting some noble mansion or abbey. Many of these cottage-doors stood ajar, as Wolf passed by, and it was easy for him to observe their quaintly-furnished interiors: the china dogs upon the mantelpieces, the grandfather's clocks, the highly-coloured lithographs of war and religion, the shining pots and pans, the well-scrubbed deal tables, the deeply-indented wooden steps leading to the rooms above. Almost all of them had large flagstones, of the same mellow, yellowish tint, laid between the doorstep and the path; and in many cases this stone was as deeply hollowed out, under the passing feet of the generations, as was the actual doorstep which rose above it.

Beyond these cottages his road led him past the low wall of the parish church. Here he stopped for a while to view the graves and to enjoy the look of that solid and yet proud edifice whose massive masonry and tall square tower gathered up into themselves so many of the characteristics of that country-side.

At last he had passed the last house of the village and was

drifting leisurely along a lonely country road. The hedges were already in full leaf; but many of the trees, especially the oaks and ashes, were yet quite bare. The ditches on both sides of the road contained gleaming patches of celandines.

After walking for about two miles, Wolf became conscious that the lively agglomeration of West-country trade was about to reveal itself. The hedges became lower, the ditches shallower, the blackbirds and thrushes less voluble. Neat little villas began to appear at the roadside, with trim but rather exposed gardens, where daffodils nodded with a splendid negligence, as if ready in their royal largesse to do what they could for the patient clerks and humble shop-assistants who had weeded the earth about their proud stems.

The town of Blacksod stands in the midst of a richly-green valley, at the point where the Dorsetshire Blackmore Vale, following the loamy banks of the River Lunt, carries its umbrageous fertility into the great Somersetshire plain.

Blacksod is not only the centre of a large agricultural district, it is the energetic and bustling emporium of many small but enterprising factories. Cheeses are made here and also shoes. Sausages are made here and also leather gloves. Ironmongers, saddlers, shops dealing in every sort of farm-implement and farm-produce, abound in the streets of Blacksod side by side with haberdashers, grocers, fishmongers; and up and down its narrow pavements farmers and labourers jostle with factory-hands and burgesses.

Soon there began to be manifested certain signs of borough traffic. Motor-cars showed themselves, and even motor-lorries. Bakers' carts and butchers' carts came swiftly past him. He overtook maids and mothers returning from shopping, with perambulators where the infant riders were almost lost beneath the heaps of parcels piled up around them. He observed a couple of tramps taking off their boots under the hedge, their long, brown, peevish fingers untwisting dirty linen, their furtive, suspicious eyes watching the passers-by with the look of sick jackals.

And then he found himself in an actual street. It was a new street, composed of spick-and-span jerry-built houses, each exactly like the other. But it gave Wolf a mysterious satisfaction. The neatness, the abnormal cleanliness of the brickwork and of the wretched sham-Gothic ornamentation did not displease him. The little gardens, behind low, brightly-painted, wooden palings, were delicious to him, with their crocuses and jonquils and budding polyanthuses.

He loved the muslin curtains over the parlour-windows, and the ferns and flower-pots on the window-sills. He loved the quaint names of these little toy houses—names like Rosecot, Woodbine, Bankside, Primrose Villa. He tried to fancy what it would be like to sit in the bow-window of any one of these, drinking tea and eating bread-and-honey, while the spring afternoon slowly darkened towards twilight.

JOHN COWPER POWYS *Wolf Solent*, 1929

Labourers' Leisure

THE only definite holidays for the men during the year were Christmas Day, Good Friday, and the local fair day.

On fair days the men drove the sale sheep to the fair in the early morning, and were then finished for the day. This fair was a business one in the morning, and a pleasure fair in the evening. In addition to sheep selling it was the recognized hiring fair. Men in search of a new situation wore the badge of their calling in their hats. A carter wore a plait of whipcord, a shepherd a tuft of wool, and cowmen sported some hair from a cow's tail.

Men were hired from Michaelmas, October the eleventh, for the year, usually by verbal agreement, the essential features of this being noted down in the farmer's pocket book. All sorts of things came under review during the discussion of these agreements. You might agree with a man subject to a favourable character from his present employer, to find on inquiry that although he was all right, his wife was of a quarrelsome disposition. This might be a hopeless drawback. A farmer doesn't just employ a man, and remain in ignorance of his life during non-working hours. He has to live with him, and these domestic differences can upset the whole farm. In many cases the cottage available might be one of a pair having a common front door opening on to a passage between the two houses. Some blocks of cottages had only one copper and washhouse, so that washing days must occur in rotation. Still if it happened that you had a single cottage available a bad-tempered wife did not matter.

I can remember one carter agreeing with my father subject to the cottage chimney not smoking. "I've a lived in a smoky

32 Lancashire Cotton Mills To-day
From a painting by Sir Charles Holmes

'ouse fer seven year, zur, and my missus do say as 'ow she bain't goin' to another less she do know the fire do draw nice and suent. You do know 'ow 'tis wi' wimmenvolk?" He and his wife journeyed over a few days afterwards to inspect the chimney, which, I remember, proved satisfactory, and the man worked for my father for several years.

The pleasure fair in the evening was a whirl of roundabouts, swinging boats, coconut shies, shooting galleries, and side-shows and cheapjacks of all kinds, the whole place being lit up in the evening with reeking naphtha flares. Here the rural youth made high holiday.

Later on in the evening the crowd would be packed shoulder to shoulder, there would be confetti in profusion, and some horse-play amongst the younger labourers. But even in the midst of all this riot you would find the older men talking about their work. Wedged by the side of a shooting gallery, one shepherd would say to another: "Our swedes be good t'year, and we'm got plenty o' hay, so we shall do all right thease winter, I 'low. How be you fitted fer grub thease season?" "Oh, I 'low we shall manage. Wonder where my missus be? I do want to get whoam. We be shiftin' flock to-morrow."

Women and boys might enjoy this yearly revel, but the older men's interest was in the land and its needs.

A. G. Street *Farmer's Glory*, 1932

A Black Spot

Even in East Durham, this village of Shotton is notorious. If I had been completely alone when I saw it I think that now I should be accusing myself of creating a weird Shotton fantasy, as a symbol of greedy, careless, cynical, barbaric industrialism. But my friend the lecturer was there, I know, and I can remember talking to several people; so some of it must be true. Imagine then a village consisting of a few shops, a public-house, and a clutter of dirty little houses, all at the base of what looked at first like an active volcano. This volcano was the notorious Shotton "tip," literally a man-made smoking hill. From its peak ran a colossal aerial flight to the pithead far below. It had a few satellite pyramids, mere dwarfs compared with this giant; and down one of them a very dirty little boy was tobogganing. The "tip" itself towered to the sky and its vast dark bulk, steaming and smoking at various levels, blotted out all the landscape at the back of the village. Its lowest slope was only a few yards from the miserable cluster of houses. One seemed to be looking at a Gibraltar made of coal dust and slag. But it was not merely a matter of sight. That monster was not smoking there for nothing. The atmosphere was thickened with ashes and sulphuric fumes; like that of Pompeii, as we are told, on the eve of its destruction. I do not mean that by standing in one particular place you could find traces of ash in the air and could detect a whiff of sulphur. I mean that the whole village and everybody in it was buried in this thick reek, was smothered in ashes and sulphuric fumes. Wherever I stood they made me gasp and cough. Out of one of the hovels there a queer, toothless, mumbling old fellow came, pointing and peering and leering, first at the "tip" and then at us, but neither of us could understand what he was saying. Perhaps he was the high priest or prophet of the belching black god up there. We retreated a few yards into the roadway, where we found the landlord of the inn standing at his door. He did not know the height of the giant "tip," but said that the atmosphere was always as bad as it was then and that sometimes it was a lot worse. And it had always been like that in his time.

It was hard to believe that Shotton and, let us say, Chipping Campden in the Cotswolds were both in the southern half of this island of ours, not more than a good day's motor journey from one another, both under the same government. No doubt it was fortunate for England that you could dig down at Shotton and find coal. But it did not seem to have been very fortunate for Shotton. The Cotswolds were to be congratulated, it seems, on their lack of coal deposits. All this part of Durham, I reflected, had done very well in its time for somebody, but not, somehow, for itself. There had been a nasty catch in this digging-for-coal business. Not for everybody, of course: the ground landlords and royalty owners had not done badly out of it, and I did not notice anybody resembling one of them hanging about Shotton. I fancy they take their sulphur elsewhere and in another form. "Is there anything else you'd like to see?" my companion asked. I thanked him. "No," I continued, "there's nothing more I want to see here. Not for a few more years, I think."

J. B. PRIESTLEY *English Journey*, 1934

Landscape

THE treatment of landscape in English literature indicates roughly the changing temper of each cultural era. The mediæval mind sees in the face of nature chiefly wonders, outward signs of an inscrutable creation. With the renascence there begins cultivation of the pastoral scene, often a plagiarism of Italian climes and conventions: sylvan England becomes peopled with naiads, oreads and dryads of classical descent. Then, as science finds foothold and man aspires to control his environment, ordered gardens and regimented shrubberies supplant less amenable aspects of the wild countryside. The age of reason, modifying nature with art, favours landscape gardens as the most grateful scene, but with a business eye to its estate management, admits smiling Ceres' golden realm a close second. After the first flush of romanticism vistas of awe, natural or artificial, catch the public fancy, which by the nineteenth century has assumed a self-conscious delight in the picturesque. As the age of industry devours more of England with its blackening stride, remoter moors and desolate mountains receive the tourist's benison, until nature has few secret places left untrodden. There is at length recognition of the homely virtues of field and wood and stream, newly significant for those who would stand and stare awhile amid the bewildering hustle of an automatic age. Preservation societies now strive to bequeath some tracts of our country as it all once was to an otherwise incredulous posterity.

In the middle ages it was unusual for a writer to comment on the landscape, unless it held a marvel or a mystery. One did not visit the Peak district for the view or indeed travel at all for the sake of scenery. Arduous enough it was to traverse the fens and heaths and forests between neighbouring towns. So Ranulph Higden, speaking of the wonders of Britain in his *Polychronicon*, selects first the Peak because "There bloweth so strong a wind out of the fissures of the earth that it casteth up again clothes that one casteth in," goes on to mention Cheddar where "There is a great hollowness under the earth. Often many men have been therein, and walked about within, and seen rivers and streams, but nowhere could they find an end," and describes a wood near to Wimborne in Dorset whose trees turn to stone if they fall into a nearby pool and lie there a year. Of the beauty of these places he has nothing to say. Chaucer, again, expresses little curiosity about English mountains, lakes, moors and coasts as scenery, dismissing his setting as "a mersshy contree called Holderness" or "His woning was ful fair upon an heeth, with grene trees shadwed was his place," and reserving wealth of description only for such paradisal visions as the garden in the Romaunt of the Rose.

By the sixteenth century, however, the spirit of exploration has infected even stay-at-home Englishmen. One of the first to investigate our countryside was John Leland, who spent six years to such account that, as he said "There is almost neyther cape nor baye, haven, creke or pere, ryver or confluence of ryvers, breches, washes, lakes, meres, fenny waters, mountaynes, valleys, mores, hethes, forestes, woodes, cyties, burges, castels, pryncypall manor places, monasterys and colleges, but I have seane them." Although encyclopædic in endeavour, Leland did not achieve an artistic survey: he was content to see without noticing more than the bare facts. Interest in landscape was not his bent: he was prone to such record as: "There lyith a greate valley under the Castelle of Rokingham, very plentifull of corne and grasse. The Forest of Rokingham after the old perambulation is about 20 miles yn length, and in bredthe 5 or 4 miles in sum places, and in sum lesse. There be dyvers lodges for Kepers of the falow dere yn it." Nevertheless his itinerary method caught the imagination of poets. With Drayton the renascence influence appears at work investing all his natural features with a genius loci: but although the confluence of rivers becomes the marriage of prince and nymph, there are scenic descriptions in the *Polyolbion* of some effect:

"Upon the utmost end of Cornwall's furrowing beak
Where Bresan from the land the tilting waves doth break
The shore let her transcend, the promont to descry,
And view about the point the unnumber'd fowl that fly . . .
Whence, climbing to the cleeves, herself she firmly sets
The Bourns, the Brooks, the Becks, the Rills, the Rivelets
Exactly to derive; receiving in her way
That straight'ned tongue of land, where, at Mt. Michael's bay
Rude Neptune, cutting in, a cantle forth doth take;
And, on the other side, Hayle's vaster mouth doth make
A chersonese thereof, the corner clipping in . . .

Incidentally Drayton's geography is not always exact: he declared that Ingleborow Hill, Pendle and Penigent were the highest mountains between Tweed and Trent, going so far as to deny Skiddo the right to peer over Penigent and omitting the claims of Crossfell altogether. Yet his work provides a more intimate sense of England than the artificial pastoral of Spenser, whose country settings are the downs, St. Bridget's bower and "The salt Medway, that trickling stremis adowne the dales of Kent." Spenser loves detail, the dainty perfection of the season when

"Flora calleth forth eche flower
And bids make readie Maias boure."

His decor under the greenwood tree belongs to the same idyllic world as the *Forest of Arden*. He applies to the countryside the art which Bacon expends on his garden. Here is the scientific discipline that man strives to impose on nature. "For gardens, the contents ought not to be well under thirty acres of ground, and to be divided into three parts: a green in the entrance; a heath or desert in the going forth; and the main garden in the midst. For the heath, I wish it to be framed, as much as may be to a natural wildness. Trees I would have none in it; but some thickets made only of sweetbriar and honeysuckle, and some wild vine amongst: and the ground set with violets, strawberries and primroses. For these are sweet and prosper in the shade . . ." Thomas Nashe in *The Unfortunate Traveller*, 1594, wrote with wonder of the Italian pleasaunces: "to tell you of the rare pleasures of their gardens, theyr bathes, theyr vineyards, theyr galleries, were to write a seconde part of the gorgeous Gallerie of gallant devices." It was left to Evelyn to carry this art to perfection in England: his work on the garden of Albury Hall has been noticed.

Travel gained in popularity in the next century: in 1608 Thomas Coryate marched from Odcombe, Somerset, to Venice, two thousand miles in one pair of shoes. His percipience, it seems, was on a similarly pedestrian level. He saw some of the grandest vistas in Europe and yet his Crudities present the country thus: "I observed also likewise in most places not only of this territory but also in most of the other parts of high Germany neare to any Towne or Village, an extraordinary great quantity of cabbages, coleworts, turnips and radishes, which are sowen in their open fields, where are to be seene hundreds of acres sowen in one of their fields." For the rest Coryate's interest lies rather in buildings, ceremonies and character. In an English Itinerary his contemporary Fynes Moryson is hardly less practical. "The woods at this day are rather frequent and pleasant than vast, being exhausted for fire, and with iron mills, so as the quantity of wood and charcoal for fire is much diminished, in respect of the old abundance; and in some places, as in the Fens, they burn turf and the very dung of cows." Such pre-occupation with the cultivated or useful aspects of the land becomes more intelligible when it is recalled that up to the Restoration only half the kingdom was claimed for arable and pasture, while the rest consisted of moor, forest and fen. Many routes which in Macaulay's time passed through an endless succession of orchards, hayfields and beanfields, ran then through nothing but heath and swamp and warren. It was thus natural for Bunyan to view the Chilterns as "a most pleasant Mountainous Country, beautified with Woods, Vineyards, Fruits of all sorts; Flowers also, with Springs of Fountains, very delectable to behold." This affinity of the pleasant with the productive recurs, slightly modified, in Evelyn's diary record of scenes that have delighted him. Of Darneford Magna he says: "We passed over the goodly plaine, or rather sea of carpet, which I think for evenness, extent, verdure and innumerable flocks to be one of the most delightful prospects in nature." By this time a goodly prospect is also considered as one of the appurtenances of a pretty town, such as Grantham, a noble castle, as Warwick, or a fine house, as Wilton, which has "a flower garden not inelegant, But after all, that which renders the seate delightful is its being so neare the downes and noble plaines about the country contiguous to it." More rare is the celebration of the view for its own sake (mark of a temperament especially given to sensitive observation), and the deliberate seeking out of vantage points. "Ascending to a great height above (the Malvern Hills) to the Trench dividing England from South Wales, we had the prospect of all Herefordshire, Radnor, Brecknock, Monmouth, Worcester, Gloucester, Shropshire, Warwick, Derbyshire and many more. We could discern Tewxbery, King's-rode towards Bristol &c. so I esteeme it one of the goodliest vistas in England." No doubt Langland saw this same panorama but he did not think fit to retail it.

In the selections chosen it will be noted that de Foe maintains the attitude to landscape just considered, and that Dr. Johnson views the scenes of his travels as the environment of human society rather than as prospects of æsthetic satisfaction. The eighteenth century developed taste, but it had to proceed by way of literature and art before it reached nature. The reviser of Camden's *Britannia*, which itself had superseded Leland, began in 1738 to indicate scenes suited for admiration in such decorous phrases as "From this Castle and hill (Huntingdon) there is a large prospect upon a lovely Meadow, and encompass'd by the Ouse, call'd Portsholm, extream large, and such a one as the Sun beholds not one more glorious, especially in the Spring, when as the Poet speaks: 'Ver pingit vario gemmantia prata colore'." The naturalist Thomas Pennant made known the beauties of Scotland in his tours 1771–5, while William Gilpin, vicar of Boldre in the New Forest, wrote a treatise on English woodlands. More advanced admirers of nature, like the poet Gray, visited the Lake District, and were duly awe-struck. In her novels Mrs. Radcliffe employed striking scenery to enhance the hypnotic attractions of her atmosphere of horror. Even after the Lake poets and their circle had tempered awe with familiarity, making of chaotic Nature a bosom friend, the cult of the picturesque had many disciples. To them Jane Austen beautifully applied the ridicule of common sense, whereas Peacock in his semi-sympathetic vein of satire, revealed himself as an explorer of the Thames and a lover of the Welsh mountains.

In mid-nineteenth century, when the path of industry is growing grimly clear, wild nature ceases to denote privation and becomes a sanctuary. Consolation is found in communion with her such as is not felt amid the works of man. This subjective, sometimes mystical, emotion imbued the novels of the Brontës, whilst Borrow by the tenor of his life and the avowed purport of his writings popularised the attitude. "What a beautiful country is England! People run abroad to see beautiful countries, and leave their own behind unknown, unnoticed—their own the most beautiful! And then, again, what a country for adventures! especially to those who travel on foot or on horseback." was the theme of Romany Rye. Later holders of a similar creed have been Lawrence, with his conjuring of the racially primitive spirit of Wales, and Walpole, reliant upon Cumberland to invest his trilogy with robust, yet sometimes austere simplicity. Reaction to the new Black Death has helped to produce those week-end treks of factory workers in search of light, air, space and freedom: the guide book to unfrequented and unspoiled plots of England has never before been so much in demand. Priestley's graphic picture of the Midlands should leave no doubt of the reason why. Once again Hayslope, Loamshire, reveals a charm that not all the suburbs in the country can rival: landscape has been equated with living space.

Amid this search for rural peace there is less room for the pioneer, but an ever more appreciative following for the connoisseur. By a sweep of bronzed corn rolling up to a misty lavender sky, with wooded combe and russet pan-tiled farm on the flank, is rewarded his August stay in the solitary, timeless wolds of Lincolnshire. March is the month for striding across the moors and riggs of Northumberland, where Hadrian's wall strikes from Borcovicus camp over Crag Lough bluff and by the Nine Nicks of Thirlwall to Amboglanna. Some may be satisfied with Horace Walpole's "dumpling hills of Northamptonshire," some with nothing less than Striding Edge under January snow and a glittering sky: for one, morning light across the water-meadows of the Vale of Avalon, for another, the level glory of a vast plain as evening comes to the Hambletons, is the prospect only short of perfection: those also make converts for whom the "heathy, furzy, briary wilderness" of Egdon Heath has appeared sublime. Perhaps, then, it is permissible still to ask with Thackeray, "This charming, friendly English landscape—is there anything in the world like it?"

Bagshot Heath

From Farnham, that I might take in the whole county of Surrey, I took the coach-road, over Bagshot Heath, and that great forest, as 'tis call'd of Windsor: Those that despise Scotland, and the north part of England, for being full of vast and barren land, may take a view of this part of Surrey, and look upon it as a foil to the beauty of the rest of England; or a mark of the just resentment shew'd by Heaven upon the Englishmen's pride; I mean the pride they shew in boasting of their country, its fruitfulness, pleasantness, richness, the fertility of the soil, &c. whereas here is a vast tract of land, some of it within seventeen or eighteen miles of the capital city; which is not only poor, but even quite steril, given up to barrenness,

33 Tonbridge Castle and the River Medway in 1795
After Joseph Farington, R.A.

horrid and frightful to look on, not only good for little, but good for nothing; much of it is a sandy desert, and one may frequently be put in mind here of *Arabia Deserta*, where the winds raise the sands, so as to overwhelm whole caravans of travellers, cattle and people together; for in passing this heath, in a windy day, I was so far in danger of smothering with the clouds of sand, which were raised by the storm, that I cou'd neither keep it out of my mouth, nose or eyes; and when the wind was over, the sand appear'd spread over the adjacent fields of the forest some miles distant, so as that it ruins the very soil. This sand indeed is check'd by the heath, or heather, which grows in it, and which is the common product of barren land, even in the very Highlands of Scotland; but the ground is otherwise so poor and barren, that the product of it feeds no creatures, but some very small sheep, who feed chiefly on the said heather, and but very few of these, nor are there any villages, worth mentioning, and but few houses, or people for many miles far and wide; this desert lyes extended so much, that some say, there is not less than a hundred thousand acres of this barren land that lyes all together, reaching out every way in the three counties of Surrey, Hampshire and Berkshire; besides a great quantity of land, almost as bad as that between Godalming and Petersfield, on the road to Portsmouth, including some hills, call'd the Hind Head and others.

DANIEL DE FOE *A Tour through England*, 1724

Borrodale

OCTOBER 3. Wind at S.E.; a heavenly day. Rose at 7, and walked out under the conduct of my landlord to *Borrodale*. The grass was covered with a hoar frost, which soon melted and exhaled in a thin blueish smoke. Crossed the meadows obliquely, catching a diversity of views among the hills over the lake and islands, and changing prospect at every ten paces; left *Cockshut* and *Castle-hill* (which we formerly mounted) behind me, and drew near the foot of *Walla-crag*, whose bare and rocky brow, cut perpendicularly down above 400 feet, as I guess, awefully overlooks the way; our path here tends to the left, and the ground gently rising, and covered with a glade of scattering trees and bushes on the very margin of the water, opens both ways the most delicious view that my eyes ever beheld.

Behind you are the magnificent heights of *Walla-crag*; opposite lie the thick hanging woods of Lord Egremont, and *Newland* valley, with green and smiling fields embosomed in the dark cliffs; to the left the jaws of *Borrodale*, with that turbulent chaos of mountain behind mountain, rolled in confusion; beneath you, and stretching far away to the right, the shining purity of the *Lake*, just ruffled by the breeze enough to shew it is alive, reflecting rocks, woods, fields, and inverted tops of mountains, with the white buildings of *Keswick*, *Crosthwait* church, and *Skiddaw* for a background at a distance.

Soon after we came under *Gowder* crag, a hill more formidable to the eye and to the apprehension than that of *Lodoor;* the rocks a-top, deep-cloven, perpendicularly, by the rains, hanging loose and nodding forwards, seem just starting from their base in shivers; the whole way down, and the road on both sides, is strewed with piles of the fragments, strangely thrown across each other, and of a dreadful bulk. The place reminds one of those passes in the Alps, where the guides tell you to move on with speed and say nothing, lest the agitation of the air should loosen the snows above, and bring down a mass that would overwhelm a caravan. I took their counsel here and hastened on in silence.

Met a civil young farmer overseeing his reapers (for it is oat-harvest here), who conducted us to a neat white house in the village of Grange, which is built on a rising ground in the midst of a valley. Round it the mountains form an awful amphitheatre, and through it obliquely runs the Derwent clear as glass, and shewing under its bridge every trout that passes. Beside the village rises a round eminence of rock, covered entirely with old trees, and over that more proudly towers Castle-crag invested also with wood on its sides, and bearing on its naked top some traces of a fort said to be Roman. By the side of the hill, which almost blocks up the way, the valley turns to the left and contracts its dimensions, till there is hardly any road but the rocky bed of the river. The wood of the mountain increases, and their summits grow loftier to the eye, and of more fantastic forms: among them appear *Eagle's-Cliff*, *Dove's Nest*, *Whitedale-pike*, &c. celebrated names in the annals of Keswick. The dale opens about four miles higher till you come to *Sea-Whaite* (where lies the way mounting the hills to the right, that leads to the *Wadd-mines*): all farther access is here barred to prying mortals, only there is a little path winding over the Fells, and for some weeks in the year passable to the Dale's-men; but the mountains know well that these innocent people will not reveal the mysteries of their ancient kingdom, the reign of Chaos and Old Night: only I learned that this dreadful road, dividing again, leads one branch to *Ravenglas*, and the other to *Hawkshead*. For me, I went no farther than the farmer's at *Grange*.

THOMAS GRAY *Journal*, October 3rd, 1769

Seascape

SEPTEMBER 3.—Walked on the beach, watching the retiring and returning waves, and attending to the bursting thunder of the surge.

Afterwards stood on a fortified point below the castle, immediately and high over the beach, commanding a vast marine horizon, with a long tract of the French coast, a white line bounding the blue waters. Below, on the right, Dover curves picturesquely along the sea-bay; the white and green cliffs rising closely over it, except near the castle, where they give place to the hills, that open to a green valley, with enclosures and a pretty village, beyond which it winds away. The most grand and striking circumstances, as we stood on the point, were—the vast sea-view—the long shades on its surface of soft green, deepening exquisitely into purple; but, above all, that downy tint of light blue, that sometimes prevailed over the whole scene, and even faintly tinged the French coast, at a distance. Sometimes, too, a white sail passed in a distant gloom, while all between was softly shadowed; the cliffs above us broken and encumbered with fortifications; the sea viewed beyond them, with vessels passing from behind; the solemn sound of the tide breaking immediately below, and answered, as it were, at measured intervals, along the whole coast; this circumstance inexpressibly grand; the sound more solemn and hollow than when heard on the beach below. A fleet of merchantmen, with a convoy, passed and spread itself over the channel.

Walked towards Shakespeare's Cliff; the fleet still in view. Looked down from the edge of the cliffs on the fine red gravel margin of the sea. Many vessels on the horizon and in mid-channel. The French coast, white and high, and clear in the evening gleam. Evening upon the sea becoming melancholy, silent and pale. A leaden-coloured vapour rising upon the horizon, without confounding the line of separation; the ocean whiter, till the last deep twilight falls, when all is one gradual, inseparable, indistinguishable, grey.

ANN RADCLIFFE *Journal*, 1797

The Highlands

WE were now in the bosom of the Highlands, with full leisure to contemplate the appearance and properties of mountainous regions, such as have been, in many countries, the last shelters of national distress, and are everywhere the scenes of adventures, stratagems, surprises and escapes.

The height of mountains philosophically considered is properly computed from the surface of the next sea; but as it affects the eye or imagination of the passenger, as it makes either a spectacle or an obstruction, it must be reckoned from the place where the rise begins to make a considerable angle with the plain. These mountains may be properly enough measured from the inland base; for it is not much above the sea. As we advanced at evening towards the western coast, I did not observe the declivity to be greater than is necessary for the discharge of the inland waters.

Of the hills many may be called with Homer's Ida *abundant in springs*, but few can deserve the epithet which he bestows upon Pelion by *waving their leaves*. They exhibit very little variety; being almost wholly covered with dark heath, and even that seems to be checked in its growth. What is not heath is nakedness, a little diversified by now and then a stream rushing down the steep. An eye accustomed to flowery pastures and waving harvests is astonished and repelled by this wide extent of hopeless sterility. The appearance is that of matter incapable of form or usefulness, dismissed by nature from her care and disinherited of her favours, left in its original elemental state, or quickened only with one sullen power of useless vegetation.

It will very readily occur, that this uniformity of barrenness can afford very little amusement to the traveller.

As the day advanced towards noon, we entered a narrow valley, not very flowery, but sufficiently verdant. Our guides told us that the horses could not travel all day without rest or meat, and intreated us to stop here, because no grass would be found in any other place. The request was reasonable and the argument cogent. We therefore willingly dismounted and diverted ourselves as the place gave us opportunity.

I sat down on a bank, such as a writer of Romance might have delighted to feign. I had indeed no trees to whisper over my head, but a clear rivulet streamed at my feet. The day was calm, the air soft, and all was rudeness, silence and solitude. Before me, and on either side, were high hills, which by hindering the eye from ranging, forced the mind to find entertainment for itself. Whether I spent the hour well I know not; for here I first conceived the thought of this narration.

We were in this place at ease and by choice, and had no evils to suffer or to fear; yet the imaginations excited by the view of an unknown and untravelled wilderness are not such as arise in the artificial solitude of parks and gardens, a flattering notion of self-sufficiency, a placid indulgence of voluntary delusions, a secure expansion of the fancy, or a cool concentration of the mental powers. The phantoms which haunt a desert are want, and misery, and danger; the evils of dereliction rush upon the thoughts; man is made unwillingly acquainted with his own weakness, and meditation shows him only how little he can sustain, and how little he can perform. There were no traces of inhabitants, except perhaps a rude pile of clods called a summer hut, in which a herdsman had rested in the favourable seasons. Whoever had been in the place where I then sat, unprovided with provisions and ignorant of the country, might, at least before the roads were made, have wandered among the rocks till he had perished with hardship, before he could have found either food or shelter. Yet what are these hillocks to the ridges of Taurus, or these spots of wildness to the deserts of America?

SAMUEL JOHNSON *A Journey to the Western Islands*, 1775

Winter Prospect

ALFOXDEN, February 24th.

Went to the hill-top. Sat a considerable time overlooking the country towards the sea. The air blew pleasantly round us. The landscape wildly interesting. The Welsh hills capped by a huge range of tumultuous white clouds. The sea, spotted with white, of a bluish grey in general, and streaked with darker lines. The near shores clear; scattered farm houses, half-concealed by green mossy orchards, fresh straw lying at the doors; haystacks in the fields. Brown fallows, the springing wheat, like a shade of green over the brown earth, and the choice meadow plots, full of sheep and lambs, of a soft and vivid green; a few wreaths of blue smoke, spreading along the ground; the oaks and beeches in the hedges retaining their yellow leaves; the distant prospect on the land side, islanded with sunshine; the sea, like a basin full to the margin; the dark fresh-ploughed fields; the turnips of a lively rough green. Returned through the wood. February 26th.

Coleridge came in the morning, and Mr. and Mrs. Cruikshank; walked with Coleridge nearly to Stowey after dinner. A very clear afternoon. We lay sidelong upon the turf, and gazed on the landscape till it melted into more than natural loveliness. The sea very uniform, of a pale greyish blue, only one distant bay, bright and blue as a sky; had there been a vessel sailing up it, a perfect image of delight. Walked to the top of a high hill to see a fortification. Again sat down to feed upon the prospect; a magnificent scene, curiously spread out for even minute inspection, though so extensive that the mind is afraid to calculate its bounds. A winter prospect shows every cottage, every farm, and the forms of distant trees, such as in summer have no distinguishing mark. On our return, Jupiter and Venus before us. While the twilight still overpowered the light of the moon, we were reminded that she was shining bright above our heads, by our faint shadows going before us. We had seen her on the tops of the hills, melting into the blue sky.

DOROTHY WORDSWORTH *Journal*, 1798

The Devon Coast

WE set off together on foot, Coleridge, John Chester and I. We passed Dunster on our right, a small town between the brow of a hill and the sea. I remember eyeing it wistfully as it lay below us: contrasted with the woody scene around, it looked as clear, as pure, as "embrowned" and ideal as any landscape I have seen since, of Gaspar Poussin's or Domenichino's. We had a long day's march—(our feet kept time to the echoes of Coleridge's tongue)—through Minehead and by the Blue Anchor, and on to Linton, which we did not reach till near midnight, and where we had some difficulty in making a lodgment. We however knocked the people of the house up at last, and we were repaid for our apprehensions and fatigue by some excellent rashers of fried bacon and eggs.

The view in coming along had been splendid. We walked for miles and miles on dark brown heaths overlooking the Channel, with the Welsh hills beyond, and at times descended into little sheltered valleys close by the sea-side, with a smuggler's face scowling by us, and then had to ascend conical hills with a path winding up through a coppice to a barren top, like a monk's shaven crown, from one of which I pointed out to Coleridge's notice the bare masts of a vessel on the very edge of the horizon and within the red-orbed disk of the setting sun, like his own spectre-ship in the *Ancient Mariner*.

At Linton the character of the sea-coast becomes more marked and rugged. There is a place called the *Valley of Rocks* (I suspect this was only the poetical name for it), bedded among precipices overhanging the sea, with rocky caverns beneath, into which the waves dash, and where the sea-gull for ever wheels its screaming flight. On the tops of these are huge stones thrown transverse, as if an earthquake had tossed them there, and behind these is a fretwork of perpendicular rocks, something like the *Giant's Causeway*.

A thunder-storm came on while we were at the inn, and Coleridge was running out bare-headed to enjoy the commotion of the elements in the *Valley of Rocks*, but as if in spite, the clouds only muttered a few angry sounds, and let fall a few refreshing drops.

William Hazlitt — *Essays*, 1798

Skiddaw

We have seen Keswick, Grasmere, Ambleside, Ulswater, and a place at the other end of Ulswater—I forget the name—to which we travelled on a very sultry day, over the middle of Helvellyn. We have clambered up to the top of *Skiddaw*, and I have waded up the bed of Lodore. In fine, I have satisfied myself, that there is such a thing as that which tourists call *romantic*, which I very much suspected before: they make such a spluttering about it, and toss their splendid epithets around them, till they give as dim a light as at four o'clock next morning the lamps do after an illumination. Mary was excessively tired, when she got about half way up Skiddaw, but we came to a cold rill (than which nothing can be imagined more cold, running over cold stones), and with the reinforcement of a draught of cold water, she surmounted it most manfully. O, its fine black head, and the bleak air atop of it, with a prospect of mountains all about and about, making you giddy; and then Scotland afar off, and the border countries so famous in song and ballad! It was a day that will stand out, like a mountain, I am sure, in my life. But I am returned (I have now been come home near three weeks—I was a month out), and you cannot conceive the degradation I felt at first, from being accustomed to wander free as air among mountains, and bathe in rivers without being controul'd by anyone, to come home and *work*. I felt very *little*. I had been dreaming I was a very great man. But that is going off, and I find I shall conform in time to that state of life to which it has pleased God to call me. Besides, after all, Fleet Street and the Strand are better places to live in for good and all than amidst Skiddaw. Still, I turn back to those great places where I wandered about, participating in their greatness. After all, I could not *live* in Skiddaw. I could spend a year, two, three years among them, but I must have a prospect of seeing Fleet Street at the end of that time, or I should mope and pine away, I know. Still, Skiddaw is a fine creature. . . .

CHARLES LAMB *Letters*, 1802

Plain or Picturesque?

EDWARD returned to them with fresh admiration of the surrounding country: in his walk to the village, he had seen many parts of the valley to advantage; and the village itself, in a much higher situation than the cottage, afforded a general view of the whole which had exceedingly pleased him. This was a subject which ensured Marianne's attention, and she was beginning to describe her own admiration of these scenes, and to question him more minutely on the objects that had particularly struck him, when Edward interrupted her by saying, "You must not inquire too far, Marianne—remember I have no knowledge in the picturesque, and I shall offend you by my ignorance and want of taste, if we come to particulars. I shall call hills steep, which ought to be bold; surfaces strange and uncouth, which ought to be irregular and rugged; and distant objects out of sight, which ought only to be indistinct through the soft medium of a hazy atmosphere. You must be satisfied with such admiration as I can honestly give. I call it a very fine country—the hills are steep, the woods seem full of fine timber, and the valley looks comfortable and snug—with rich meadows and several neat farmhouses scattered here and there. It exactly answers my idea of a fine country, because it unites beauty with utility—and I dare say it is a picturesque one too, because you admire it; I can easily believe it to be full of rocks and promontories, grey moss and brushwood, but these are all lost on me. I know nothing of the picturesque."

"It is very true," said Marianne, "that admiration of landscape scenery is become a mere jargon. Everybody pretends to feel and tries to describe with the taste and elegance of him who first defined what picturesque beauty was. I detest jargon of every kind, and sometimes I have kept my feelings to myself, because I could find no language to describe them in but what was worn and hackneyed out of all sense and meaning."

"I am convinced" said Edward, "that you really feel all the delight in a fine prospect that you profess to feel. I like a fine prospect but not on picturesque principles. I do not like crooked, twisted, blasted trees. I admire them much more if they are tall, straight and flourishing. I do not like ruined, tattered cottages. I am not fond of nettles, or thistles or heath blossoms. I have more pleasure in a snug farmhouse than a watch-tower—and a troop of tidy, happy villagers please me better than the finest banditti in the world."

JANE AUSTEN *Sense and Sensibility*, 1811

Huntingdon

BETWEEN this place and Huntingdon is the village of Caxton, which very much resembles almost a village of the same size in *Picardy*, where I saw the women dragging harrows to harrow in the corn. Certainly this village resembles nothing English, except some of the rascally rotten boroughs in Cornwall and Devonshire, on which a just Providence seems to have entailed its curse. The land just about here does seem to be really bad. The face of the country is naked. The few scrubbed trees that now and then meet the eye, and even the quick-sets, are covered with a yellow moss. All is bleak and comfortless; and, just on the most dreary part of this most dreary scene, stands almost opportunely, "*Caxton Gibbet*," tendering its friendly one arm to the passers-by.

The country changes but little till you get quite to Huntingdon. The land is generally quite open, or in large fields. Strong wheat-land, that wants a good deal of draining. Very few turnips of any sort are raised; and, of course, few sheep and cattle kept. Few trees, and those scrubbed. Few woods, and those small. Few hills, and those hardly worthy of the name. All which, when we see them, make us cease to wonder, that this country is so famous for *fox-hunting*. Such it has doubtless been, in all times, and to this circumstance Huntingdon, that is to say, Huntingdun, or Huntingdown, unquestionably owes its name; because *down* does not mean *unploughed* land, but open and *unsheltered* land, and the Saxon word is *dun*.—When you come down near to the town itself, the scene suddenly, totally, and most agreeably, changes. The *River Ouse* separates Godmanchester from Huntingdon, and there is, I think, no very great difference in the population of the two. Both together do not make up a population of more than about five thousand souls. Huntingdon is a slightly built town, compared with Lewes, for instance. The houses are not in general so high, nor made of such solid and costly materials. The shops are not so large and their contents not so costly. There is not a show of so much business and so much opulence. But Huntingdon is a very clean and nice place, contains many elegant houses, and the environs are beautiful. Above and below the bridge, under which the Ouse passes, are the most beautiful, and by far the most beautiful, meadows that I ever saw in my life. The meadows at Lewes, at Guildford, at Farnham, at Winchester, at Salisbury, at Exeter, at Gloucester, at Hereford, and even at Canterbury, are nothing, compared with those of Huntingdon in point of beauty. Here are no reeds, here is no sedge, no unevenness of any sort. Here are *bowling-greens* of hundreds of acres in extent, with a river winding through them, full to the brink. *One* of these meadows is the *race-course;* and so pretty a spot, so level, so smooth, so green, and of such an extent I never saw, and never expected to see. From the bridge you look across the valleys, first to the west and then to the east; the valleys terminate at the foot of rising ground, well set with trees, from amongst which church spires raise their heads here and there. I think it would be very difficult to find a more delightful spot than this in the world. To my fancy (and every one to his taste) the prospect from this bridge far surpasses that from Richmond Hill.—All that I have yet seen of Huntingdon I like exceedingly. It is one of those pretty, clean, unstenched, unconfined places that tend to lengthen life and make it happy.

William Cobbett — *Rural Rides*, 1830

A "Romantic" Scene

Miss Susannah Touchandgo had read the four great poets of Italy, and many of the best writers of France. About the time of her father's downfall, accident threw into her way *Les Rêveries du Promeneur Solitaire:* and from the impression which these made on her, she carried with her into retirement all the works of Rousseau. The society of children, the beauties of nature, the solitude of the mountains, became her consolation, and, by degrees, her delight. The gay society from which she had been excluded remained on her memory only as a disagreeable dream. She imbibed her new monitor's ideas of simplicity of dress, assimilating her own with that of the peasant girls in the neighbourhood; the black hat, the blue gown, the black stockings, the shoes tied on the instep.

Miss Susannah often wandered among the mountains alone, even to some distance from the farm-house. Sometimes she descended into the bottom of the dingles, to the black rocky beds of the torrents, and dreamed away hours at the feet of the cataracts. One spot in particular, from which she had at first shrunk with terror, became by degrees her favourite haunt. A path turning and returning at acute angles, led down a steep wood-covered slope to the edge of a chasm, where a pool, or resting-place of a torrent, lay far below. A cataract fell in a single sheet into the pool; the pool boiled and bubbled at the base of the fall, but through the greater part of its extent lay calm, deep, and black, as if the cataract had plunged through it to an unimaginable depth without disturbing its eternal repose. At the opposite extremity of the pool, the rocks almost met at their summits, the trees of the opposite banks intermingled their leaves, and another cataract plunged from the pool into a chasm on which the sunbeams never gleamed. High above, on both sides, the steep woody slopes of the dingle soared into the sky; and from a fissure in the rock, on which the little path terminated, a single gnarled and twisted oak stretched itself over the pool, forming a fork with its boughs at a short distance from the rock. Miss Susannah often sat on the rock, with her feet hanging over the abyss; and at length she accustomed herself to lie along upon its trunk, with her side on the mossy boll of the fork, and an arm round one of the branches. From this position a portion of the sky and the woods was reflected in the pool, which, from its bank, was but a mass of darkness.

There was, in the novelty and strangeness of the position, an excitement which never wholly passed away, but which became gradually subordinate to the influence, at once tranquillising and elevating, of the mingled eternity of motion, sound, and solitude.

THOMAS PEACOCK *Crotchet Castle*, 1831

Moorland

WHITCROSS is no town, nor even a hamlet; it is but a stone pillar set up where four roads meet: white-washed, I suppose, to be more obvious at a distance and in darkness. Four arms spring from its summit: the nearest town to which these point is, according to the inscription, distant ten miles; the farthest, above twenty. From the well-known names of these towns I learn in what county I have lighted; a north-midland shire, dusk with moorland, ridged with mountain: this I see. There are great moors behind and on each hand of me; there are waves of mountains far beyond that deep valley at my feet. The population here must be thin, and I see no passengers on these roads: they stretch out east, west, north, and south—white, broad, lonely; they are all cut in the moor, and the heather grows deep and wild to their very verge. Yet a chance traveller might pass by; and I wish no eye to see me now: strangers would wonder what I am doing, lingering here at the sign-post, evidently objectless and lost.

I struck straight into the heath; I held on to a hollow I saw deeply furrowing the brown moorside; I waded knee-deep in its dark growth; I turned with its turnings, and finding a moss-blackened granite crag in a hidden angle, I sat down under it. High banks of moor were about me; the crag protected my head; the sky was over that.

Some time passed before I felt tranquil even here: I had a vague dread that wild cattle might be near, or that some sportsman or poacher might discover me. If a gust of wind swept the waste, I looked up, fearing it was the rush of a bull; if a plover whistled, I imagined it a man. Finding my apprehensions unfounded, however, and calmed by the deep silence that reigned as evening declined at nightfall, I took confidence.

I touched the heath: It was dry, and yet warm with the heat of the summer day. I looked at the sky; it was pure: a kindly star twinkled just above the chasm ridge. The day fell, but with

34 Borrowdale and the Derwent River
After J. B. Pyne, 1853

35 Snowdon
After P. J. de Loutherbourg, R.A., 1805

36 The North Devon Coast at Watermouth
After W. Westall, R.A., 1823

37 Langley Weir on the Upper Thames
After Joseph Farington, R.A., 1795

propitious softness; no breeze whispered. Nature seemed to me benign and good; I thought she loved me, outcast as I was; and I, who from man could anticipate only mistrust, rejection, insult, clung to her with filial fondness.

CHARLOTTE BRONTË *Jane Eyre*, 1847

A Sea-gorge

SUCH are those delightful glens, which cut the high table-land of the confines of Devon and Cornwall, and opening each through its gorge of down and rock, towards the boundless Western Ocean. Each is like the other, and each is like no other English scenery. Each has its upright walls, inland of rich oak-wood, nearer the sea of dark green furze, then of smooth turf, then of weird black cliffs which range out right and left far into the deep sea, in castles, spires, and wings of jagged iron-stone. Each has its narrow strip of fertile meadow, its crystal trout stream winding across and across from one hill-foot to the other; its grey stone mill, with the water sparkling and humming round the dripping wheel; its dark rock pools above the tide mark, where the salmon-trout gather in from their Atlantic wanderings, after each autumn flood: its ridge of blown sand, bright with golden trefoil and crimson lady's finger; its grey bank of polished pebbles, down which the stream rattles toward the sea below. Each has its black field of jagged shark's-tooth rock which paves the cove from side to side, streaked with here and there a pink line of shell sand, and laced with white foam from the eternal surge, stretching in parallel lines out to the westward, in strata set upright on edge, or tilted towards each other at strange angles by primeval earthquakes; —such is the "Mouth"—as those coves are called; and such the jaw of teeth which they display, one rasp of which would grind abroad the timbers of the stoutest ship. To landward, all richness, softness, and peace; to seaward, a waste and howling wilderness of rock and roller, barren to the fisherman, and hopeless to the shipwrecked mariner.

CHARLES KINGSLEY *Westward Ho!* 1855

"Loamshire"

THE Green lay at the extremity of the village, and from it the road branched off in two directions, one leading farther up the hill by the church, and the other winding gently down towards the valley. On the side of the Green that led towards the church, the broken line of thatched cottages was continued nearly to the churchyard gate; but on the opposite, north-western side, there was nothing to obstruct the view of gently-swelling meadow, and wooded valley, and dark masses of distant hill. That rich undulating district of Loamshire to which Hayslope belonged, lies close to a grim outskirt of Stonyshire, overlooked by its barren hills as a pretty blooming sister may sometimes be seen linked in thc arm of a rugged, tall, swarthy brother; and in two or three hours' ride the traveller might exchange a bleak treeless region, intersected by lines of cold grey stone, for one where his road wound under the shelter of woods, or up swelling hills, muffled with hedgerows and long meadow-grass and thick corn; and where at every turn he came upon some fine old country-seat, nestled in the valley or crowning the slope, some homestead with its long length of barn and its cluster of golden ricks, some grey steeple looking out from a pretty confusion of trees and thatch and dark-red tiles. It was just such a picture as this last that Hayslope Church had made to the traveller as he began to mount the gentle slope leading to its pleasant uplands, and now from his station near the Green he had before him in one view nearly all the other typical features of this pleasant land. High up against the horizon were the huge conical masses of hill, like giant mounds intended to fortify this region of corn and grass against the keen and hungry winds of the north; not distant enough to be clothed in purple mystery, but with sombre greenish sides visibly specked with sheep, whose motion was only revealed by memory, not detected by sight; wooed from day to day by the changing hours, but responding with no change in themselves—left for ever grim and sullen after the flush of morning, the winged gleams of the April noonday, thc parting crimson glory of the ripening summer sun. And directly below them the eye rested on a more advanced line of hanging woods, divided by bright patches of pasture or furrowed crops, and not yet deepened into the uniform leafy curtains of high summer, but still showing the warm tints of the young oak and the tender green of the ash and lime. Then came the valley, where the woods grew thicker, as if they had rolled down and hurried together from the patches left smooth on the slope, that they might take the better care of the tall mansion which lifted its parapets and sent its faint blue summer smoke among them. Doubtless there was a large sweep of park and a broad glassy pool in front of that mansion, but the swelling slope of meadow would not let our traveller see them from the village green. He saw instead a foreground which was just as lovely—the level sunlight lying like transparent gold among the gently-curving stems of the feathered grass and the tall red sorrel, and the white umbels of the hemlocks lining the bushy hedgerows.

GEORGE ELIOT *Adam Bede*, 1859

Mud Flats

THE air felt cold upon the river, but it was a bright day, and the sunshine was very cheering. The tide ran strong, I took care to lose none of it, and our steady stroke carried us on thoroughly well. By imperceptible degrees, as the tide ran out, we lost more and more of the nearer woods and hills, and dropped lower and lower between the muddy banks, but the tide was yet with us when we were off Gravesend. I purposely passed within a boat or two's length of the floating Custom House, and so out to catch the stream, alongside of two emigrant ships, and under the bows of a large transport with troops on the forecastle looking down at us. And soon the tide began to slacken, and the craft lying at anchor to swing, and presently they had all swung round, and the ships that were taking advantage of the new tide to get up to the Pool, began to crowd upon us in a fleet, and we kept under the shore, as much out of the strength of the tide now as we could, standing carefully off from low shallows and mud-banks.

Our oarsmen were so fresh, by dint of having occasionally let her drive with the tide for a minute or two, that a quarter of an hour's rest proved full as much as they wanted. We got ashore among some slippery stones while we ate and drank what we had with us, and looked about. It was like my own marsh country, flat and monotonous, and with a dim horizon; while the winding river turned and turned, and the great floating buoys upon it turned and turned, and everything else seemed stranded and still. For, now, the last of the fleet of ships was round the last low point we had headed; and the last green barge, straw-laden, with a brown sail, had followed; and some ballast-lighters, shaped like a child's first rude imitation of a boat, lay low in the mud; and a little squat shoal-lighthouse on open piles, stood crippled in the mud, and slimy stones stood out of the mud, and red landmarks and tidemarks stuck out of the mud, and an old landing-stage, and an old roofless building slipped into the mud, and all about us was stagnation and mud.

We pushed off again, and made what way we could. By that time the river had lifted us a little, so that we could see above the bank. There was the red sun, on the low level of the shore, in a purple haze, fast deepening into black; and there was the solitary flat marsh; and far away there were the rising grounds, between which and us there seemed to be no life, save here and there in the foreground a melancholy gull.

CHARLES DICKENS *Great Expectations*, 1860

Snowdon

SNOWDON or Eryri is no single hill, but a mountainous region, the loftiest part of which, called Y-Wyddfa, nearly four thousand feet above the level of the sea, is generally considered to be the highest point of Southern Britain. The name Snowdon was bestowed upon this region by the early English on account of its snowy appearance in winter; Eryri by the Britons, because in the old time it abounded with eagles, Eryri in the ancient British language signifying an eyrie or breeding-place of eagles.

Snowdon is interesting on various accounts. It is interesting for its picturesque beauty. Perhaps in the whole world there is no region more picturesquely beautiful than Snowdon; a region of mountains, lakes, cataracts, and groves, in which nature shows herself in her most grand and beautiful forms.

To the Welsh, besides being the hill of the Awen or Muse, it has always been the hill of hills, the loftiest of all mountains, the one whose snow is the coldest, to climb to whose peak is the most difficult of all feats; and the one whose fall will be the most astounding catastrophe of the last day.

To view this mountain I and my little family set off in a *calèche* on the third morning after our arrival at Bangor. We were far from being the only visitors to the hill this day; groups of people, or single individuals, might be seen going up or descending the path as far as the eye could reach. The path was remarkably good, and for some way the ascent was anything but steep. On our left was the Vale of Llanberis, and on our other side a broad hollow, or valley of Snowdon, beyond which were two huge hills forming part of the body of the grand mountain, the lowermost of which our guide told me was called Moel Elia, and the uppermost Moel y Cynghorion. On we went until we had passed both these hills, and come to the neighbourhood of a great wall of rocks constituting the upper region of Snowdon, and where the real difficulty of the ascent commences. Feeling now rather out of breath we sat down on a little knoll with our faces to the south, having a small lake near us, on our left hand, which lay dark and deep, just under the great wall.

Here we sat for some time resting and surveying the scene which presented itself to us, the principal object of which was the north-eastern side of the mighty Moel y Cynghorion, across the wide hollow or valley, which it overhangs in the shape of a sheer precipice some five hundred feet in depth.

Getting up we set about surmounting what remained of the ascent, and in little more than twenty minutes from the time when we arose from our resting-place under the crags, we stood, safe and sound, though panting, upon the very top of Snowdon, the far-famed Wyddfa. There we stood, in a cold bracing atmosphere, though the day was almost stiflingly hot in the regions from which we had ascended, enjoying a scene inexpressibly grand, comprehending a considerable part of the mainland of Wales, the whole of Anglesey, a faint glimpse of part of Cumberland; the Irish Channel, and what might be either a misty creation or the shadowy outline of the hills of Ireland. Peaks and pinnacles and huge moels stood up here and there, about us and below us, partly in glorious light, partly in deep shade. Manifold were the objects which we saw from the brow of Snowdon, but of all the objects which we saw, those which filled us with delight and admiration, were numerous lakes and lagoons, which, like sheets of ice, or polished silver, lay reflecting the rays of the sun in the deep valleys at his feet.

GEORGE BORROW *Wild Wales*, 1862

Vale of the Wylye

IT is a green valley—the greenness strikes one sharply on account of the pale colour of the smooth, high downs on either side—half a mile to a mile in width, its crystal current showing like a bright serpent for a brief space in the green, flat meadows, then vanishing again among the trees. So many are the great shade trees, beeches and ashes and elms, that from some points the valley has the appearance of a continuous wood—a contiguity of shade. And the wood hides the villages, at some points so effectually that looking down from the hills you may not catch a glimpse of one and imagine it to be a valley where no man dwells. As a rule you do see something of human occupancy—the red or yellow roofs of two or three cottages, a half-hidden, grey church tower, or column of blue smoke, but to see the villages you must go down and look closely, and even so you will find it difficult to count them all. On one occasion I caught sight of a quaint, pretty little church standing by itself in the middle of a green meadow, where it looked very solitary with no houses in sight and not even a cow grazing near it. The river was between me and the church, so I went upstream, a mile and a half, to cross by the bridge, then doubled back to look for the church, and couldn't find it! Yet it was no illusory church; I have seen it again on two occasions, but again from the other side of the river, and I must certainly go back some day in search of that lost church, where there may be effigies, brasses, sad, eloquent inscriptions, and other memorials of ancient tragedies and great families now extinct in the land.

This is perhaps one of the principal charms of the Wylye—the sense of beautiful human things hidden from sight among the masses of foliage. Yet another lies in the character of the villages. Twenty-five or twenty-eight of them in a space of twenty miles; yet the impression left on the mind is that these small centres of population are really few and far between. For not only are they small, but of the old, quiet, now almost obsolete type of village, so unobtrusive as to affect the mind soothingly, like the sight of trees and flowery banks and grazing cattle. The churches, too, as is fit, are mostly small and ancient and beautiful, half hidden in their tree-shaded churchyards, rich in associations which go back to a time when history fades into myth and legend.

There are, I imagine, few places in England where the humble homes of the people have so great a charm. Undoubtedly they are darker inside, and not so convenient to live in as the modern box-shaped, red-brick, slate-roofed cottages, which have spread a wave of ugliness over the country; but they do not offend—they please the eye. They are smaller than the modern-built habitations; they are weathered and coloured by sun and wind and rain and many lowly vegetable forms to a harmony with nature. They appear related to the trees amid which they stand, to the river and meadows, to the sloping downs at the side, and to the sky and clouds over all. And, most delightful feature, they stand among, and are wrapped in, flowers as in a garment—rose and vine and creeper and clematis. They are mostly thatched, but some have tiled roofs, their deep, dark red clouded and stained with lichen and moss; and these roofs, too, have their flowers in summer. They are grown over with yellow stonecrop, that bright cheerful flower that smiles down at you from the lowly roof above the door, with such an inviting expression, so delighted to see you no matter how poor and worthless a person you may be or what mischief you may have been at, that you begin to understand the significance of a strange vernacular name of this plant—welcome-home-husband-though-never-so-drunk.

W. H. Hudson *A Shepherd's Life*, 1910

The Eye of the Beholder

A leisurely and dusty tramp, plump equatorially and slightly bald, with his hands in his pockets and his lips puckered to a contemplative whistle, strolled along the river bank between Uppingdon and Potwell. It was such a profusely budding spring day, and greens such as God had never permitted in the world before in human memory (though, indeed, they come every year and we forget) were mirrored vividly in a mirror of equally unprecedented brown. For a time the wanderer stopped and stood still, and even the thin whistle died away from his lips as he watched a water-vole run to and fro upon a little headland across the stream. The vole plopped into the water, and swam and dived, and only when the last ring of its disturbance had vanished did Mr. Polly resume his thoughtful course to nowhere in particular.

After a lapse of fifteen years he rediscovered this interesting world, about which so many people go incredibly blind and bored. He went along country roads while all the birds were piping and chirruping and cheeping and singing, and looked at fresh new things, and felt as happy and irresponsible as a boy with an unexpected half-holiday. He came to country inns and sat for unmeasured hours talking of this and that to those sage carters who rest for ever in the taps of country inns, while the big, sleek, brass-jingling horses wait patiently outside with their wagons. He got a job with some van people who were wandering about the country with swings and a steam roundabout, and remained with them three days, until one of their dogs took a violent dislike to him, and made his duties unpleasant. He talked to tramps and wayside labourers. He snoozed under hedges by day, and in outhouses and hayricks at night, and once, but only once, he slept in a casual ward. He felt as the etiolated grass and daisies must do when you move the garden roller away to a new place.

He gathered a quantity of strange and interesting memories.

He crossed some misty meadows by moonlight and the mist lay low on the grass, so low that it scarcely reached above his waist, and houses and clumps of trees stood out like islands in a milky sea, so sharply defined was the upper surface of the mist-bank. He came nearer and nearer to a strange thing that floated like a boat upon this magic lake, and behold, something moved at the stern, and a rope was whisked at the prow, and it had changed into a pensive cow, drowsy-eyed, regarding him. . . .

He saw a remarkable sunset in a new valley near Maidstone, a very red and clear sunset, a wide redness under a pale, cloudless heaven, and with the hills all round the edge of the sky a deep purple blue and clear and flat, looking exactly as he had seen mountains painted in pictures. He seemed transported to some strange country, and would have felt no surprise if the old labourer he came upon leaning silently over a gate had addressed him in an unfamiliar tongue.

H. G. Wells *Mr. Polly*, 1910

Downland

There is a valley in South England remote from ambition and from fear, where the passage of strangers is rare and unperceived, and where the scent of the grass in summer is breathed only by those who are native to that unvisited land. The roads to the Channel do not traverse it; they choose upon either side easier passes over the range. One track alone leads up through it to the hills, and this is changeable: now green where men have little occasion to go, now a good road where it nears the homesteads and the barns. The woods grow steep above the slopes; they reach sometimes the very summit of the heights, or, when they cannot attain them, fill in and clothe the coombes. And, in between, along the floor of the valley, deep pastures and their silence are bordered by lawns of chalky grass and the small yew trees of the Downs.

The clouds that visit its sky reveal themselves beyond the one great rise, and sail, white and enormous, to the other, and sink beyond that other. The wind, when it reaches such fields, is no longer a gale from the salt, but fruitful and soft, an inland breeze; and those whose blood was nourished here feel in that wind the fruitfulness of our orchards and all the life that all things draw from the air.

In this place, when I was a boy, I pushed through a fringe of beeches that made a complete screen between me and the world, and I came to a glade called No Man's Land. I climbed beyond it, and I was surprised and glad, because from the ridge of that glade I saw the sea. To this place very lately I returned.

The many things that I recovered as I came up the countryside were not less charming than when a distant memory had enshrined them, but much more. Much also that I had forgotten now returned to me as I approached—a group of elms, a little turn of the parson's wall, a small paddock beyond the graveyard close, cherished by one man, with a low wall of very old stone guarding it all round. And all these things fulfilled and amplified my delight, till even the good vision of the place, which I had kept so many years, left me and was replaced by its better reality.

HILAIRE BELLOC *Hills and the Sea*, 1906

The "Metallic Midlands"

I CLIMBED a steep little hillside, and then smoked a pipe or two sitting by the remains of the Keep of Dudley Castle. The view from there is colossal. On the Dudley side, you look down and across at roofs and steeply mounting streets and pointing factory chimneys. It looked as if a great slab of Birmingham had been torn away and then tilted up there at an angle of about forty-five degrees. The view from the other side, roughly, I suppose, to the north-east, was even more impressive. There was the Black Country unrolled before you like a smouldering carpet. You looked into an immense hollow of smoke and blurred buildings and factory chimneys. There seemed to be no end of it. In the vague middle, dominating everything, was an enormous round white tower, which I afterwards learned was a new gasometer. It looked bigger than anything else in sight, and as nothing had dimension that could be measured, it was any size you liked to imagine it. You could think of it, without unduly straining your fancy, as the temple of some horrible new religion. The only sounds that arrived from this misty immensity below came from the tangle of railway lines that gleamed in the foreground of the scene, and these noises were so clear that they might have been picked out and then amplified. There was the scream of a locomotive; there was the clanking of the bumped wagons; there was the long pu-u-ushing of a train gathering speed. I never remember hearing these railway sounds so clearly. Nothing else came from that enormous hollow. You could easily believe that there were no people down there, that a goods locomotive was probably the most playful inhabitant of the region. I was glad that I did not know the names of the towns down there in the smoke; I felt that I was not looking at this place and that, but at the metallic Midlands themselves, at a relief map of a heavy industry, at another and greater exhibition of the 'fifties. No doubt at all that the region had a sombre beauty of its own. I thought so then, and I thought so later, when I had seen far more of its iron face lit with hell fire. But it was a beauty you could appreciate chiefly because you were not condemned to live there.

I descended into the vast smoky hollow and watched it turn itself into so many workshops, grimy rows of houses, pubs and picture theatres, yards filled with rusted metal, and great patches of waste ground. There was a cynical abundance of these patches of waste ground, which were as shocking as raw sores and open wounds. In my own West Riding, industry of the grimmest and most uncompromising kind has long been allowed to work its will on the countryside. There, however, the countryside itself is grim and uncompromising. Sometimes the mills, the rows of little houses, the cobbled streets, all seem like natural out-croppings of the Pennine rock. Huddersfield and Rochdale, Keighley and Nelson, may look grim, but the high lands that still separate them look even grimmer. But here in these Midlands, the countryside is mild and friendly. It is on the border of Arden itself. Industry has ravished it; drunken storm troops have passed this way; there are signs of atrocities everywhere; the earth has been left gaping and bleeding; and what were once bright fields have been rummaged and raped into these dreadful patches of waste ground. And nothing I saw there, not even the slums, impressed me more painfully.

The places I saw had names, but these names were merely so much alliteration: Wolverhampton, Wednesbury, Wednesfield, Willenhall and Walsall. You could call them all wilderness, and have done with it.

J. B. PRIESTLEY *English Journey*, 1934

Borrowdale Revisited

HE had crossed the fields, passed the little cottages of Seatoller and the yews, and started up the hill to Honister. On the left of him Hause Gill, tumbling in miniature cataracts with the recent rain, on the right of him the ever-opening fells. He drew great gulps of air into his lungs. That was for him, that unenclosed fell. As soon as he reached a point where the moss ran unbroken to the sky all his troubles dropped away from him and he was a man. There was no place in the world for open country like this stretch of ground in Northern England and Scotland, for it was man's country: it was neither desert nor icy waste; it had been on terms with man for centuries and was friendly to man. The hills were not so high that they despised you; their rains and clouds and becks and heather and bracken, gold at a season, green at a season, dun at a season, were yours; the air was fresh with kindliness, the running water sharp with friendship, and when the mist came down it was as though the hill put an arm around you and held you even though it killed you. For kill you it might. There was no sentimentality here. It had its own life to lead and, as in true friendship, kept its personality. It had its own tempers with the universe and, when in a rolling rage, was not like to stop and inquire whether you chanced to be about or no. Its friendship was strong, free, unsentimental, breathing courage and humour. And the fell ran from hill to hill, springing to the foot, open to the sky, cold to the cheek, warm to the heart, unchanging in its fidelity. As he breasted the hill and turned back to look across Borrowdale the sky began to break.

He stared, as though the scene were new to him, to Glaramara and then over Armboth to the Helvellyn range. It was new to him: never before had it held those shapes and colours nor would it again: with every snap of the shuttle it changed.

Now across the Helvellyn line the scene was black and against the black hung the soft white clouds. Borrowdale glittered in sun like a painted card, flat, emerald and shining. Above his head all the sky was in motion: beyond him over Honister tenebrous shadows thrust upward to one long line of saffron light that lay like a path between smoking clouds. All the fell smelt of rain and young bracken, and two streams ran in tumult across the grass, finding their way to the beck. The sunlight was shut off from Borrowdale, which turned instantly dead grey like a mouse's back; then the sun burst out as though with a shout over the low fells that lay before the Gavel. A bird on a rock above the beck began to sing.

SIR HUGH WALPOLE *Rogue Herries*, 1930

38 The Lower Reaches of the Thames in 1796: the View from Upnor, looking to Sheerness
After Joseph Farington, R.A.

39 The Beaufort Hunt Lawn Meet at Badminton, *ca.* 1860
After W. and H. Barraud

The Field

ONE test of the importance of any activity is the extent to which terms and metaphors belonging to it have interpenetrated our everyday language. On the evidence of the spoken and written word and the usage of all ranks of society, there can be little question of the predominance in English of those terms which derive from the field of sport. Whether a man "gives rein to" his passion or "holds it in leash," is "hot on the scent" or on "a wild-goose chase," whether he "rushes his fences" or "follows the field," he is using the language of Jorrocks. It is scarcely necessary to turn to its special literature to illustrate our tradition in the field: from earliest times sport has been part of the inherited genius of English writers. Dr. Johnson boasted "I have contrived wonderfully well to be idle without sports." Who will deny it? But he was the outstanding exception that proves the rule.

It remains true that many excuses for idleness have been made in the name of sport. The Austinian monk, a fair prelate who

> "yaf nat of that text a pulled hen,
> That seith, that hunters be nat holy men;"

and who asked why he should study in his cloister and grow stupid over his book, wins our, as he won Chaucer's tolerance.

> "Therfore he was a pricasour aright;
> Grehoundes he hadde, as swifte as fowel in flight;
> Of priking and of hunting for the hare
> Was al his lust, for no cost wolde he spare."

Chaucer, too, glorifies the chase in his story of the Cock and the Fox, in whose pursuit hens, ducks, geese, dogs, cows, hogs, men and maid-servants, even a swarm of bees vociferously joined: amid the din view-hallos and hunting horns could hardly be heard, although

> "They yelleden as feenden doone in helle . . .
> Of bras they broughten bemes, and of box,
> Of horn, of boon, in which they blew and pouped,
> And therwithal they shryked and they houped;
> It semed as that heven sholde falle."

Nor in the same period as this free-for-all style of hunting, were the interests of the specialist sportsman neglected. Dame Juliana Berners, born about 1388, devoted part of *Boke of St. Albans* to a treatise in English verse on the Art of Hawking. It might still be read in Wilton library towards the end of the seventeenth century.

As yet, however, the gentleman did not take up one sport to the exclusion of the rest: he had a choice of exercise in many fields. Among the pastimes "that be fitte for courtlie Ientlemen" were advocated "To ride cumlie, to run faire at the tilte or ring; to plaie at all weapons; to shoote faire in bow, or surelie in gon; to vaut lustely: to runne: to leape: to wrestle: to swimme: To daunce cumlie: to sing, and playe of instruments cunnyngly: to Hawke: to hunte: to playe at Tennes." To shoot fair in bow was Roger Ascham's own hobbyhorse and in 1545 he designed a comprehensive essay *Toxophilus* for the inculcation of this exacting art. His precepts were detailed, ranging from calculation of the wind to choosing of the wood, and at times amusing. In particular his observations upon stance may be appreciated in this age of golfers: "Some shooteth his head forward, as though he would bite the mark; another stareth with his eyes, as though they should fly out; another winketh with one eye and looketh with the other; some make a face with writhing their mouth and countenance so, as though they were doing you wot what. . . . In drawing some fet such a compass, as though they would turn about and bless all the field; others heave their hand now up now down, that a man cannot discern whereat they would shoot; another waggeth the upper end of his bow one way, the nether end another way. Another cowereth down, and layeth out his buttocks, as though he should shoot at crows." Besides his callisthenic interest in archery, Ascham enjoyed the "honest diversion" of Alectryomachia, the battle of the cock-pit. It is patent that the sportsmen of the sixteenth century were of catholic taste: no sport was condemned because of the pain or destruction of animals it involved, nor could it be held in low repute when at Kenilworth the learned Queen Elizabeth was entertained with bear-baiting and looked with much complaisance on the "bloody cynarctomachy."

Among the simpler folk football and wrestling were already popular. Thomas Tusser mentioned the former as being allowed on the meadows in December and supposed to settle the roots of grass and destroy the moss. Known as "camping" the game appealed to

> "The sturdie plowman, lustie, stronge and bolde" who
> "Overcommeth the winter with driving the football
> Forgetting labour and many a grievous fall."

Michael Drayton noticed both sports in his account of Devon and Cornwall

> "whose people were of old
> Known by one general name upon this point that dwell,
> All other of this isle in wrastling that excell:
> With collars be they yok'd, to prove the arm at length,
> Like bulls set head to head, with mere deliver strength:
> Or by the girdles grasp'd, they practise with the hip,
> The forward, backward, falx, the mare, the turn, the trip,
> When stript into their shirts, each other they invade
> Within a spacious ring, by the beholders made
> According to the law. Or when the ball to throw,
> And drive it to the goal, in squadrons forth they go;
> And to avoid the troops (their forces that forelay),
> Through dikes and rivers make, in this robustious play."

The game of those days had fewer rules but apparently no less following than its modern counterpart. By an adverse critic it was called rather "a friendly kind of fight, a bloody and murdering practice, than a fellowly sport or pastime." According to Philip Stubbes football players in 1583 had "sleights to meet one betwixt two, to dash him against the heart with their elbows, to hit him under the short ribs with their gripped fists, and with their knees to catch him upon the hip, and to pick him upon his neck, with an hundred such murdering devices." The ball seems to have been almost an irrelevance to the fray.

No less compelling in this robustious age was the cry of the hounds. The pages of Gervase Markham and George Turberville offer perfect counsel to the huntsman, whether he would have his hounds "matched in mouth like bells" or was intent to make them snuff more keenly by applying vinegar to their nostrils. Indeed to Markham "Hunting is a curious search or conquest of one beast over another, pursued by a natural instinct of enmity, and accomplished by the diversities and dignities of smells only." The hound is able to distinguish and follow the stag, buck, roe, hare, fox, badger, otter and boar. Shakespeare adds tribute to this prized faculty in *The Taming of the Shrew*:

LORD:

"Sawest thou not, boy, how Silver made it good
At the hedge-corner in the coldest fault?
I would not lose the dog for twenty pound."

HUNTSMAN:

"Why, Belman is as good as he, my lord:
He cried upon it at the merest loss,
And twice today picked out the dullest scent:
Trust me, I take him for the better dog."

Shrewder still, however, is the ostler, whose nose for prey rivals that of the wiliest hound: "He will tell you, if he find you credulous, that your horse hurts at withers, or he is hoof-bound; but refer all unto him, and you shall be sure to pay both saddler and farrier for nothing." Clitus Alexandrinus, pen-name of the writer of *Whimzies* in 1631, goes on to declare "not a barber in Europe can set a better edge on his razor than he can set on a horse's teeth, to save his provender." The proverb is: "The master's eye feeds his horse: but the ostler's starves him."

Both literature and sport would have been the poorer had not Izaak Walton turned from ironmongery to angling and in 1653 at the age of sixty published his quiet classic. With Walton sport enters the realms of art; the angler "sees nature through the glass of culture" and composes an idyll, in which poetry and piety have equal place. "No life, my honest scholar, no life so happy and so pleasant, as the life of a well-governed angler; for when the Lawyer is swallowed up with business, and the Statesman is preventing or contriving plots, then we sit on cowslip-banks, hear the birds sing, and possess ourselves in as much quietness as these silent silver streams, which we now see glide so quietly by us. Indeed my good scholar, we may say of angling, as Dr. Boteler said of strawberries, 'Doubtless God could have made a better berry, but doubtless God never did: and so (if I might be Judge) God never did make a more calm, quiet, innocent recreation than Angling.'" Amid the pictures of riverside inns, gipsy singing and milkmaids' choruses there is, however, expert knowledge at work. The chapter on "How to fish for and to dress the Chavender or Chub" remains to-day unsuperseded. Yet although Walton's methods of baiting are no less valuable than Charles Cotton's account of clear-worm fishing or his description of flies, the especial value of *The Compleat Angler* can only be realised by a reading of the whole: as a study of old English country life it has few rivals. Even so, the same decade can claim another admirable work, which offsets the country by a day-to-day journal of town life. Pepys' *Diary* deals as a rule with the world of courts, theatres and fashionable rendezvous, but Pepys shews between-whiles the instinctive interest in a new game. On April 2nd, 1660, he went to St. James' Park and saw "The Duke of York playing at Pele Mele, the first time that I ever saw the sport. It is derived from *Paille maille*, French . . . a game, wherein a round box is with a mallet struck through a high arch of iron (standing, at either end of an alley, one) which he that can do at the fewest blows, or at the number agreed on, wins." It might seem that decorum had begun to oust derring-do.

The eighteenth century, however, did not transform the popular attitude to bloodier sports. An advertisement of this period reads: "At His Majesty's Bear Garden at Hockley in the Hole, on Monday, 19th of September, 1730, a mad bull is to be dressed up with fireworks over him, and turned loose with the man in the ground. Also a bull to be let loose at the same time, and a cat to be tied to the bull's tail. Note.—The doors will be opened at four, as the sports begin at five exactly, because the diversion will last long, and the days grow short." French travellers in England, Misson and de Saussure, attended both bull-baitings and cock-fighting, while le Blanc in 1737 found cause for much caustic comment in the favourite sport of all country gentlemen. "The fox-hunter is an animal very frequently met with in Great Britain and particularly in the Northern counties; we must own it resembles a man very much, at least externally, and has even the use of speech, though it commonly halloes more than it speaks. . . . What makes it imagined fox-hunters are not men, is, that in the midst of a civilised nation renowned for sciences, they are entirely ignorant what education, learning and politeness are. . . . The fox-hunter knows no glory except that of running as fast as the animal whose declared enemy he is, no pleasure but hunting, no virtue but hard drinking. . . . He drinks two favourite healths at meals, which is, perhaps, the only rule he observed; the first is to all honest fox-hunters in Great Britain, protestants or catholics, without exception—the title of hunter reconciles them all; the second bumper is confusion to the minister." The type is recognisable as "our English Bumpkin Country Gentleman" whose "rustick, illiberal sports of guns, dogs and horses" Lord Chesterfield delighted to despise. The hunt might boast George III for patron, but politer taste affected the cult of racing. This century sent elegant concourses to Newmarket and saw the inauguration of Epsom, Ascot and Derby day.

It is now left to the reader to judge the merits and demerits of the field from the forum of novelists' views that follow. Fielding, with good-humoured severity, declared: "The English never enquire into the merit of any diversion when they hear it is very much frequented." It is not only to the women-gladiators, bear-baiters or bruisers that his rebuke may be applied. Most of our writers, however, from Mary Mitford to John Masefield have shewn their awareness of the lasting kinship of sport with the English character: some sportsmen, even, have gained a place in literature through their love of the field. The *Hunting Tours* of "Nimrod" or Charles Apperley and the *Thoughts on Hunting* of Peter Beckford would deserve quotation had not a successor no less than Surtees immortalised their tradition. The popularity of Sassoon's *Memoirs* illustrates its vigorous survival. The early vogue of golf noted by Smollett (James I was the first English monarch to play), the continued existence of the Elizabethan quintain in Barsetshire society, and the hint of a reviving interest in archery are included to set in perspective the accepted pastimes of shooting, coursing, cricket and hunting. Cricket can compare with football for antiquity: in Saxon times "creag" was played with a bent wooden bat. County games drew crowds two hundred years ago and in 1747 Horace Walpole received village "cricketalia" as an accepted custom. Even ladies' matches were not unusual and perhaps were no more demure than Rowlandson's hoydenish caricature of the game.

Shooting, like hunting, has had its critics, chiefly on the ground of the cost, the merely personal accomplishment and the interference with humbler folk's liberties. The Caroline Statute had authorised only those of the rank of heir-apparent to an esquire and upwards, or holders of land worth at least £100 per annum to keep dogs and shooting weapons or to employ gamekeepers. Game laws and rights have always added incentive to trespass, as *The Gamekeeper at Home* and the novels of H. E. Bates testify. To Cobbett, however, the situation seemed a burning injustice. When the farmers had raised an outcry against the damage done to their fields by foxhunters, Parliament had produced an act prohibiting the chase until after crops were gathered; why, then, should peasants lose their access to woods and heaths, merely because one stock-jobber wished to emulate the bag of birds made by another? From mediæval monk to industrial magnate men still transgressed in the name of sport. And yet Cobbett enjoyed a day with gun or beagles as well as any man: he would resent the charge of running with the hare and hunting with the hounds, but he could not deny his nature. His tribute to sport is the result of upbringing as well as predilection: it is the Englishman's underpraise of his favourite activity. "In the country where all circumstances seem calculated to cause never-ceasing concord with its accompanying dullness, there would be no relief at all, were it not for the game."

The Humane Huntsman

Sir Roger, being at present too old for fox-hunting, to keep himself in action, has disposed of his beagles and got a pack of stop-hounds. What these want in speed, he endeavours to make amends for by the deepness of their mouths and the variety of their notes, which are suited in such manner to each other, that the whole cry makes up a complete concert.

Sir Roger is so keen at this sport, that he has been out almost every day since I came down; and upon the chaplain's offering to lend me his easy pad, I was prevailed on yesterday morning to make one of the company.

After we had rid about a mile from home, we came upon a large heath, and the sportsmen began to beat. They had done so for some time, when, as I was at a little distance from the rest of the company, I saw a hare pop out from a small furze-brake almost under my horse's feet. I marked the way she took, which I endeavoured to make the company sensible of by extending my arm; but to no purpose, till Sir Roger, who knows that none of my extraordinary motions are insignificant, rode up to me, and asked me, if puss was gone that way? Upon my answering, yes, he immediately called in the dogs, and put them upon the scent. As they were going off, I heard one of the country-fellows muttering to his companion, "that 'twas a wonder they had not lost all their sport, for want of the silent gentleman's crying Stole away."

This, with my aversion to leaping hedges, made me withdraw to a rising ground, from whence I could have the pleasure of the whole chace, without the fatigue of keeping in with the hounds. The hare immediately threw them about a mile behind her; but I was pleased to find, that instead of running straight forwards, or in hunter's language, "flying the country," as I was afraid she might have done, she wheeled about, and described a sort of a circle round the hill where I had taken my station, in such a manner as gave me a very distinct view of the sport. I could see her first pass by, and the dogs sometime afterwards unravelling the whole track she had made, and following her through all her doubles. I was at the same time delighted in observing that deference which the rest of the pack paid to each particular hound, according to the character he had acquired amongst them. If they were at a fault, and an old hound of reputation opened but once, he was immediately followed by the whole cry; while a raw dog, or one who was a noted liar, might have yelped his heart out, without being taken notice of.

The hare now, after having squatted two or three times, and been put up again as often, came still nearer to the place where she was at first started. The dogs pursued her, and these were followed by the jolly knight, who rode upon a white gelding, encompassed by his tenants and servants, and cheering his hounds with all the gaiety of five and twenty. One of the sportsmen rode up to me, and told me, that he was sure the chace was almost at an end, because the old dogs, which had hitherto lain behind, now headed the pack. The fellow was in the right. Our hare took a large field just under us, followed by the full cry in view. I must confess the brightness of the weather, the cheerfulness of every thing around me, the chiding of the hounds, which was returning upon us in a double echo from two neighbouring hills, with the hallooing of the sportsmen, and the sounding of thc horn, lifted my spirits into a most lively pleasure, which I freely indulged because I was sure it was innocent. If I was under any concern, it was on the account of the poor hare, that was now quite spent, and almost within the reach of her enemies; when the huntsman getting forward threw down his pole before the dogs. They were now within eight yards of that game which they had been pursuing for almost as many hours; yet on the signal before-mentioned they all made a sudden stand, and though they continued opening as much as before, durst not once attempt to pass beyond the pole. At the same time Sir Roger rode forward, and alighting, took up the hare in his arms; which he soon after delivered up to one of his servants with an order, if she could be kept alive, to let her go in his great orchard; where it seems he has several of these prisoners of war, who live together in a very comfortable captivity. I was highly pleased to see the discipline of the pack, and the good nature of the knight, who could not find in his heart to murder a creature that had given him so much diversion.

E. BUDGELL *The Spectator*, 1711

Golf

I NEVER saw such a concourse of genteel company at any races in England as appeared on the course of Leith. Hard by, in the fields called the Links, the citizens of Edinburgh divert themselves at a game called golf, in which they use a curious kind of bats tipped with horn, and small elastic balls of leather, stuffed with feathers, rather less than tennis-balls, but of a much harder consistence. This they strike with such force and dexterity from one hole to another, that they will fly to an incredible distance. Of this diversion the Scots are so fond, that when the weather will permit, you may see a multitude of all ranks, from the senator of justice to the lowest tradesman, mingled together, in their shirts, and following the balls with the utmost eagerness. Among others, I was shown one particular set of golfers, the youngest of whom was turned of fourscore. They were all gentlemen of independent fortunes, who had amused themselves with this pastime for the best part of a century, without having ever felt the least alarm from sickness or disgust; and they never went to bed, without having each the best part of a gallon of claret in his belly. Such uninterrupted exercise, co-operating with the keen air from the sea, must, without all doubt, keep the appetite always on edge, and steel the constitution against all the common attacks of distemper.

TOBIAS SMOLLETT *Humphrey Clinker*, 1771

The Ring

THE day was fine for a December morning. The grass was wet, and the ground miry, and ploughed up with multitudinous feet, except that, within the ring itself, there was a spot of virgin-green closed in and unprofaned by vulgar tread, that shone with dazzling brightness in the mid-day sun. For it was now noon, and we had an hour to wait. This is the trying time. It is then the heart sickens, as you think what the two champions are about, and how short a time will determine their fate.

The swells were parading in the white box-coats, the outer ring was cleared with some bruises on the heads and shins of the rustic assembly (for the cockneys had been distanced by the sixty-six miles); the time drew near, I had got a good stand; a bustle, a buzz ran through the crowd, and from the opposite side entered Neate, between his second and bottle-holder. He rolled along, swathed in his loose great coat, his knock-knees bending under his huge bulk; and, with a modest cheerful air, threw his hat into the ring.

He then just looked round, and began quietly to undress; when from the other side there was a similar rush and an opening made, and the Gas-man came forward with a conscious air of anticipated triumph, too much like the cock-of-the-walk. He strutted about more than became a hero, sucked oranges with a supercilious air, and threw away the skin with a toss of his head, and went up and looked at Neate, which was an act of supererogation. The only sensible thing he did was, as he strode away from the modern Ajax, to fling out his arms, as he wanted to try whether they would do their work that day.

By this time they had stripped and presented a strong contrast in appearance. If Neate was like Ajax, "with Atlantean shoulders, fit to bear" the pugilistic reputation of all Bristol, Hickman might be compared to Diomed, light, vigorous, elastic, and his back glistened in the sun, as he moved about, like a panther's hide. There was now a dead pause—attention was awestruck. Who, at that moment, big with a great event, did not draw his breath short—did not feel his heart throb? All was ready. They tossed up for the sun, and the Gas-man won. They were led up to the scratch—shook hands, and went at it.

In the first round every one thought it was all over. After making play a short time, the Gas-man flew at his adversary like a tiger, struck five blows in as many seconds, three first, and then following him as he staggered back, two more, right and left, and down he fell, a mighty ruin. There was a shout, and I said, "There is no standing this." Neate seemed like a lifeless lump of flesh and bone, round which the Gas-man's blows played with the rapidity of electricity or lightning, and you imagined he would only be lifted up to be knocked down again. It was as if Hickman held a sword or a fire in that right hand of his, and directed it against an unarmed body.

They met again, and Neate seemed, not cowed, but particularly cautious. I saw his teeth clenched together and his brows knit close against the sun. He held out both his arms at full length straight before him, like two sledge-hammers, and raised his left an inch or two higher. The Gas-man could not get over this guard—they struck mutually and fell, but without advantage on either side. It was the same in the next round; but the balance of power was thus restored—the fate of the battle was suspended. No one could tell how it would end.

WILLIAM HAZLITT *Essays*, 1798

Sportsmen's Characters

THE great business of life, in the country, appertains, in some way or other, to *the game*, and especially at this time of the year. If it were not for the game, a country life would be like an *everlasting honeymoon*, which would, in about half a century, put an end to the human race.

This, happily, supplies the place of all other sources of alternate dispute and reconciliation; it keeps all in life and motion, from the lord down to the hedger. When I see two men, whether in a market-room, by the way-side, in a parlour, in a church-yard, or even in the church itself, engaged in manifestly deep and most momentous discourse, I will, if it be any time between September and February, bet ten to one that it is, in some way or other, about *the game*.

There is, however, an important distinction to be made between *hunters* (including coursers) and *shooters*. The latter are, as far as relates to their exploits, a disagreeable class compared with the former; and the reason of this is, their doings are almost wholly their own; while, in the case of the others, the achievements are the property of the dogs. Nobody likes to hear another talk *much* in praise of his own acts, unless those acts have a manifest tendency to produce some good to the hearer; and shooters do talk *much* of their own exploits, and those exploits rather tend to *humiliate* the hearer. Then, a *greater shooter* will, nine times out of ten, go so far as almost to *lie a little;* and though people do not tell him of it, they do not like him the better for it; and he but too frequently discovers that they do not believe him: whereas, hunters are mere followers of the dogs, as mere spectators; their praises, if any are called for, are bestowed on the greyhounds, the hounds, the fox, the hare, or the horses. There is a little rivalship in the riding, or in the behaviour of the horses; but this has so little to do with the personal merit of the sportsmen, that it never produces a want of good fellowship in the evening of the day. A shooter who has been *missing* all day, must have an uncommon share of good sense not to feel mortified while the slaughterers are relating the adventures of that day; and this is what cannot exist in the case of the hunters. Bring me into a room, with a dozen men in it, who have been sporting all day; or rather let me be in an adjoining room, where I can hear the sound of their voices, without being able to distinguish the words, and I will bet ten to one that I tell whether they be hunters or shooters.

WILLIAM COBBETT *Rural Rides*, 1830

Village Cricket

I DOUBT if there be any scene in the world more animating or delightful than a cricket-match: I do not mean a set match at Lord's Ground for money, hard money, between a certain number of gentlemen and players, as they are called—people who make a trade of that noble sport, and degrade it into an affair of bettings, and hedgings, and cheatings, it may be, like boxing or horse-racing; nor do I mean a pretty *fête* in a gentleman's park, where one club of cricketing dandies encounter another such club, and where they show off in graceful costume to a gay marquee of admiring belles, who condescend so to purchase admiration, and while away a long summer morning in partaking cold collations, conversing occasionally, and seeming to understand the game—the whole being conducted according to ball-room etiquette, so as to be exceedingly elegant and exceedingly dull. No! the cricket that I mean is a real solid old-fashioned match between neighbouring parishes, where each attacks the other for honour and a supper, glory and half-a-crown a man. If there be any gentleman amongst them, it is well—if not, it is so much the better. Your gentleman cricketer is in general rather an anomalous character. Elderly gentlemen are obviously good for nothing; and your beaux are, for the most part, hampered and trammelled by dress and habit; the stiff cravat, the pinched-in waist, the dandy-walk—oh, they

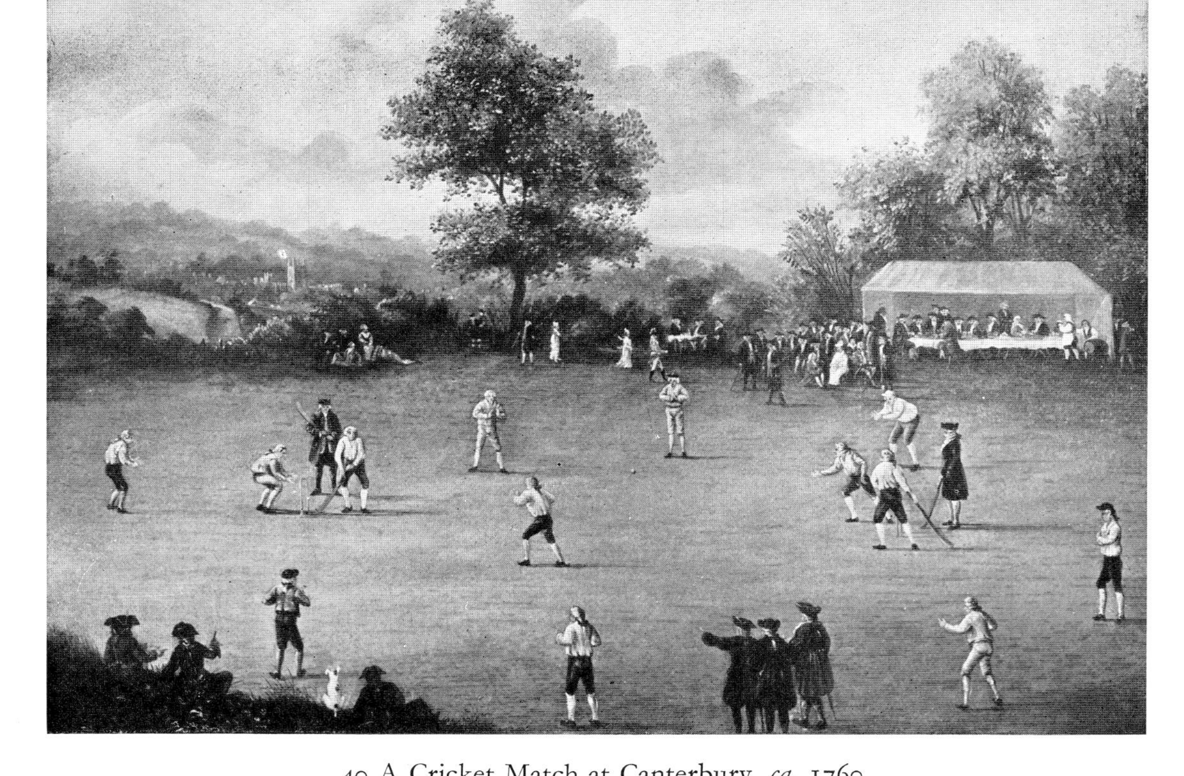

40 A Cricket Match at Canterbury, *ca.* 1760
From a painting by Henry Hodgins, in the Collection of Sir Jeremiah Colman, Bt.

41 "Mr. Pickwick Slides"

42 A Country Pastime for Ladies: Archery

will never do for cricket! Now, our country lads, accustomed to the flail or the hammer (your blacksmiths are capital hitters), have the free use of their arms; they know how to use their shoulders; and they can move their feet too—they can run; then they are so much better made, so much more athletic, and yet so much lissomer—to use a Hampshire phrase, which deserves at least to be good English. Here and there, indeed, one meets with an Old Etonian, who retains his boyish love for that game which formed so considerable a branch of his education; some even preserve their boyish proficiency, but in general it wears away like the Greek, quite as certainly, and almost as fast; a few years of Oxford, or Cambridge, or the continent, are sufficient to annihilate both the power and the inclination. No! a village match is the thing—where our highest officer—our conductor (to borrow a musical term) is but a little farmer's second son; where a day-labourer is our bowler, and a blacksmith our long-stop; where the spectators consist of the retired cricketers, the veterans of the green, the careful mothers, the girls, and all the boys of two parishes, together with a few amateurs, little above them in rank, and not at all in pretension; where laughing and shouting, and the very ecstasy of merriment and good-humour prevail: such a match, in short, as I attended yesterday, at the expense of getting twice wet through, and as I would attend to-morrow, at the certainty of having that ducking doubled.

MARY MITFORD *Our Village*, 1832

Winter Sports

WHILE Mr. Pickwick was delivering himself of the sentiment just recorded, Mr. Weller and the fat boy, having by their joint endeavours cut out a slide, were exercising themselves thereupon, in a very masterly and brilliant manner. Sam Weller, in particular, was displaying that beautiful feat of fancy-sliding which is currently denominated "knocking at the cobbler's door," and which is achieved by skimming over the ice on one foot, and occasionally giving a postman's knock upon it with the other. It was a good long slide, and there was something in the motion which Mr. Pickwick who was very cold with standing still, could not help envying.

Mr. Pickwick paused, considered, pulled off his gloves and put them in his hat; took two or three short runs, balked himself as often, and at last took another run, and went slowly and gravely down the slide, with his feet about a yard and a quarter apart, amidst the gratified shouts of all the spectators.

"Keep the pot a-bilin', sir!" said Sam; and down went Wardle again, and then Mr. Pickwick, and then Sam, and then Mr. Winkle, and then Mr. Bob Sawyer, and then the fat boy, and then Mr. Snodgrass, following closely upon each other's heels, and running after each other with as much eagerness as if their future prospects in life depended on their expedition.

It was the most intensely interesting thing, to observe the manner in which Mr. Pickwick performed his share in the ceremony; to watch the torture of anxiety with which he viewed the person behind, gaining upon him at the imminent hazard of tripping him up; to see him gradually expend the painful force he had put on at first, and turn slowly round on the slide, with his face towards the point from which he had started; to contemplate the playful smile which mantled on his face when he had accomplished the distance, and the eagerness with which he turned round when he had done so, and ran after his predecessor, his black gaiters tripping pleasantly through the snow, and his eyes beaming cheerfulness and gladness through his spectacles. And when he was knocked down (which happened upon the average every third round), it was the most invigorating sight that can possibly be imagined, to behold him gather up his hat, gloves, and handkerchief, with a glowing countenance, and resume his station in the rank, with an ardour and enthusiasm that nothing could abate.

The sport was at its height, the sliding was at the quickest, the laughter was at the loudest, when a sharp smart crack was heard. There was a quick rush towards the bank, a wild scream from the ladies, and a shout from Mr. Tupman. A large mass of ice disappeared; the water bubbled up over it; Mr. Pickwick's hat, gloves, and handkerchief were floating on the surface; and this was all of Mr. Pickwick that anybody could see.

CHARLES DICKENS *Pickwick Papers*, 1837

The Meet

THE greatest day of all was that on which Sir Huddlestone Fuddlestone's hounds met upon the lawn at Queen's Crawley.

That was a famous sight for little Rawdon. At half-past ten, Tom Moody, Sir Huddlestone Fuddlestone's huntsman, was seen trotting up the avenue, followed by the noble pack of hounds in a compact body—the rear being brought up by the two whips clad in stained scarlet frocks—light hard-featured lads on well-bred lean horses, possessing marvellous dexterity in casting the points of their long heavy whips at the thinnest part of any dog's skin who dares to straggle from the main body, or to take the slightest notice, or even so much as wink, at the hares and rabbits starting under their noses.

Next comes boy Jack, Tom Moody's son, who weighs five stone, measures eight-and-forty inches, and will never be any bigger. He is perched on a large raw-boned hunter, half-covered by a capacious saddle. This animal is Sir Huddlestone Fuddlestone's favourite horse—the Nob. Other horses, ridden by other small boys, arrive from time to time, awaiting their masters, who will come cantering on anon.

Tom Moody rides up to the door of the Hall, where he is welcomed by the butler, who offers him drink, which he declines. He and his pack then draw off into a sheltered corner of the lawn, where the dogs roll on the grass, and play or growl angrily at one another, ever and anon breaking out into furious fight, speedily to be quelled by Tom's voice, unmatched at rating, or the snaky thongs of the whips.

Many young gentlemen canter up on thoroughbred hacks, spatterdashed to the knee, and enter the house to drink cherry brandy and pay their respects to the ladies, or, more modest and sportsmanlike, divest themselves of their mud-boots, exchange their hacks for their hunters, and warm their blood by a preliminary gallop round the lawn. Then they collect round the pack in the corner, and talk with Tom Moody of past sport, and the merits of Sniveller and Diamond, and of the state of the country and of the wretched breed of foxes.

Sir Huddlestone presently appears mounted on a clever cob, and rides up to the Hall, where he enters and does the civil thing by the ladies, after which, being a man of few words, he proceeds to business. The hounds are drawn up to the Hall door and little Rawdon descends amongst them, excited, yet half alarmed by the caresses which they bestow upon him, at the thumps he receives from their waving tails, and at their canine bickerings, scarcely restrained by Tom Moody's tongue and lash.

Meanwhile, Sir Huddlestone has hoisted himself unwieldily on the Nob: "Let's try Sowster's Spinney, Tom," says the

Baronet. "Farmer Mangle tells me there are two foxes in it." Tom blows his horn and trots off, followed by the pack, by the whips, by the young gents from Winchester, by the farmers of the neighbourhood, by the labourers of the parish on foot, with whom the day is a great holiday; Sir Huddlestone bringing up the rear with Colonel Crawley, and the whole *cortège* disappears down the avenue.

WILLIAM MAKEPEACE THACKERAY *Vanity Fair*, 1847

Tilting

MISS THORNE left the toxophilites to their bows and arrows, and returned towards the house. But as she passed by the entrance to the small park, she thought that she might, at any rate, encourage the yeomen by her presence, as she could not induce her more fashionable guests to mix with them in their manly amusements. Accordingly she once more betook herself to the quintain post.

Here to her great delight she found Harry Greenacre ready mounted, with his pole in his hand, and a lot of comrades standing round him, encouraging him to the assault. She stood at a little distance and nodded to him in token of her good pleasure.

"Shall I begin, ma'am?" said Harry, fingering his long staff in a rather awkward way, while his horse moved uneasily beneath him, not accustomed to a rider armed with such a weapon.

"Yes, yes," said Miss Thorne, standing triumphant as the queen of beauty, on an inverted tub which some chance had brought thither from the farm-yard.

"Here goes then," said Harry, as he wheeled his horse round to get the necessary momentum of a sharp gallop. The quintain post stood right before him, and the square board at which he was to tilt was fairly in his way. If he hit that duly in the middle and maintained his pace as he did so, it was calculated that he would be carried out of reach of the flour bag, which, suspended at the other end of the cross bar on the post, would swing round when the board was struck. It was also calculated that if the rider did not maintain his pace, he would get a blow from the flour bag just at the back of his head, and bear about him the signs of his awkwardness to the great amusement of the lookers-on.

Harry Greenacre did not object to being powdered with flour in the service of his mistress and therefore gallantly touched his steed with his spur, having laid his lance in rest to the best of his ability. But his ability in this respect was not very great, and his appurtenances probably not very good; consequently he struck his horse with his pole unintentionally on the side of the head as he started. The animal swerved and shied, and galloped off wide of the quintain. Harry, well accustomed to manage a horse, but not to do so with a twelve-foot rod on his arm, lowered his right hand to the bridle and thus the end of the lance came to the ground, and got between the legs of the steed. Down came rider and steed and staff. Young Greenacre was thrown some six feet over the horse's head, and poor Miss Thorne almost fell off her tub in a swoon.

ANTHONY TROLLOPE *Barchester Towers*, 1857

The Chase

"HOOP!" cheered Facey, delighted with his prowess. He didn't care a copper for his Bedford cords, nor yet for his new coat-laps.

Meanwhile the hounds shot away with renewed melody, renovating the roadsters, and making the country ring with their energy. The face of the landscape now changed, inclining upwards towards the dark frowning hills, which divided the vale from the moorlands above. The enclosures, too, got larger and larger—twenty, thirty, and forty acres each—while the surface was more openly exposed, flat, and expansive, with very weak hedges, and few hollows for concealment or out-of-sight running. The hounds now showed to great advantage, striving and racing for the mastery. A sheet would cover them.

"Dash it! but they are a rare lot!" muttered Facey, eyeing their performances. "And didn't cost much either," chuckled he, thinking how he got them. "*Forrard! forrard!*" cheered he, fanning the flame of their ardour. So they went screeching and pressing to the front—now Prosperous leading, now Terrible, now Tuneable. Dash it! He didn't know whether the Beaufort or the Belvoir were the best. Didn't think even Bondsman himself could beat some of the former. Monstrous lucky he was to get them.

Facey next views the fox stealing steadily over what was once Coltsfoot Common, with an attendant canopy of crows hovering over him, indicating his course. "*Yow! yow! yow!*" went the bustling hounds. "Caw! caw! caw!" went the birds. So the poor fox had a double set of pursuers.

On he went, however, steadily and perseveringly. He had beat the old Larkspur hounds twice, and did not see why he should not beat Mr. Romford's. But nearer and nearer came the notes of the pack, commingling with the vociferous cawing of the black gentry above. It was hard to say which seemed the most inveterate against the unfortunate fox. Still, the many-caverned rocks were close at hand, and if he could but gain them, they might work for a week before they got him out. There they girded the horizon in frowning altitude, the dark interstices looking most inviting for a refuge. Facey saw the difficulty. If the fox and hounds held on at the same pace, the fox would inevitably gain the rocks and beat the hounds. This was not to be desired, especially on a first day after a good run. So clapping spurs to Pull-Devil-Pull-Baker, now, indeed, made into Placid Joe, he capped them on from scent to view; and, after a smart race, the Belvoir Dreadnought pulled the fox down by the brush, just as he was ascending the first reef of rocks.

"WHO-HOOP!" shrieked Romford, in a voice that made the hills ring and reverberate. "*Who-hoop!*" repeated he, throwing himself from his horse, and diving into the midst of the pack, to extricate the fox from their fangs. Up he held him triumphantly, with the baying pack jumping and frolicking around. "Take my horse away now," cried Facey to Swig, and the coast being then clear, Facey advanced a few steps to where a soft mossy bank seemed to invite the performance of the last obsequies of the chase. There, on the bright green cushion, he cast the nut-brown fox.

ROBERT SURTEES *Mr. Facey Romford's Hounds*, 1865

A Gamekeeper

HE is an ash-tree man, as a certain famous writer would say; hard, tough, unconquerable by wind or weather, fearless of his fellows, yielding but by slow and imperceptible degrees to the work of time. His neck has become the colour of mahogany, sun and tempest have left their indelible marks upon his face; and he speaks from the depths of his broad chest, as men do who talk much in the open air, shouting across the fields and through the copses. There is a solidity in his very footstep, and he stands like an oak. He meets your eye full and unshrinkingly, yet without insolence; not as the labourers do, who either stare with sullen ill-will or look on the earth. In brief, freedom and constant contact with nature have made him every inch a man; and here in this nineteenth century of civilised effeminacy may be seen some relic of what men were in the old feudal days when they dwelt practically in the woods. The shoulder of his coat is worn a little where the gun rubs, and so is his sleeve; otherwise he is fairly well dressed.

Perfectly civil to every one, and with a willing manner towards his master and his master's guests, he has a wonderful knack of getting his own way. Whatever the great house may propose in the shooting line, the keeper is pretty certain to dispose of in the end as he pleases; for he has a voluble "silver" tongue, and is full of objections, reasons, excuses, suggestions, all delivered with a deprecatory air of superior knowledge which he hardly likes to intrude upon his betters, much as he would regret to see them go wrong. So he really takes the lead, and in nine cases in ten the result proves he is right, as minute local knowledge naturally must be when intelligently applied.

He is very "great" on dogs (and, indeed, on all other animals); his opinion is listened to and taken by everybody round about who has a dog, and sometimes he has three or four under treatment for divers ills. By this knowledge many "tips" are gained, and occasionally he makes a good thing by selling a pup at a high price. He may even be seen, with his velveteen jacket carefully brushed, his ground-ash stick under his arm, and hat in hand, treading daintily for fear of spoiling the carpet with his shoe, in the anteroom, gravely prescribing for the ailing pug in which the ladies are interested.

He has his faults: notably, a hastiness of temper towards his undermen, and towards labourers and wood-cutters who transgress his rules. He is apt to use his ground-ash stick rather freely without thought of consequences, and he has got into trouble more than once in that way. When he takes a dislike or suspicion of a man, nothing will remove it; he is stubbornly inimical and unforgiving, totally incapable of comprehending the idea of loving an enemy. He hates cordially in the true pagan fashion of old. He is full of prejudices, and has some ideas which almost amount to superstitions; and though he fears nothing, has a vague feeling that sometimes there is "summat" inexplicable in the dark and desolate places. Such is this modern man of the woods.

RICHARD JEFFERIES *The Gamekeeper at Home*, 1879

Poaching Methods

IT is a popular belief that the village poacher is an idle, hang-dog ne'er-do-well, with a spice of sneaking romance in his disposition—the Bohemian of the hamlet, whose grain of genius has sprouted under difficulties, and produced weeds instead of wheat. This is a complete fallacy, in our day at least.

The real man is often a sober and to all appearance industrious individual, working steadily during the day at some handicraft in the village, as black-smithing, hedge-carpentering —*i.e.* making posts and rails, etc.—cobbling, tinkering, or perhaps in the mill; a somewhat reserved, solitary workman of superior intelligence and frequently advanced views as to the "rights of labour." He has no appetite for thrilling adventure; his idea is simply money, and he looks upon his night-work precisely as he does upon his day-labour.

His great object is to avoid suspicion, knowing that success will be proportionate to his skill in cloaking his operations; for in a small community, when a man is "suspect," it is comparatively easy to watch him, and a poacher knows that if he is watched he must sooner or later be caught. Secrecy is not so very difficult; for it is only with certain classes that he need practise concealment; his own class will hold their peace. If a man is seen at his work in the day, if he is moderate in his public-house attendance, shows himself at church, and makes friends with the resident policeman (not as a confederate, but to know his beat and movements), he may go on for years without detection.

Perhaps the most promising position for a man who makes a science of it is a village at the edge of a range of downs, generally fringed with large woods on the lower slopes. He has then ground to work alternately, according to the character of the weather and the changes of the moon. If the weather be wet, windy, or dark from the absence of the moon, then the wide open hills are safe; while, on the other hand, the woods are practically inaccessible, for a man must have the eyes of a

43 The Hunt in Full Cry, *ca.* 1830
After James Pollard

44 A Staffordshire Squire and his Keeper pheasant-shooting in 1812
From a painting of John Levett of Wychnor, by James Ward, R.A.

45 Poachers
From a print of ca. 1830

cat to see to do his work in the impenetrable blackness of the plantations. So that upon a bright night the judicious poacher prefers the woods, because he can see his way, and avoids the hills, because, having no fences to speak of, a watcher may detect him a mile off.

A judicious man rarely uses a gun, for the reason that noise is inconvenient, and a gun is an awkward tool to carry concealed about the person, even when taken to pieces. There is a certain prejudice in rural places against a labouring man possessing a gun; it is sure to draw suspicion upon him. A professional poacher is pre-eminently a trapper, relying chiefly upon the dexterous employment of the snare. If he does shoot, by preference he chooses a misty day, knowing that the sound of the report travels scarcely half the distance through fog; and he beats the meadows rather than the preserves, where the discharge would instantly attract attention, while in the meadows or ploughed fields it may pass unnoticed as fired by a farmer with leave to kill rabbits.

When the acorns are ripe and the pheasants wander great distances from the plantations, along the hedgerows, is his best time for shooting; no keepers at that period can protect them. He also observes where the partridges which roost on the ground assemble nightly as it grows dark, easily ascertaining the spot by their repeated calls to each other, and sometimes knocks over three or four at a shot.

Occasionally, also, early in the season, before the legitimate sportsman perhaps has stepped into the stubble, and while the coveys are large, he sees a good chance, and with two or even three ounces of shot makes havoc among them. He invariably fires at his game sitting, first, because he cannot lose an opportunity, and, next, because he can kill several at once. He creeps up behind a hedge, much as the sportsman in Rubens' picture in the National Gallery is represented, stooping to get a view, himself unseen, at the brown birds on the ground. With the antique firelock such a practice was necessary; but nothing in our day so stamps a man a poacher as this total denial of "law" to the game.

RICHARD JEFFERIES *The Gamekeeper at Home*, 1879

At the Races

THEY had fine but somewhat cloudy westerly weather for the races, with enough wind to blow out the flags on the jumps and tents, and enough sun to make the scene delightful. The tents, enclosures and carriage-stands were on a low slope called The Rummers (possibly from a now vanished inn) above the flattish fields of Yell Brook, which made the "four miles of fair hunting country" of the course. Near the enclosures there were booths selling nut-toffee, Italian cream in pink and white slabs, and brandy-balls. The turf between the booths was often stuck about with paper zinnias and dahlias on sticks. There were also amusement-booths, a try-your-strength machine, at which you smote a disc with a mallet; a try-your-skill machine, at which you prodded a loop of leather with a dart; and a try-your-luck machine, which dealt you a hand of cards from which you did not profit. There was a small hurdled ring, where men in loud check suits, often hung about with bright tin medals, called to the world to come and do business with your old friends, who paid first past the post, and whose mottoes were reliability, courtesy and prompt payment. Someone at a rifle booth kept crying: "Step up, step up and shoot the glittering globes." The spitting cracks of the little caps were almost continuous. Men passed by crying: "Cards of the races." The hunt terrier-man in faded scarlet, which he had worn as huntsman on the great Pyeford Bridge day, thirty years before, was offering his poem on that event at sixpence a copy. The lines of the carriages kept lengthening out; all sorts were there, from the four-in-hand to the farm-cart, in line after line, some with shafts up, some with shafts down, the horses secured in the intervals, with rugs over their backs and their heads tossing at the nose-bags.

All the countryside was there: the middle period folk as actors, the old and the young as spectators. The old men were there in great numbers, leaning on their Sunday sticks. Nearly all wore knee-breeches and gaiters. Their coats reached far down and were very baggy over the hips, with inner pockets on each side big enough to hold three rabbits. They wore old tall hats that had belonged to the grandfathers of the present squires, and each of them could have told a history of that countryside such as does not come into history-books. They could do a bit of work still at foalings and calvings, pig-killings, mole-catchings, and rick-thatchings. Some of them sang (and danced) the old songs, pointing the stresses with their pipe-stems: and knew odd versions of the Mummer's Play, which ended with the killing of a beast. All remembered the good old days of public hangings, whippings, duckings, stockings and gibbetings; when bastards (so it was thought) could be drowned and wives sold; when few could read or write (indeed most of them could only make their mark); when men were hanged or transported for being present when someone set fire to a rick; and mowing was done with a scythe and threshing with a flail. George Childrey, moving about the course before the races began, stopped to talk to many of these old men, whom he now saw for the first time for seven years.

There came a movement among the crowd as the hunt servants, who were to keep the course, moved down to their places. After them came seven farmers, on horses of greatly varying quality, for the first race. George watched them draw into line, pause, and spring into motion at the start; he noticed one very powerful horse on the near side of the field, eating up the going like a glutton, and promptly backed him in his heart to win. He saw them go over the first fence and pass away into the country, where his pick lost twenty lengths at the turn. He then walked over to the water-jump, from which it was but a hundred yards to the straight. In a few minutes the riders came into sight, only three of them left, old J. leading on a failing horse, the strong horse well up, and the third fifty yards behind. Old J.'s horse was done, but old J. put him at the leap. He went at it, swerved into it, seemed to turn over sideways, and sent old J. into the water. This made the second horse refuse. As the rider brought him round with an oath and a blow for a second attempt, the third man got safely across and won as he pleased.

"A rotten bit of luck," a man said. "Young Kissop had the race won, but for that brute baulking him; and there goes my sov."

JOHN MASEFIELD *The Hawbucks*, 1929

The Challenge

I MUST tell you a little about the life of "the girt old stag of Stumberleap Wood," as he was called by the farmer. Several times I saw him, before the stag-hunting season, once in the Badgeworthy valley in June, when his coat was glowing ruddy-gold, for he was fat with young corn and roots plundered from moorland farms.

And during the rutting season I saw him coming down from the hills before an October gale, driving a herd of hinds. Three young male deer followed the herd, and sometimes one would approach too near a hind, when Stumberleap would charge back and the young deer would race away. The old stag was gaunt with sinew and muscle, in shape of body not unlike a donkey, but taller; the hair of his flanks was shaggy with mud, and he was thin with so much travelling and fighting. They say on the moor that at such a time a stag's blood is black and poisonous, and that he eats nothing for weeks. The grey gale fell upon the valley, the oaks shuddered in the rainy wind, and as I crouched under a rock Stumberleap was seen against the sky. His head was thrown back as he roared a challenge to any other stag that might be in the goyal. Then bending his neck he dug his antlers into the boggy ground and tore up grasses and sods, which the wind flung away. Again he bellowed. So brazen was the note above the wind that terror entered into me, and fearing lest when he crossed my scent he might charge back and drive the brow-point through my body into the trunk which sheltered me, I climbed the tree. The bark was rough with lichen, and I scrambled along a branch in order to watch, as another bellow had answered Stumberleap. Immediately he roared back, and trotted forward, and, while I sat on the creaking bough a strange stag came forward to meet him. The points of the stranger's antlers made the outline of a crown, whereas Stumberleap's was a forked head. Both stags jumped round feinting for an opening to stab and point. While the gale passed over the sombre moor they thrust and drew back to watch, but suddenly Stumberleap leapt up, and plunged down his head, and the horns clashed. With fury they wrestled and swayed, breaking the soft leaf-mould at the hill's edge with their slot, until the crown-headed stag (who for three days and nights had hardly eaten or slept, for every breeze that drew across his nostrils had made him more feverish to travel and seek the hinds of his rivals) was so buffeted that he was thrown down the slope. Again the antlers clashed, and a young hind stole back from the herd and butted him in the flank. She had been conquered by Stumberleap, and loved him. The stranger seemed to lose strength, and after a minute he backed away and ran into the undergrowth. Stumberleap threw up his head, stretched his thick neck, and bellowed; then rose on his hind legs and sniffed. I saw the instant alertness in the fine eyes of the head upheld. He scented man. The deer were gone, and the rain and the wind blurred all things in my sight.

HENRY WILLIAMSON *The Old Stag*, 1926

Old Style Football

Now it was time for the great Football game. Everyone streamed towards the upper down where the game was to be. The goals were distant nearly half a mile the one from the other. There were few rules, if any; all cunning and trickery were at advantage, but brute force was the greatest power of all. There were fifty players a-side to start with, although before the game ended there were nearly a hundred a-side. It was a match between the Uldale men and the Keswick men, wide latitude allowed for district partisanship.

It was a superb sight to see the hundred men—farmers, labourers, townsmen, woodsmen, sailors from the coast, dalesmen, shepherds—stripped to their small-clothes, rush together with great shouts of joy and triumph. The ball rose into the air and at once the battle began, clumps of men binding together, arms locked, rushing head down to meet other heads with a great crash of neck and shoulder. . . .

Here now was a mêlée in the grand old style, no quarter asked and no quarter given. Over the ball in a wriggling, writhing heap twenty men were lying, and over these another thirty were striving, while behind them were the outguards, arriving from every part of the field, and, if they could not reach the central scrimmage, wrestling and boxing on their own. So that now there was a grand and noble sight, this central mass of heaving men, detached groups of fighters, and the spectators shouting, roaring, the dogs barking as though they were mad. . . . .

But the ball was out again. Three men had it and were racing towards the Uldale goal. All Uldale drew its breath; soon most of the remaining audience, save the very aged, were rushing into the field to join the game.

David too. He had been all this time like a dog straining at the leash. Now stripping off his mulberry coat and flowered vest, he rushed into the fray. Peel's two sons were with him. Together they raced the field, and David, as he ran, felt that this was truly the grandest moment of his life, with the wind brushing his cheeks, the mountains crowding to meet him, the turf strong and resilient beneath his feet.

He touched the ball; it passed to young Isaac Peel, then over to Rumney Peel, back to himself again. He could feel the field streaming behind him. Two men were in their way. David feinted; the ball obeyed him like a living thing, and now the three of them, sharing for an instant a comradeship that was as true and strong as though long companionship had made it, were away, away with only the hills to meet them.

Skiddaw smiled; Blencathra clapped his hands; all the rosy clouds sang together; and to the roar of the approving world, the ball slipped between the posts.

SIR HUGH WALPOLE *Rogue Herries*, 1930

The Poacher at Work

LUKE BISHOP stood on the river-path, staring at the water. The rain was freckling the water-surface finely, and the wind, blowing against the current, startled it here and there into a frenzy of little waves. They were like ripples of dark ice that repeatedly melted and froze and dissolved again into the flow of the stream. Luke stood with his head down. He was quite still. He seemed fascinated by the rain on the water and the endless rippling and smoothing of the soundless little waves.

All the time the river-keeper was watching him. Luke saw it, without moving, from the corner of his eyes. His stare at the water was a mere pretence. He saw in reality neither the river nor the rain, but only the keeper, standing farther upstream, half-concealed by a bush of hawthorn, beyond the bridge. He had been aware of the keeper for some time. Now he wondered if the keeper, in turn, knew that he was aware. And he stood still, a little apprehensive, trying to make up his mind. But the keeper did not stir.

Finally Luke walked on, moving with a casual slouch, turning up his jacket collar with one hand. Along the river, beyond the keeper, a solitary heron had been flapping slowly above the white flocks of seagulls and the shallow patches of flood water. It began to come down stream, flapping heavily into the rain. Luke lifted his head to watch it as though in abrupt alarm, ignoring the keeper altogether.

The trick did not work. The keeper continued to stand with

steadfast patience, hidden by the bush, waiting. The heron passed overhead. Luke turned to watch its flight down the river, his back to the keeper, his eyes on the bird until it had passed from sight. And again when he turned to walk on, the keeper was still there. His very motionlessness was a sort of hostility. Luke continued to walk on, coming to the bridge at last. Once on the bridge he was safe. Lounging on the stone parapet he took up an attitude of sprawling contempt, half-challenging the keeper to move or show himself. But again nothing happened. And now, from the bridge, the keeper looked suddenly ridiculous, the bush no longer hiding him completely, his head bent in discomfort against the increasing rain. Half-taking off his cap Luke pulled it sharply back on his head again with a slick gesture of defiance. A moment later, leaning over the parapet, he saw the dim reflection of both the bush and the keeper in the stream. He spat at them and walked on . . . .

On the first night he was nervous with misgivings and excitement. Things for some reason were not right. His footsteps seemed loud and harsh in the dead winter grass, the ferrets were restless in his pocket, the stars were curiously bright. He discovered he was trembling. He kept working over and over in his mind the routine of spreading and pegging the nets, introducing the ferrets, waiting for the first rabbit. He felt that he had forgotten something. He kept trying to remember what it was, and while he was still trying to remember what it was he began to execute the first movement of opening the nets, pegging them, pausing in alert and mechanical attitudes of listening. For a moment or two it was all unconscious. He had the net outspread and the first peg driven in the earth before he came to himself, aroused by the sudden damp proximity of the earth, the smell of bruised grass, the feel of it on his hands. And he stood astonished by his own lightness and quickness, by the ease with which it had all come back to him. It was a masterpiece, a licker. His fears began to recede and become meaningless. He was working with great rapidity. On the land he was inclined to be a slow worker, deliberate. He moved about the nets with amazing agility and silence, working without thinking, his movement instinctive. It was not until he had the net laid and the ferret in his hands that he paused at all. He had the ferret-string tied to his leg. He listened for one moment before releasing the ferret into the burrow. The night was very quiet;

there was not even the sound of a distant train. He let go the ferret and waited. The silence seemed to expand into the darkness in infinite circles, like rings on a pool. Then it was broken by a sudden rush and struggle almost under his hands, the wild struggle of the first rabbit escaping into the imprisonment of the net. In a moment he had the rabbit in his hands. Then he felt the headbone hard on his hands as he struck it. And then for a single second a running of excitement through his blood before the wild rush and struggle began in the net again.

H. E. BATES *The Poacher*, 1935

The Road

HISTORY has no more living witness than the road and its natural signpost, the inn. One may still ride into Roman times by Ermine Street, walk with mediæval piety along Pilgrims' Way, climb the Cleveland hills by the same drovers' track that the border raiders used, or take the Kisdon corpse road to an ancient cemetery. It is not difficult to find counterparts to the bibula and tabernæ at the sign of the Chequers, although to-day's landlord may have overlooked its derivation from the Roman game of chess. Among existing inns tradition claims primogeniture for The Fighting Cocks of St. Albans. Some doubt may arise of its date 795, but a German ambassador, who recorded his stay in 1129 at the Fountain, Canterbury, complimented an inn that was almost certainly already a centenarian. The Angel, Grantham, hospitable since 1213, housed Richard III while he signed Buckingham's death warrant: an Elizabethan novelist set the scene of diabolical murder at The Ostrich, Colnbrook, opened about 1106: and the New Inn, Gloucester, after a century and a half of existence, made ready to welcome Shakespearean drama. It is tempting to call many halts on the road, for few inns are without some claim to fame and any relics, rooms or architectural features of antiquarian interest are generally preserved. The road, however, lies ahead and the inn was made for the traveller.

Under Hadrian's direction and since Macadam's day, the road, on the whole, has been adequate to its traffic: throughout the rest of our country's history it has been both inadequate and ill-maintained. The arteries of the Roman occupation, military and trade routes from London to York, South Wales and Cornwall, were built to last. They outlasted their engineers: many were in use in the middle ages, supplemented by newer roads between castles or abbeys, but the later system of repair proved their eventual ruin. Repair depended on the goodwill of those to whom the adjoining land belonged, on the devotion of friars and the Guild of the Holy Cross; like hospitality it was not a compulsion but a pious charity.

Throughout the manorial period roads were only kept open by landowners, going from one country seat to another to collect revenues, and by workmen on the monastic estates. Langland recommends to merchants, as an act meriting salvation, the repairing of "wikked wayes" and also hopes that they may

"brygges to-broke by the heye weyes
Amende in some manere wise."

Bridges, again, were the gift of private benefactors or the care of religious brotherhoods, and even if soundly built were not always endowed. Sir Hugh of Clopton's fifteenth-century bridge over the Avon at Stratford, long in use, replaced a poor timber affair which endangered its passengers at every flood. Fourteenth-century bridges still standing are the three-branched one at Crowland, the single span of Danby bridge over the Esk in Yorkshire, and the famous bridge with a chapel at Wakefield. There were sporadic attempts at maintenance by tariff charges, but most bridges were allowed to wear away until they collapsed. Although work on the roads was one of the last duties of a peasant to be remitted, and in spite of the Highway Act of 1555 by which each parish was required to maintain roads under locally selected surveyors, for whom parishioners must do six days' statutory labour on pain of a 12d. fine for each day's absence, the travellers of the time record indifferent thoroughfares. Surveyors were apt to mend first roads that fronted their own fields, the rich might cancel their portions, and then stone was not always locally available. Of such an important route as that from Boroughbridge to Carlisle Leland remarks: "The way on Wattelyngestrete from Borow Bridge to Catericke 16 miles. Thens X good miles to Gretey, then V miles to Bowes, a very excedinge poore thorowghe fayre, and VIII myle to Burgh on Stane More, and V so to Appleby." His verdict held good long afterwards.

Except by kings and nobility a journey at this period was usually made either on horseback or on foot. Carriages, slow and ponderous, were costly luxuries and litters were chiefly for ladies. The favoured traveller and the swiftest was the mounted messenger: standing wheat was no obstacle to his right of way and fines could be exacted from those who caused him hindrance. In the fifteenth century even a sick man of some substance would take to horse, as Margaret Paston's letter to her husband shows: "I pray you if your sore be whole, and so that ye may endure to ride, when my father comes to London, that ye will ask leave, and come home, when the horse shall be sent home again, for I hope ye should be kept as tenderly here as ye be at London." Until Elizabeth's reign coaches were rare in England. By 1622, however, John Taylor could say "This is a rattling, rowling and rumbling age. The world runs on wheels." For the benefit of poorer people, to whom the fare of one shilling per five miles was prohibitive, and who would not find it necessary to cover the hundred and nine miles between London and Bath in three days, he published *The Carriers' Cosmography*. Cross-country journeys were made in trading waggons by agreement with driver. "The carrier is his own hackney man, for he lets himself out to travel as well as his horses: he is a great afflicter of the highways and beats them out of measure," declared Earle. In 1663 the tonnage of these waggons was limited and the Turnpike Act introduced to ensure that travellers paid for the upkeep of the roads at the parish toll-gates. This act provoked resentment and even riots, but in time improved the condition of the busier highways. As yet many people clung to the horse, suffering all the discomforts of our climate but enjoying independence. One September day Samuel Pepys was "up early and begun our march: the way about Puckridge very bad, and my wife in the very dirty last place of all, got a fall, but no hurt, though some dirt. At last she begun poor wretch to be tired." Nevertheless they rode to Cambridge, Sturbridge, Brampton, Huntingdon, Baldwick and Stevenage, and six days later, "rose and set forth, but found a most sad alteration in the roads, by reason of last night's rains, they being now all dirty and washy, though not deep." De Foe protested in an *Essay on Projects*, 1697. He proposed a national levy of £3,000 for eight years—in vain. In his *Tour through Great Britain* he anathematised bad roads and singled out that from Hatfield to Stevenage and Baldock as containing sloughs and holes through which no horse could wade. If turnpikes were enforced he anticipated that travel would be easier to man and horse than it had ever been since the Romans laid their solid causeways. Yet for another half century highways continued to "lie in a most shameful manner in most parts of the kingdom." In 1727 King George II and Queen Caroline had their coach upset and were thrown into the road on their way from London to Kew: they took all night to complete the journey.

Not all the dangers of the roads, however, lay in their ruts and quags: they were the habitual lurking place for vagrants and adventurers of every kind. The Canterbury Pilgrims were a mixed bag, and the pardoner a persuasive impostor with his "holy relics" of pigs' bones: no doubt other charlatans accosted them, sham pilgrims or escaped peasants, idle hermits or outlaws turned brigand. The tricks and impostures of these mountebanks were exposed by Robert Copland in *The Hye Way to the Spyttel House*, 1531, and again by Thomas Harman, who added a glossary of thieves' slang to his *Caveat or Warening for Common Corsetors, vulgarly called Vagabones*. The "Abraham man" feigned madness, the "washman" produced artificial sores by spickwort or ratsbane: Harman denounces them as "Lewtering Luskes, lazy Lorells, rowsey ragged rabblement of rakehells," and forewarns all honest travellers. Shakespeare transformed his vagabond into an Autolycus, that trafficker in sheets and "snapper up of unconsidered trifles" or a "Poor Turlygood, Poor Tom," the Bedlam beggar: the Gadshill robbery of Falstaff and his abettors was doubtless repeated by many a ruffler on Blackheath. William Harrison believed that in 1587 there were above ten thousand persons of this class, hookers, whipjacks, jarkmen, priggers and their womenfolk: doxies, dells, morts and kinchingcoes: only martial law could check their practices. Three hundred years before Edward I had faced this problem and by the statute of Westminster decreed that the edge of the highways should be cleared for a distance of two hundred feet on each side, in such a manner that there remained neither coppice nor brushwood, hollow nor ditch which might serve as shelter for malefactors. But now the same convenience of the road which sheltered travellers might also harbour his menace. The innkeeper and the ostler were frequently in partnership with the highwayman, or even employed to play the part themselves. They made "such packs with slipper merchants which hunt after prey," said Harrison, "that many an honest man is spoiled of his goods as he travelleth to and fro, in which feat also the counsel of the tapsters or drawers of drink and chamberlains is not seldom behind or wanting." The Ostrich Inn at Colnbrook, known then as The Crane, was once infamous for its host's crime. It appears from Thomas Deloney's account that any man travelling alone and with a great store of money was given a particular bedroom above the kitchen most fairly furnished. The bed, cunningly carved, was fixed to the floor, and the bedclothes sewed fast to the bedstead: it stood upon a trap-door directly over a great vat which they used for brewing. "The men appointed for the slaughter, were laid in this bed, and in the dead time of the night, when they were sound a sleepe, by plucking out the yron pinnes (of the trap-door) downe would the man fall out of his bed into the boyling caldron, and all the cloaths that were upon him: where being suddenly scalded and drowned, he was never able to cry or speake one word." Sixty victims are reputed thus to have been dispatched.

The inn had replaced that charitable mode of hospitality extended by monasteries, castles and guest houses as a religious duty. When a king travelled and found himself at nightfall remote from a castle, his marshal marked the best houses of the town with chalk and required accommodation for the whole retinue. Travelling knights were received by an abbot or at country houses, where they sat with the lord at high table: the guest house, attached to a monastery, was open to people of a lower order. Wayfarers' dole of bread and beer is still offered by the Hospital of St. Cross near Winchester. Inns served the middle class of merchants, small landowners, college officials: in 1331 for 2s. 3¼d. three fellows of Merton, Oxford, found a day's simple food and lodging for themselves and four servants. At the cross-roads of important highways alehouses were advertised by a projecting pole or bush: the pardoner took a corny draught at the "ale-stake" before beginning his tale of drunkenness. Langland introduces us to the ale-wife who for poor people mixed pudding-ale with the penny-a-gallon quality. The inn flourished as travel increased: up to 1550 any man could open a house, but "hostelers and herbergers" were required to sell food at reasonable prices. After the licensing acts inn-keepers provided lodging for travellers, tavern-keepers victuals but no shelter, and alehouses supplied only liquor for the inhabitants of the town. Among inn-keepers a sense of personal hospitality still lingered. At the Tabard we remember:

> "Grete chere made our hoste us everichon
> And to the soper set us anon;
> And after soper pleyen he bigan
> And spake of mirthe amonges othere thinges
> Whan that we hadde maad our rekeninges."

Mistress Quickly not only kept open house for Sir John, but bandaged his cuts and provided his shirts as well. In 1617 Fynes Moryson declared that "The world affords not such Inns as

England hath, either for good and cheap entertainment at the guests own pleasure, or for humble attendance on passengers." In mid-century this entertainment seems often to have been of a different order. Each guest was supposed to lie in clean sheets, in which no man had been lodged since they came from the laundress: but on one "merry" occasion Pepys concluded his bedfellow "to be the eldest blood and house of Clerkes because that all the fleas came to him and not to me." At its best doubtless the inn deserved Johnson's fulsome tribute.

The lure of the road ever proved stronger than its trials. The eighteenth century was one of travel and journals of travel. The principal highways of the country had in 1698 been surveyed by John Ogilby, Cosmographer to Charles II, and on them Fielding, Smollett and Boswell set their heroes out to encounter the stuff of humanity. Of driving rapidly in a post-chaise Dr. Johnson declared: "Life has not many things better than this." Yet at sixty-five he was equally ready to venture his bulk on horseback in the Hebrides. The adventurous or the curious made the horse as ubiquitous as is the bicycle to-day: nor was the fashion confined to men. In 1702 Celia Fiennes completed her *Rides through England on a Side-saddle*. Although for long foot-travellers held inferior status and were subject to discrimination at inns, being refreshed only in the kitchen if they were not refused outright, their numbers and fame increased. Coryate and Ben Jonson, who walked to Scotland in 1618, Bunyan and George Fox, whose itinerant preaching once took him to Pendle summit, were notable pedestrians, while the professional feats of Foster Powell, who in 1773 covered the 402 miles from London to York and back in six days, drew attention to a new cult. For the innovating poets and essayists to walk was the only way justly to observe the countryside: Keats, Coleridge and Wordsworth, Hazlitt, De Quincey and Carlyle were afoot in Scotland, Cumberland and Wales, and many fine things were written at their inns. It was said of Wordsworth "with these identical legs he must have traversed a distance of 175,000 to 180,000 English miles—a mode of exertion, which, to him, stood in the stead of alcohol and all other stimulants whatsoever to the animal spirits, to which, indeed, he was indebted for a life of unclouded happiness, and we for much of what is most excellent in his writings." There were only needed Borrow and Stevenson to play the roles of high priests to the cult.

Traditionally more conservative, the novelists celebrated the great age of the stage coach. "Next after a fox-hunt, the finest sight in England is a stage coach just ready to start." The words are Cobbett's, but the sentiment belongs no less to Dickens and Thackeray. Dickens' heroes are constantly on the road and hardly less often at inns: Barnaby Rudge at The Maypole puts his claim against The Uncommercial Traveller, Pickwick on the road replies to the critics of the Dover mail: and George Eliot might well have been asked to act as arbiter. In an age running to railways, Surtees admits their existence only to decry it—waiting-rooms, placards, branch-lines and all; Meredith also clings to the older fashion. The Jehus of the road are jealous of usurpers: yet it must suffer strange indignities to outlive these iron times. The price of survival has been paid: Lawrence thrusts his traveller into the clangour of the Midland trams, and the milestone of another age is added to the road. The way, however, is long, and trams, like tilburies, evanescent: Edward Thomas returns to trace the tracks of the Downs.

The Condition of the Roads

THE soil of all the midland part of England, even from sea to sea, is of a deep stiff clay, or marly kind, and it carries a breadth of near 50 miles at least, in some places much more; nor is it possible to go from London to any part of Britain, north, without crossing this clayey dirty part. For example, suppose we take the great northern post road from London to York, and so into Scotland; you have tolerable good ways and hard ground, 'till you reach Royston about 32, and to Kneesworth, a mile farther: But from thence you enter upon the clays, which beginning at the famous Arrington-Lanes, and going on to Caxton, Huntington, Stilton, Stamford, Grantham, Newark Tuxford (call'd for its deepness Tuxford in the Clays) holds on 'till we come almost to Bawtree, which is the first town in Yorkshire, and there the country is hard and sound, being part of Sherwood Forest.

The reason of my taking notice of this badness of the roads, through the midland counties, is this: that as these are counties which drive a very great trade with the city of London, and with one another, perhaps the greatest of any counties in England; and that, by consequence the carriage is exceeding great, and also that all the land carriage of the northern counties necessarily goes through these counties, so the roads had been plow'd so deep, and materials have been in some places so difficult to be had for repair of the roads, that all the surveyors' rates have been able to do nothing; nay, the very whole country has not been able to repair them; that is to say, it was a burthen too great for the poor farmers; for in England it is the tenant, not the landlord, that pays the surveyors of the highways.

This necessarily brought the country to bring these things before the Parliament; and the consequence has been, that turnpikes or toll-bars have been set up on the several great roads of England, beginning at London, and proceeding thro' almost all those dirty deep roads, in the midland counties especially; at which turnpikes all carriages, droves of cattle, and travellers on horseback, are oblig'd to pay an easy toll; that is to say, a horse a penny, a coach three pence, a waggon six pence, in some a shilling, and the like; cattle pay by the score, or by the head, in some places more, in some less; but in no place is it thought a burthen that ever I met with, the benefit of a good road abundantly making amends for that little charge the travellers are put to at the turnpikes.

Several of these turnpikes and tolls had been set up of late years, and great progress had been made in mending the most difficult ways, and that with such success as well deserves a place in this account and this is one reason for taking notice of it in this manner; for as the memory of the Romans, which is so justly famous, is preserv'd in nothing more visible to common observation, than in the remains of those noble causeways and highways, which they made through all parts of the kingdom, and which were found so needful, even then, when there was not the five hundredth part of the commerce and carriage that is now: How much more valuable must these new works be, tho' nothing to compare with those of the Romans, for the firmness and duration of their work?

The causeways and roads, or streetways of the Romans, were perfect solid buildings, the foundations were laid so deep, and the materials so good, however far they were oblig'd to fetch them, that if they had been vaulted and arch'd they could not have been more solid: I have seen the bottom of them dug up in several places, where I have observ'd flint-stones, chalk-stones, hard gravel, solid hard clay, and several other sorts of earth, laid in layers, like the veins of oar in a mine; a laying of clay of a solid binding quality, then flint-stones, then chalk, then upon the chalk rough ballast or gravel, 'till the whole work has been rais'd six or eight foot from the bottom; then it has been covered with a crown or rising ridge in the middle, gently sloping to the sides, that the rain might run off every way, and not soak into the work: This I have seen as fair and firm, after having stood, as we may conclude, at least 12 or 1600 years, as if it had been made but the year before.

DANIEL DE FOE *A Tour through England*, 1724

The Hazards of Travel

THERE is no such convenience as a waggon in this country, and my finances were too weak to support the expense of hiring a horse. I determined, therefore, to set out with the carriers, who transport goods from one place to another on horseback; and this scheme I accordingly put in execution on the first day of September, 1739, sitting on a pack-saddle between two baskets, one of which contained my goods in a knapsack. But by the time we arrived at Newcastle-on-Tyne, I was so fatigued with the tediousness of the carriage, and benumbed with the coldness of the weather, that I resolved to travel the rest of my journey on foot rather than proceed in such a disagreeable manner.

The ostler of the inn at which we put up, understanding I was bound for London, advised me to take my passage in a collier, which would be both cheap and expeditious, and withal much easier than to walk upwards of three hundred miles through deep roads in the winter time; a journey which he believed I had not strength enough to perform. I was almost persuaded to take his advice, when one day, stepping into a barber's shop to be shaved, the young man, while he lathered my face, accosted me thus: "Sir, I presume you are a Scotchman." I answered in the affirmative, and when I declared my name was Random, he exclaimed, in a rapture, "How! Rory Random?"—"The same," I replied, looking at him with astonishment. "What!" cried he, "don't you know your old schoolfellow Hugh Strap?"

When I communicated to him my situation and design, he did not approve of my taking a passage by sea, by reason of the danger of a winter voyage, which is very hazardous along that coast, as well as the precariousness of the wind, which might possibly detain me a great while, to the no small detriment of my fortune; whereas, if I would venture by land, he would bear me company, carry my baggage all the way, and, if we should be fatigued before we could perform the journey, it would be no hard matter for us to find on the road either return horses or waggons, of which we might take the advantage for a very trifling expense.

Having concerted the plan and settled our affairs that night, we departed next morning by daybreak, armed with a good cudgel each (my companion being charged with the furniture of us both, crammed into one knapsack), and our money sewed between the lining and waistbands of our breeches, except some loose silver for our immediate expenses on the road. We travelled all day at a round pace; but, being ignorant of the proper stages, were benighted at a good distance from any inn, so that we were compelled to take up our lodging at a small hedge alehouse, that stood on a by-road, about half a mile from the highway. There we found a pedlar of our own country, in whose company we regaled ourselves with bacon and eggs, and a glass of good ale, before a comfortable fire, conversing all the while very sociably with the landlord and his daughter, Betty—a hale, buxom lass, who entertained us with great good-humour, and in whose affection I was vain enough to believe I had made some progress. About eight o'clock we were all three, at our own desire, shown into an apartment furnished with two beds, in one of which Strap and I betook ourselves to rest, and the pedlar occupied the other, though not before he had prayed a considerable time extempore, searched into every corner of the room, and fastened the door on the inside with a strong iron screw, which he carried about with him for that use.

I slept very sound till midnight, when I was disturbed by a violent motion of the bed, which shook under me with a continual tremor. Alarmed at this phenomenon, I jogged my companion, whom, to my no small amazement, I found drenched in sweat, and quaking through every limb. He told me, with a low faltering voice, that we were undone, for there was a bloody highwayman, with loaded pistols, in the next room; then bidding me make as little noise as possible, he directed me to a small chink in the board partition, through which I could see a thickset, brawny fellow, with a fierce countenance, sitting at a table with our young landlady, having a bottle of ale and a brace of pistols before him.

46 A Stage-wagon entering Towcester, Northamptonshire, in 1836
From a drawing by G. S. Shepherd

47 A Country Lane in the Eighteenth Century

48 An Eighteenth-century Postchaise
After Thomas Rowlandson

49 A Carriage Arrival at a Regency House
After J. C. Loudon

I listened with great attention, and heard him say in a terrible tone, "D—n that son of a —, Smack, the coachman!—he has served me a fine trick indeed! But d—tion seize me, if I don't make him repent it! I'll teach the scoundrel to give intelligence to others while he is under articles with me!"

Here, as the devil would have it, the pedlar snored so loud that the highwayman, snatching his pistols, started up, crying, "Hell and d—n—n! I am betrayed! Who's that in the next room?" Mrs. Betty told him he need not be uneasy; there were only three poor wearied travellers, who, missing the road, had taken up their lodging in the house, and were asleep long ago. "Travellers!" says he, "spies, you —! But no matter, I'll send them all to hell in an instant." He accordingly ran towards our door, when his sweetheart, interposing, assured him there was only a couple of poor young Scotchmen, who were too raw and ignorant to give him the least cause of suspicion; and the third was a presbyterian pedlar of the same nation, who had often lodged in the house before.

This declaration satisfied the thief, who swore he was glad there was a pedlar, for he wanted some linen. Then, in a jovial manner, he put about the glass, mingling his discourse to Betty with caresses and familiarities, that spoke him very happy in his amours. During that part of the conversation which regarded us, Strap had crept under the bed, where he lay in the agonies of fear, so that it was with great difficulty I persuaded him our dangers were over, and prevailed on him to awake the pedlar, and inform him of what he had seen and heard.

While we were at breakfast, Betty endeavoured, by all the cunning she was mistress of, to learn whether or no we suspected our fellow-lodger whom we saw take horse; but, as we were on our guard, we answered her sly questions with a simplicity she could not distrust; when, all of a sudden, we heard the trampling of a horse's feet at the door. This noise alarmed Strap so much, whose imagination was wholly engrossed by the image of Rifle, that, with a countenance as pale as milk, he cried, "O Lord! there is the highwayman returned!"

Our landlady, staring at these words, said, "What highwayman, young man? Do you think any highwaymen harbour here?"

Though I was very much disconcerted at this piece of indiscretion in Strap, I had presence of mind enough to tell her we had met a horseman the day before, whom Strap had foolishly supposed to be a highwayman, because he rode with pistols;

and that he had been terrified at the sound of a horse's feet ever since.

She forced a smile at the ignorance and timidity of my comrade; but, I could perceive, not without great concern, that this account was not at all satisfactory to her.

TOBIAS SMOLLETT *Roderick Random*, 1748

A Ceremonious Journey

THE clock had no sooner struck seven, than the ladies were ready for their journey; and, at their desire, his lordship and his equipage were prepared to attend them. And now a matter of some difficulty arose; and this was, how his lordship himself should be conveyed: for though in stage-coaches, where passengers are properly considered as so much luggage, the ingenious coachman stows half a dozen, with perfect ease, in the place of four; for well he contrives that the fat hostess, or well-fed alderman, may take up no more room than the slim miss, or taper master—it being the nature of guts, when well squeezed, to give way, and to lie in a narrow compass; yet in these vehicles which are called, for distinction's sake, gentlemen's coaches, though they are often larger than the others, this method of packing is never attempted. His lordship would have put a short end to the difficulty by very gallantly desiring to mount his horse; but Mrs. Fitzpatrick would by no means consent to it. It was, therefore, concluded, that the Abigails should by turns, relieve each other on one of his lordship's horses, which was presently equipped with a side-saddle for that purpose.

His lordship conducted the ladies into the vehicle, as he did likewise Mrs. Honour, who, after many civilities, and more dear madams, at last yielded to the well-bred importunities of her sister Abigail, and submitted to be complimented with the first ride in the coach; in which, indeed, she would afterwards have been contented to have pursued her whole journey, had not her mistress, after several fruitless intimations, at length forced her to take her turn on horseback. The coach now, having received its company, began to move forwards, attended by many servants, and by two led-captains, who had before rode with his lordship, and who would have been dismissed from the vehicle upon a much less worthy occasion than was this of accommodating two ladies.

His lordship and his fair companions, made such good expedition, that they performed a journey of ninety miles in two days, and on the second evening arrived in London, without having encountered any one adventure on the road worthy the dignity of this history to relate. Our pen, therefore, shall imitate the expedition which it describes, and our history shall keep pace with the travellers who are its subject. Good writers will, indeed, do well to imitate the ingenious traveller in this instance, who always proportions his stay at any place to the beauties, elegances, and curiosities which it affords. At Esher, at Stowe, at Wilton, at Estbury, and at Prior's Park, days are too short for the ravished imagination; while we admire the wondrous power of art in improving nature. In some of these, art chiefly engages our admiration; in others, nature and art contend for our applause; but, in the last, the former seems to triumph.

The same taste, the same imagination, which luxuriously riots in these elegant scenes, can be amused with objects of far inferior note. The woods, the rivers, the lawns of Devon and of Dorset, attract the eye of the ingenious traveller, and retard his pace; which delay he afterwards compensates by swiftly scouring over the gloomy heath of Bagshot, or that pleasant plain which extends itself westward from Stockbridge, where no other object than one single tree only in sixteen miles presents itself to the view, unless the clouds, in compassion to our tired spirits, kindly open their variegated mansions to our prospect. Not so travels the money-meditating tradesman, the sagacious justice, the dignified doctor, the warm-clad grazier, with all the numerous offspring of wealth and dullness. On they jog, with equal pace, through the verdant meadows, or over the barren heath, their horses measuring four miles and a half per hour with the utmost exactness; the eyes of the beast and of his master being alike directed forwards, and employed in contemplating the same objects in the same manner. With equal rapture the good rider surveys the proudest boasts of the architect, and those fair buildings, with which some unknown name hath adorned the rich clothing town; where heaps of bricks are piled up as a kind of monument, to show that heaps of money have been piled there before. And now, reader, as we are in haste to attend our heroine, we will leave to thy sagacity to apply all this to the Boeotian writers, and to those authors who are their opposites.

HENRY FIELDING *Tom Jones*, 1749

A Breakdown

We made a precipitate retreat from Scarborough, setting out accordingly over the moors, by the way of Whitby, and began our journey betimes, in hopes of reaching Stockton that night; but in this hope we were disappointed. In the afternoon, crossing a deep gutter made by a torrent, the coach was so hard strained, that one of the irons which connect the frame snapped, and the leather sling on the same side cracked in the middle. The shock was so great, that my sister Liddy struck her head against Mrs. Tabitha's nose with such violence that the blood flowed; and Win Jenkins was darted through a small window in that part of the carriage next the horses, where she stuck like a bawd in the pillory, till she was released by the hand of Mr. Bramble. We were eight miles distant from any place where we could be supplied with chaises, and it was impossible to proceed with the coach, until the damage should be repaired. In this dilemma, we discovered a blacksmith's forge on the edge of a small common, about half a mile from the scene of our disaster, and thither the postilions made shift to draw the carriage slowly, while the company walked a-foot; but we found the blacksmith had been dead some days; and his wife, who had been lately delivered, was deprived of her senses, under the care of a nurse hired by the parish. We were exceedingly mortified at this disappointment, which, however, was surmounted by the help of Humphrey Clinker, who is a surprising compound of genius and simplicity. Finding the tools of the defunct, together with some coals in the smithy, he unscrewed the damaged iron in a twinkling, and kindling a fire, united the broken pieces with equal dexterity and despatch. But his ingenuity was not confined to his own province of farrier and blacksmith: it was necessary to join the leather sling, which had been broken; and this service he likewise performed, by means of a broken awl, which he new-pointed and ground, a little hemp which he spun into lingels, and a few tacks which he made for the purpose. On the whole, we were in a condition to proceed in little more than one hour; but even this delay obliged us to pass the night at Gisborough. Next day we crossed the Tees at Stockton, which is a neat, agreeable town; and there we resolved to dine, with purpose to lie at Durham.

Tobias Smollett — *Humphrey Clinker*, 1771

Touring

We rode on well, till we came to the high mountain called the Rattakin, by which time both Dr. Johnson and the horses were a good deal fatigued. It is a terrible steep to climb, notwithstanding the road is formed slanting along it; however, we made it out. Going down the hill on the other side was no easy task. As Dr. Johnson was a great weight, the two guides agreed that he should ride the horses alternately. Hay's were the two best, and the Doctor would not ride but upon one or other of them, a black or a brown. But, as Hay complained much after ascending the *Rattakin*, the Doctor was prevailed with to mount one of Vass's greys. As he rode upon it down hill, it did not go well; and he grumbled.

It grew dusky; and we had a very tedious ride for what was called five miles; but I am sure would measure ten. We had no conversation. I was riding forward to the inn at Glenelg, on the shore opposite to Sky, that I might take proper measures, before Dr. Johnson, who was now advancing in dreary silence, Hay leading his horse, should arrive.

As we passed the barracks at Bernéra I looked at them wishfully, as soldiers have always everything in the best order: but there was only a serjeant and a few men there. We came on to the inn at Glenelg. There was no provender for our horses; so they were sent to grass, with a man to watch them. A maid shewed us upstairs into a room damp and dirty, with bare walls, a variety of bad smells, a coarse black greasy fir table, and forms of the same kind; and out of a wretched bed started a fellow from his sleep, like Edgar in King Lear, "*Poor Tom's a cold.*"

This inn was furnished with not a single article that we could either eat or drink; but Mr. Murchison, factor to the Laird of Macleod in Glenelg, sent us a bottle of rum and some sugar, with a polite message, to acquaint us, that he was very sorry that he did not hear of us till we had passed his house, otherwise he should have insisted on our sleeping there that night. Our bad accommodation here made me uneasy, and almost fretful. I sent for fresh hay, with which we made beds for ourselves, each in a room equally miserable. Like Wolfe, we had a "*choice of difficulties.*" Dr. Johnson made things easier by comparison. At M'Queen's, last night, he observed, that few were so well lodged in a ship. To-night he said, we were better than if we had been upon the hill. He lay down buttoned up in his great coat. I had my sheets spread on the hay, and my clothes and great coat laid over me, by way of blankets.

JAMES BOSWELL *Journal of a Tour to the Hebrides with Samuel Johnson, LL.D.*, 1785

The English Inn

WE (Johnson and Boswell) dined at an excellent inn at Chapel-house, where he expatiated on the felicity of England in its taverns and inns, and triumphed over the French for not having, in any perfection, the tavern life. "There is no private house," said he, "in which people can enjoy themselves so well as at a capital tavern. Let there be ever so great plenty of good things, ever so much grandeur, ever so much elegance, ever so much desire that everybody should be easy ; in the nature of things it cannot be: there must always be some degree of care and anxiety to entertain his guests; the guests are anxious to be agreeable to him; and no man, but a very impudent dog indeed, can as freely command what is in another man's house, as if it were his own. Whereas at a tavern there is a general freedom from anxiety. You are sure you are welcome: and the more noise you make, the more trouble you give, the more good things you call for, the welcomer you are. No servants will attend you with the alacrity which waiters do, who are incited by the prospect of an immediate reward in proportion as they please. No, Sir; there is nothing which has yet been contrived by man, by which so much happiness is produced as by a good inn or tavern." He then repeated, with great emotion, Shenstone's lines:—

"Who'er has travell'd life's dull round,
Where'er his stages may have been,
May sigh to think he still has found
The warmest welcome at an inn."

JAMES BOSWELL *The Life of Samuel Johnson, LL.D.*, 1791

Country Roads

FROM East-Meon, I did not go on to Froxfield church, but turned off to the left to a place (a couple of houses) called *Bower*. Near this I stopped at a friend's house, which is in about as lonely a situation as I ever saw.

At Bower I got instructions to go to Hawkley, but accompanied with most earnest advice not to go that way, for that it was impossible to get along. The roads were represented as so bad; the floods so much out; the hills and bogs so dangerous; that, really, I began to *doubt;* and, if I had not been brought up amongst the clays of the Holt Forest and the bogs of the neighbouring heaths, I should certainly have turned off to my right, to go over Hindhead, great as was my objection to going that way. "Well, then," said my friend at Bower, "if you *will* go that way, by G—, you must go down *Hawkley Hanger;*" of which he then gave me *such* a description! But even this I found to fall short of the reality. I inquired simply, whether *people were in the habit* of going down it; and the answer being in the affirmative, on I went through green lanes and bridle-ways till I came to the turnpike-road from Petersfield to Winchester, which I crossed, going into a narrow and almost untrodden green lane, on the side of which I found a cottage. Upon my asking the way to *Hawkley*, the woman at the cottage said, "Right up the lane, sir: you'll come to a *hanger* presently: you must take care, sir: you can't ride down: will your horses *go alone*?"

On we trotted up this pretty green lane; and indeed, we had been coming gently and generally uphill for a good while. The lane was between highish banks and pretty high stuff growing on the banks, so that we could see no distance from us, and could receive not the smallest hint of what was so near at hand. The lane had a little turn towards the end; so that, out we came, all in a moment, at the very edge of the hanger! And never, in all my life, was I so surprised and so delighted! I pulled up my horse, and sat and looked; and it was like looking from the top of a castle down into the sea, except that the valley was land and not water. Those who had so strenuously dwelt on the dirt and dangers of this route, had said not a word about beauties, the matchless beauties of the scenery. These hangers are woods on the sides of very steep hills. The trees and underwood *hang*, in some sort, to the ground, instead of *standing on* it. Hence these places are called *Hangers*. From the summit of that which I had now to descend, I looked down upon the villages of Hawkley, Greatham, Selborne and some others.

Men, however, are not to have such beautiful views as this without some trouble. We had had the view; but we had to go down the hanger. We had, indeed, some roads to get along, as we could, afterwards; but we had to get down the hanger first. The horses took the lead, and crept partly down upon their feet and partly upon their hocks. It was extremely slippery too; for the soil is a sort of marl, or, as they call it here, maume, or mame, which is, when wet, very much like *grey soap*. In such a case it was likely that I should keep in the rear, which I did, and I descended by taking hold of the branches of the underwood, and so letting myself down. When we got to the bottom, I bade my man, when he should go back to Uphusband, tell the people there that *Ashmansworth Lane* is not the *worst* piece of road in the world. Our worst, however, was not come yet, nor had we by any means seen the most novel sights.

After crossing a little field and going through a farmyard, we came into a lane, which was, at once, road and river. We found a hard bottom, however; and when we got out of the water, we got into a lane with high banks. The banks were quarries of white stone, like Portland stone, and the bed of the road was of the same stone: and, the rains having been heavy for a day or two before, the whole was as clean and as white as the steps of a fundholder or dead-weight doorway in one of the squares of the Wen. Here were we, then, going along a stone road with stone banks, and yet the underwood and trees grew well upon the tops of the banks. In the solid stone beneath us, there were a horse-track and wheel-tracks, the former about three and the latter about six inches deep. How many many ages it must have taken the horses' feet, the wheels, and the water, to wear down this stone so as to form a hollow way! The horses seemed alarmed at their situation; they trod with fear; but they took us along very nicely, and, at last, got us safe into the indescribable dirt and mire of the road from Hawkley Green to Greatham. Here the bottom of all the land is this solid white stone, and the top is that *mame*, which I have before described. The hop-roots penetrate down into this stone. How deep the stone may go I know not; but, when I came to look up at the end of one of the piers, or promontories, mentioned above, I found that it was all of this same stone.

At Hawkley Green I asked a farmer the way to Thursley. He pointed to one of two roads going from the green; but, it appearing to me that that would lead me up to the London road and over Hindhead, I gave him to understand that I was resolved to get along, somehow or other, through the "low countries." He besought me not to think of it. However, finding me resolved, he got a man to go a little way to put me into the Greatham road. The man came, but the farmer could not let me go off without renewing his entreaties that I would go away to Liphook, in which entreaties the man joined, though he was to be paid very well for his trouble.

Off we went, however, to Greatham. I am thinking whether I ever did see *worse* roads. Upon the whole, I think, I have; though I am not sure that the roads of New Jersey, between Trenton and Elizabeth Town, at the breaking up of winter be worse. Talk of *shows*, indeed! Take a piece of this road! just a cut across, and a rod long, and carry it up to London. That would be something like a *show*!

William Cobbett — *Rural Rides*, 1830

Coaching Days

They have rumbled through the streets, and jolted over the stones, and at length reach the wide and open country. The wheels skim over the hard and frosty ground; and the horses, bursting into a canter at a smart crack of the whip, step along the road as if the load behind them—coach, passengers, cod-fish and oyster-barrels, and all—were but a feather at their heels. They have descended a gentle slope, and enter upon a level, as compact and dry as a solid block of marble, two miles long. Another crack of the whip, and on they speed at a smart gallop, the horses tossing their heads and rattling the harness, as if in exhilaration at the rapidity of the motion; while the coachman, holding whip and reins in one hand, takes off his hat with the other, and resting it on his knees, pulls out his handkerchief, and wipes his forehead, partly because he has a habit of doing it, and partly because it's as well to show the passengers how cool he is, and what an easy thing it is to drive four-in-hand when you have had as much practice as he has. Having done this very leisurely (otherwise the effect would be materially impaired), he replaces his handkerchief, pulls on his hat, adjusts his gloves, squares his elbows, cracks the whip again, and on they speed, more merrily than before.

A few small houses, scattered on either side of the road, betoken the entrance to some town or village. The lively notes of the guard's key-bugle vibrate in the clear cold air, and wake up the old gentleman inside, who, carefully letting down the window-sash half-way, and standing sentry over the air, takes a short peep out, and then carefully pulling it up again, informs the other inside that they're going to change directly; on which the other inside wakes himself up, and determines to postpone his next nap until after the stoppage. Again the bugle sounds lustily forth, and rouses the cottager's wife and children, who peep out at the house door, and watch the coach till it turns the corner, when they once more crouch round the blazing fire, and throw on another log of wood against father comes home; while father himself, a full mile off, has just exchanged a friendly nod with the coachman, and turned round to take a good long stare at the vehicle as it whirls away.

And now the bugle plays a lively air as the coach rattles through the ill-paved streets of a country town; and the coachman, undoing the buckle which keeps his ribands together, prepares to throw them off the moment he stops.

He throws down the reins and gets down himself, and the other outside passengers drop down also; except those who have no great confidence in their ability to get up again; and they remain where they are, and stamp their feet against the coach to warm them—looking, with longing eyes and red noses, at the bright fire in the inn bar, and the sprigs of holly with red berries which ornament the window.

But the guard has delivered at the corn-dealer's shop, the brown paper packet he took out of the little pouch which hangs over his shoulder by a leathern strap; and has seen the horses carefully put to; and has thrown on the pavement the saddle which was brought from London on the coach roof; and has assisted in the conference between the watchman and the hostler about the gray mare that hurt her off fore-leg last Tuesday; and he and Mr. Weller are all right behind, and the coachman is all right in front, and the old gentleman inside, who has kept the window down full two inches all this time, has pulled it up again, and the cloths are off, and they are all ready for starting. The coachman shouts an admonitory "Now then, gen'l'm'n," the guard re-echoes it; the old gentleman inside thinks it a very extraordinary thing that people *will* get down when they know there isn't time for it; shawls are pulled up, coat collars are readjusted, the pavement ceases, the houses disappear; and they are once again dashing along the open road, with the fresh air blowing in their faces, and gladdening their very hearts within them.

Such was the progress of Mr. Pickwick and his friends by the Muggleton Telegraph, on their way to Dingley Dell.

CHARLES DICKENS *Pickwick Papers*, 1837

The Traveller's Return

OUR Major had rendered himself so popular on board the *Ramchunder*, that when he and Mr. Sedley descended into the welcome shore-boat which was to take them from the ship, the whole crew, men and officers, the great Captain Bragg himself leading off, gave three cheers for Major Dobbin, who blushed very much, and ducked his head in token of thanks. Jos, who very likely thought the cheers were for himself, took off his gold-laced cap and waved it majestically to his friends, and they were pulled to shore and landed with great dignity at the pier, whence they proceeded to the Royal George Hotel.

Although the sight of that magnificent round of beef, and the silver tankard, suggestive of real British home-brewed ale and porter, which perennially greet the eyes of the traveller returning from foreign parts, who enters the coffee-room of the George, are so invigorating and delightful, that a man entering such a comfortable snug homely English inn, might well like to stop some days there, yet Dobbin began to talk about a post-chaise instantly, and was no sooner at Southampton than he wished to be on the road to London. Jos, however, would not hear of moving that evening. Why was he to pass a night in a post-chaise instead of a great large undulating downy feather bed, which was there ready to replace the horrid little narrow crib in which the portly Bengal gentleman had been confined during the voyage? He could not think of moving till his baggage was cleared, or of travelling until he could do so with his chillum. So the Major was forced to wait over that night, and despatched a letter to his family announcing his arrival.

Major Dobbin made his appearance the next morning very neatly shaved and dressed, according to his wont. Indeed, it was so early in the morning, that nobody was up in the house except that wonderful Boots of an inn who never seems to want sleep: and the Major could hear the snores of the various inmates of the house roaring through the corridors as he creaked about in those dim passages. Then the sleepless Boots went shirking round from door to door, gathering up at each the

Bluchers, Wellingtons, Oxonians, which stood outside. Then Jos's native servant arose and began to get ready his master's ponderous dressing apparatus, and prepare his hookah: then the maid-servants got up, and meeting the dark man in the passages, shrieked, and mistook him for the devil. He and Dobbin stumbled over their pails in the passages as they were scouring the decks of the Royal George. When the first unshorn waiter appeared and unbarred the door of the inn, the Major thought that the time for departure was arrived, and ordered a post-chaise to be fetched instantly, that they might set off.

If he had been an English nobleman travelling on a pleasure tour, or a newspaper courier bearing despatches (government messages are generally carried much more quietly), he could not have travelled more quickly. The post-boys wondered at the fees he flung amongst them. How happy and green the country looked as the chaise whirled rapidly from milestone to milestone, through neat country towns where landlords came out to welcome him with smiles and bows; by pretty roadside inns, where the signs hung on the elms, and horses and waggoners were drinking under the chequered shadow of the trees; by old halls and parks; rustic hamlets clustered round ancient grey churches—and through the charming friendly English landscape. Is there any in the world like it? To a traveller returning home it looks so kind—it seems to shake hands with you as you pass through it. Well, Major Dobbin passed through all this from Southampton to London, and without noting much beyond the milestones along the road. You see he was so eager to see his parents at Camberwell.

WILLIAM MAKEPEACE THACKERAY *Vanity Fair*, 1847

An Insolent Race

THE stage-coachmen of England, at the time of which I am speaking, considered themselves mighty fine gentry, nay, I verily believe the most important personages of the realm, and their entertaining this high opinion of themselves can scarcely be wondered at; they were low fellows, but masters at driving; driving was in fashion, and sprigs of nobility used to dress as coachmen and imitate the slang and behaviour of coachmen, from whom occasionally they would take lessons in driving as they sat beside them on the box, which post of honour any

50 A Mishap to a Mail Coach, 1825

After James Pollard

51 The Iron Road: Hebden Bridge Station, Yorkshire, in 1845

After A. F. Tait

52 The Highgate Road: a Mail Coach leaving London, 1830

After James Pollard

sprig of nobility who happened to take a place on a coach claimed as his unquestionable right; and these sprigs would smoke cigars and drink sherry with the coachmen in bar-rooms, and on the road; and, when bidding them farewell, would give them a guinea or a half-guinea, and shake them by the hand, so that these fellows, being low fellows, very naturally thought no small liquor of themselves, but would talk familiarly of their friends lords so and so, the honourable misters so and so, and Sir Harry and Sir Charles, and be wonderfully saucy to any one who was not a lord, or something of the kind; and this high opinion of themselves received daily augmentation from the servile homage paid them by the generality of the untitled male passengers, especially those on the fore part of the coach, who used to contend for the honour of sitting on the box with the coachman when no sprig was nigh to put in his claim. Oh! what servile homage these craven creatures did pay these same coach fellows, more especially after witnessing this or t'other act of brutality practised upon the weak and unoffending—upon some poor friendless woman travelling with but little money, and perhaps a brace of hungry children with her, or upon some thin and half-starved man travelling on the hind part of the coach from London to Liverpool with only eighteen pence in his pocket after his fare was paid, to defray his expenses on the road; for as the insolence of these knights was vast, so was their rapacity enormous; they had been so long accustomed to have crowns and half-crowns rained upon them by their admirers and flatterers, that they would look at a shilling, for which many an honest labourer was happy to toil for ten hours under a broiling sun, with the utmost contempt; would blow upon it derisively, or fillip it into the air before they pocketed it; but when nothing was given them, as would occasionally happen—for how could they receive from those who had nothing? and nobody was bound to give them anything, as they had certain wages from their employers—then what a scene would ensue! Truly the brutality and rapacious insolence of English coachmen had reached a climax; it was time that these fellows should be disenchanted, and the time—thank Heaven!—was not far distant. Let the craven dastards who used to curry favour with them, and applaud their brutality, lament their loss now that they and their vehicles have disappeared from the roads; I, who have ever been an enemy to insolence, cruelty, and tyranny, loathe their memory, and, what is more, am not afraid to say so, well aware of the storm of vituperation, partly learnt from them, which I may expect from those who used to fall down and worship them.

George Borrow *Romany Rye*, 1857

The Dover Mail

It was the Dover road that lay, on a Friday night late in November, before the first of the persons with whom this history has business. The Dover road lay, as to him, beyond the Dover mail, as it lumbered up Shooter's Hill. He walked uphill in the mire by the side of the mail, as the rest of the passengers did; not because they had the least relish for walking exercise, under the circumstances, but because the hill, and the harness, and the mud, and the mail, were all so heavy, that the horses had three times already come to a stop, besides once drawing the coach across the road, with the mutinous intent of taking it back to Blackheath.

With drooping heads and tremulous tails, they mashed their way through the thick mud, floundering and stumbling between whiles, as if they were falling to pieces at the larger joints. As often as the driver rested them and brought them to a stand, with a wary "Wo-ho! so-ho then!" the near leader violently shook his head and everything upon it—like an unusually emphatic horse, denying that the coach could be got up the hill. Whenever the leader made this rattle the passenger started, as a nervous passenger might, and was disturbed in mind.

Two other passengers, besides the one, were plodding up the hill by the side of the mail. All three were wrapped to the cheek-bones and over the ears, and wore jack-boots. Not one of the three could have said, from anything he saw, what either of the other two was like; and each was hidden under almost as many wrappers from the eyes of the mind, as from the eyes of the body, of his two companions. In those days travellers were very shy of being confidential on a short notice, for anybody on the road might be a robber or in league with robbers. As to the latter, when every posting-house and ale-house could produce somebody in "the Captain's" pay, ranging from the landlord to the lowest stable nondescript, it was the likeliest thing upon the cards. So the guard of the Dover mail thought to himself, that Friday night in November, one thousand, seven hundred and seventy-five, lumbering up Shooter's Hill, as he stood on his own particular perch behind the mail, beating his feet, and keeping an eye and a hand on the arm-chest before him, where a loaded blunderbuss lay at the top of six or eight loaded horse-pistols, deposited on a substratum of cutlass.

The Dover mail was in its usual genial position that the guard suspected the passengers, the passengers suspected one another and the guard, they all suspected everybody else, and the coachman was sure of nothing but the horses; as to which cattle he could with a clear conscience have taken his oath on the two Testaments that they were not fit for the journey.

"Wo-ho!" said the coachman. "So, then! One more pull and you're at the top and be damned to you, for I have had trouble enough to get you to it!—Joe!"

"Hello!" the guard replied.

"What o'clock do you make it, Joe?"

"Ten minutes, good, past eleven."

"My blood!" ejaculated the vexed coachman, "and not a-top of Shooter's yet! Tst! Yah! Get on with you!"

The emphatic horse, cut short by the whip in a most decided negative, made a decided scramble for it, and the three other horses followed suit. Once more the Dover mail struggled on, with the jack-boots of its passengers squashing along by its side. They had stopped when the coach stopped, and they kept close company with it. If any one of the three had had the hardihood to propose to another to walk on a little ahead in the mist and darkness, he would have put himself in a fair way of getting shot instantly as a highwayman.

The last burst carried the mail to the summit of the hill. The horses stopped to breathe again, and the guard got down to skid the wheel for the descent, and open the coach door to let the passengers in.

CHARLES DICKENS *A Tale of Two Cities*, 1859

The Branch Line

RAILWAYS have destroyed the romance of travelling. Bulwer himself could not make anything out of a collision, and trains, trucks, trams, and tinkling bells are equally intractable. No robbing, no fighting, no benighting, no run-away-ing. One journey is very much like another, save that the diagonal shoots across country are distinguished by a greater number of changes. But with the exception of certain level crossings, certain mountings up, certain divings down like a man changing his floor at a lodging, there is really nothing to celebrate. It's, "Away you go!" or, "Here you are!"

The Heavyside Hunt country had scarcely been screeched and whistled awake by the noise of railways. It had few requirements that way.

There were no factories, no tall chimneys, no coal pits, no potteries, no nothing. The grass grew in the streets of what they called the principal towns, where the rattle of a chaise would draw all heads to the windows. The people seemed happy and contented, more inclined to enjoy what they had than disposed to risk its possession in the pursuit of more. In fact, they might be called a three per cent. sort of people in contradistinction to the raving rapacity of modern cupidity.

It was long after dark ere the little dribbling, single line, branch railway, that Mr. Romford had adopted by means of a sort of triumphal arch on quitting the main one at Langford Green, deposited him at the quiet little town of Minshull Vernon, the nearest point to the Heavyside Hunt kennel. He had been in and out of so many trains, paced the platforms of so many stations, and read the announcements of so many waiting-rooms, that he felt as if he had traversed half the kingdom, and was thankful to get his luggage out for the last time in a quiet, unhurrying way. The train was twenty minutes behind time as it was, and the guard did not seem to care if he made it thirty before he got to the end of his short but slow journey. Minshull Vernon was a very small station, too insignificant for any advertiser save a temperance hotel-keeper and a soda-water maker to patronise. Even their placards looked worn and dejected. There wasn't a bus or a cab or a fly or a vehicle of any sort in attendance, only a little boy, who, however, was willing to carry any quantity of luggage. Such a contrast to the leaving in London.

Finding there were but two inns in the place, the White Swan, and the West-end Swell, our friend, true to his colours, patronised the latter, and was presently undergoing the usual inquiry "what would he like for supper," from a comely hostess, Mrs. Lockwood, the widow of a London groom, who in all probability had christened the house after his master. Romford wasn't a dainty man, and having narrowed the larder to the usual point of beefsteaks and mutton-chops, he said he'd have both, which he afterwards supplemented by a large cut of leathery cheese. Two pipes and two glasses of brandy-and-water, one to his own health, the other to that of the hounds, closed the performance, after which he rolled off to bed in a pair of West-end Swell slippers. He was soon undressed, in bed, and asleep.

ROBERT SURTEES *Mr. Facey Romford's Hounds*, 1865

Finding the Way

A LIGHT in a cottage invited him (Redworth) to apply for the needed directions. The door was opened by a woman, who had never heard tell of the Crossways, nor had her husband, nor any of the children crowding round them. A voice within ejaculated: "Crossways!" and soon upon the grating of a chair, an old man, whom the woman named her lodger, by way of introduction, presented himself with his hat on saying: "I knows the spot they call Crassways," and he led. Redworth understood the intention that a job was to be made of it, and submitting, said: "To the right, I think." He was bidden to come along, if he wanted "they Crassways," and from the right they turned to the left, and further sharp round, and on to a turn, where the old man, otherwise incommunicative, said: "There, down thik theer road, and a post in the middle."

"I want a house, not a post!" roared Redworth, spying a bare space.

The old man despatched a finger travelling to his nob. "Naw, there's ne'er a house. But that's crassways for four roads, if it's crassways you wants."

They journeyed backward. They were in such a maze of lanes that the old man was master, and Redworth vowed to be rid of him at the first cottage. This, however, they were long in reaching, and the old man was promptly through the garden-gate, hailing the people and securing information, before Redworth could well hear. He smiled at the dogged astuteness of a dense-headed old creature determined to establish a claim to his fee. They struck a lane sharp to the left.

"You're Sussex?" Redworth asked him, and was answered: "Naw; the Sheers."

Emerging from deliberation, the old man said: "Ah'm a Hampshireman."

"A capital county!"

"Heigh!" The old man heaved his chest. "Once!"

"Why, what has happened to it?"

"Once it were a capital county, I say. Hah! you asks me what have happened to it. You take and go and look at it now. And down heer'll be no better soon, I tells 'em. When ah was a boy, old Hampshire was a proud country, wi' the old coaches and the old squires, and Harvest Homes, and Christmas merryings.—Cutting up the land! There's no pride in livin' theer, nor anywhere, as I sees, now."

"You mean the railways."

"It's the Devil come up and abroad ower all England!" exclaimed the melancholy ancient patriot.

A little cheering was tried on him, but vainly. He saw with unerring distinctness the triumph of the Foul Potentate, nay his personal appearance "in they theer puffin' engines." The country which had produced Andrew Hedger, as he stated his name to be, would never show the same old cricketing commons it did when he was a boy. Old England, he declared, was done for.

When Redworth applied to his watch under the brilliant moonbeams, he discovered that he had been listening to this natural outcry of a decaying and shunted class full three-quarters of an hour, and The Crossways was not in sight. He remonstrated. The old man plodded along. "We must do as we're directed," he said.

Further walking brought them to a turn. They crossed the wooden bridge of a flooded stream. "Now ye have it, that may be the house, I reckon."

GEORGE MEREDITH *Diana of the Crossways*, 1885

Wayfaring

SURELY, of all possible moods, this, in which a man takes the road, is the best. Of course, if he *will* keep thinking of his anxieties, if he *will* open the merchant Abudah's chest and walk arm-in-arm with the hag—why, wherever he is, and whether he walk fast or slow, the chances are that he will not be happy. And so much the more shame to himself! There are perhaps thirty men setting forth at that same hour, and I would lay a large wager, there is not another dull face among the thirty. It would be a fine thing to follow, in a coat of darkness, one after another of these wayfarers, some summer morning, for the first few miles upon the road. This one, who walks fast, with a keen look in his eyes, is all concentrated in his own mind; he is up at his loom, weaving and weaving, to set the landscape to words. This one peers about, as he goes, among the grasses; he waits by the canal to watch the dragonflies; he leans on the gate of the pasture, and cannot look enough upon the complacent kine. And here comes another, talking, laughing, gesticulating to himself. His face changes from time to time, as indignation flashes from his eyes or anger clouds his forehead. He is composing articles, delivering orations, and conducting the most impassioned interviews, by the way. A little farther on, and it is as like as not he will begin to sing. And well for him, supposing him to be no great master in that art, if he stumble across no stolid peasant at a corner; for on such an occasion, I scarcely know which is the more troubled, or whether it is worse to suffer the confusion of your troubadour, or the unfeigned alarm of your clown. A sedentary population, accustomed, besides, to the strange mechanical bearing of the common tramp, can in no wise explain to itself the gaiety of these passers-by.

In the course of a day's walk, you see, there is much variance in the mood. From the exhilaration of the start, to the happy phlegm of the arrival, the change is certainly great. As the day goes on, the traveller moves from the one extreme towards the other. He becomes more and more incorporated with the material landscape, and the open-air drunkenness grows upon him with great strides, until he posts along the road, and sees everything about him, as in a cheerful dream. The first is certainly brighter, but the second stage is the more peaceful. A man does not make so many articles towards the end, nor does he laugh aloud; but the purely animal pleasures, the sense of physical well-being, the delight of every inhalation, of every time the muscles tighten down the thigh, console him for the absence of the others, and bring him to his destination still content.

Nor must I forget to say a word on bivouacs. You come to a milestone on a hill, or some place where deep ways meet under trees; and off goes the knapsack, and down you sit to smoke a pipe in the shade. You sink into yourself, and the birds come round and look at you; and your smoke dissipates upon the afternoon under the blue dome of heaven; and the sun lies warm upon your feet, and the cool air visits your neck and turns aside your open shirt. If you are not happy, you must have an evil conscience. You may dally as long as you like by the roadside. It is almost as if the millennium were arrived, when we shall throw our clocks and watches over the housetop, and remember time and seasons no more. Not to keep hours for a lifetime is, I was going to say, to live for ever. You have no idea, unless you have tried it, how endlessly long is a summer's day, that you measure out only by hunger, and bring to an end only when you are drowsy.

But it is at night, and after dinner, that the best hour comes. If the evening be fine and warm, there is nothing better in life than to lounge before the inn door in the sunset, or lean over the parapet of the bridge, to watch the weeds and the quick fishes. It is then, if ever, that you taste Joviality to the full significance of that audacious word. Your muscles are so agreeably slack, you feel so clean and so strong and so idle, that whether you move or sit still, whatever you do is done with pride and a kingly sort of pleasure. You fall in talk with anyone, wise or foolish, drunk or sober. And it seems as if a hot walk purged you, more than of anything else, of all narrowness and pride, and left curiosity to play its part freely, as in a child or a man of science. You lay aside all your own hobbies, to watch provincial humours develop themselves before you, now as a laughable farce, and now grave and beautiful like an old tale.

ROBERT LOUIS STEVENSON *Virginibus Puerisque*, 1881

The Tram Route

THERE is in the Midlands a single-line tramway system which boldly leaves the county town and plunges off into the black, industrial countryside, up hill and down dale, through the long ugly villages of workmen's houses, over canals and railways, past churches perched high and nobly over the smoke and shadows, through stark, grimy, cold little market-places, tilting away in a rush past cinemas and shops down to the hollow where the collieries are; then up again, past a little rural church, under the ash trees, on in a rush to the terminus, the last little ugly place of industry, the cold little town that shivers on the edge of the wild, gloomy country beyond. There the green and creamy coloured tram-car seems to pause and purr with curious satisfaction. But in a few minutes—the clock on the turret of the Co-operative Wholesale Society's Shops gives the time—away it starts once more on the adventure. Again there are the reckless swoops downhill, bouncing the loops: again the chilly wait in the hill-top market-place: again the breathless slithering round the precipitous drop under the church: again the patient halts at the loops, waiting for the outcoming car: so on and on, for two long hours, till at last the city looms beyond the fat gas-works, the narrow factories draw near, we are in the sordid streets of the great town, once more we sidle to a standstill at our terminus, abashed by the great crimson and cream-coloured city cars, but still perky, jaunty, somewhat dare-devil, green as a jaunty sprig of parsley out of a black colliery garden.

To ride on these cars is always an adventure. Since we are in war-time, the drivers are men unfit for active service: cripples and hunchbacks. So they have the spirit of the devil in them. The ride becomes a steeplechase. Hurray! we have leapt in a clear jump over the canal bridges—now for the four-lane corner. With a shriek and a trail of sparks we are clear again. To be sure, a tram often leaps the rails—but what matter! It sits in a ditch till other trams come to haul it out. It is quite common for a car, packed with one solid mass of living people, to come to a dead halt in the midst of unbroken blackness, the heart of nowhere on a dark night, and for the driver and the girl conductor to call: "All get off—car's on fire!" Instead, however, of rushing out in a panic, the passengers stolidly reply: "Get on—get on! We're not coming out. We're stopping where we are. Push on, George." So till flames actually appear.

The reason for this reluctance to dismount is that the nights are howlingly cold, black, and windswept, and a car is a haven of refuge. From village to village the miners travel, for a change of cinema, of girl, of pub. The trams are desperately packed. Who is going to risk himself in the black gulf outside, to wait perhaps an hour for another tram, then to see the forlorn notice "Depot Only," because there is something wrong! Or to greet a unit of three bright cars all so tight with people that they sail past with a howl of derision. Trams that pass in the night.

D. H. Lawrence — *England, my England*, 1922

Old Roads

In the middle of the wood is a four-went way, and the grassy or white roads lead where you please among tall beeches or broad, crisp-leaved shining thorns and brief open spaces given over to the mounds of ant and mole, to gravel pits and heather. Is this the Pilgrim's Way, in the valley now, a frail path chiefly through oak and hazel, sometimes over whin and whinberry and heather and sand, but looking up at the yews and beeches of the chalk hills? It passes a village pierced by straight clear waters—a woodland church—woods of the willow wren—and then, upon a promontory, alone, within the greenest mead rippled up to its walls by but few graves, another church, dark, squat, small-windowed, old, and from its position above the world having the characters of church and beacon and fortress, calling for all men's reverence. Up here in the rain it utters the pathos of the old roads behind, wiped out as if writ in water, or worn deep and then deserted and surviving only as tunnels under the hazels. I wish they could always be as accessible as churches are, and not handed over to land-owners—like Sandsbury Lane near Petersfield—because straight new roads have taken their places for the purposes of tradesmen and carriage people, or boarded up like that discarded fragment, deep-sunken and overgrown, below Colman's Hatch in Surrey. For centuries these roads seemed to hundreds so necessary, and men set out upon them at dawn with hope and followed after joy and were fain of their whiteness at evening: few turned this way or that out of them except into others as well worn (those who have turned aside for wantonness have left no trace at all), and most have been well content to see the same things as those who went before and as they themselves have seen a hundred times. And now they, as the sound of their feet and the echoes, are dead, and the roads are but pleasant folds in the grassy chalk. Stay, traveller, says the dark tower on the hill, and tread softly because your way is over men's dreams; but not too long; and now descend to the west as fast as feet can carry you, and follow your own dream, and that also shall in course of time lie under men's feet; for there is no going so sweet as upon the old dreams of men.

EDWARD THOMAS *The South Country*, 1909

Relics and Rituals

IT is a sophisticated nation that investigates its own ritual. As the age of materialism is more devoted *à la recherche du temps perdu*, so the renascence of culture awakens interest in the rites of an illiterate past. The common practices of common people are not remarkable so long as they are universal: when intellect leaps ahead they become a social study. The Elizabethans then were the first seriously to annotate the ritual of their own and preceding centuries. The forced development of city culture rapidly left behind traditional modes of country life, and so enabled critics to contemplate a period to which they only half belonged.

The rites of May, celebrated in almost every age, will serve to illustrate this critical attitude. As symbol of the beginning of summer the Celts chose a living tree, and around it held festive dances to arouse the spirit within. A pole was an early substitute for the tree, but greenery has always remained characteristic of May time. In the Shepheard's Calendar, Spenser asks:

"Is not thilke the mery moneth of May,
When love-lads masken in fresh array?
How falles it, then, we no merier bene,
Ylike as others, girt in gawdy greene?
Yougthes folke now flocken in every where,
To gather May buskets and smelling brere;
And home they hasten the postes to dight
And all the kirke pillours eare day light,
With Hawthorne buds, and swete Eglantine,
And girlonds of roses, and Sopps in wine."

After that they are off to the green wood to crown the King and Queen of the May amid dance and song. Such a ceremony early peoples deemed fitting to propitiate the spirit of fertile growth and Spenser offered no disparagement. But the more sophisticated observer Philip Stubbes makes other matter of a village festivity. "They have twenty or forty yoke of oxen, every ox having a sweet nose-gay of flowers placed on the tip of his horns; and these oxen draw home this May-pole (this stinking idol rather), which is covered all over with flowers and herbs, bound round about with strings from the top to the bottom, and sometimes painted with variable colours, with two or three hundred men, women and children following it with great devotion. And thus being reared up with handkerchiefs and flags streaming on the top, they straw the ground about it, set up summer-halls, bowers and arbours hard by it; and then they fall to banquet and feast, to leap and dance about it as the heathen people did at the dedication of their idols, whereof this is a perfect pattern, or rather the thing itself." If the author of this *Anatomie of Abuses* in 1583 seems to have overshot the mark, there is a further instance of the forces at work to uproot old customs, from a treatise of different bias eighty years later. John Evelyn's *Sylva* was more than a manual of plantation, it was an impassioned appeal to all tree-lovers. After approving the punishments ordained for stealers and destroyers of wood, Evelyn reinforces his charge against them: "And here we cannot but perstringe those riotous assemblies of idle people, who under pretence of going a Maying (as they term it), do oftentimes cut down and carry away fine straight trees, to set up before some alehouse or revelling place, where they keep their drunken Bacchanalia . . . occasioning so much waste and spoil as we find is done to trees at that season, under this wanton pretence, by breaking, mangling and tearing down of branches and entire arms of trees, to adorn their wooden idol." A newly scientific age is out of sympathy with folk beliefs, but it is testimony to the persistence of primitive instinct against all the assaults of rational minds, that Mary Mitford was able to enjoy her May-day undespoiled. In our time sentiment and sense of ritual combine to encourage Shipston-on-Stour to hold her annual festivity.

Rites of farm and countryside have sometimes a more practical end. The significance of the corn-spirit at sowing and reaping is clear enough: but with Plough Monday and Harvest Home other habits were ingrafted. Tusser, in 1571, catalogues the Farmer's feast days and adds:

> "For all this good feasting yet art thou not loose
> till thou give the ploughman in harvest his goose.
> Though goose go in stubble, yet passe not for that,
> let goose have a goose be shee leane be shee fat."

The goose was probably a bonus to the ploughman for his

unaccustomed work with the pitchfork, perhaps forfeited if he overthrew the cart with his sheaves. On Plough Monday there was competition between ploughmen and maid-servants, a cock going as prize to whoever was first with their implements ready for work. In *Lorna Doone* the harvest ceremony of a century later is portrayed, with parson cutting first swathe and special chorus sung before supper: its social purpose becomes evident in Mary Webb's description of the Love Carriage. Formerly a small community must be united for the year's most important work: nowadays the mechanical reaper and binder and the tractor have almost abolished such needs.

The first day of summer and Midsummer Eve, the end and the rebirth of the year, are occasions which can be identified most closely with the work of country-folk. The pagan bonfires of summer sun-worship were transferred to the hearth in Christmas celebrations: the days of toil in the field were succeeded by times of ease and plenty in the home. So Christmas day had a double importance: "a good fire heats all the house, and a full alms-basket makes the beggars prayers. The masquers and mummers make the merry sport: but if they lose their money, their drum goes dead. . . . Musicians now make their instruments speak out, and a good song is worth hearing. . . . It is now Christmas, and not a cup of drink must pass without a carol; the beasts, fowl and fish come to general execution; and the corn is ground to dust for the bakehouse and the pastry. . . . The Lord of Misrule is no mean man for his time, and guests of the high table must lack no wine." Thus in 1626 Nicholas Breton gives the view of the eternal peasant. The Mellstock waits and the mummers of Egdon Heath lived by the same lights in Hardy's *Wessex*. Against enjoyment, however, there is rarely wanting a puritanical opposition. In his catalogues of abuses Stubbes cannot spare the Lord of Misrule, whom "all the wild-heads of the parish, conventing together, choose (as) a Grand-Captain (of all mischief) . . . and him they crown with great solemnity, and adopt for their king. . . . Thus all things set in order, then have they their hobby-horses, dragons and other antics, together with their bawdy pipers and thundering drummers to strike up the devil's dance withal. Then march these heathen company towards the church and churchyard, their pipers piping, their drummers thundering, their stumps dancing, their bells jingling, their handkerchiefs swinging about their heads like madmen, their hobby-horses and other monsters skirmishing among the throng. . . . And thus these terrestrial furies spend the Sabbath day." So is life in merry England, like bully Bottom, translated.

Ritual of early times is now often remembered only by relics or monuments that have weathered the centuries. The sun-temple of Stonehenge was no dead dolmen for Borrow: Wayland's smithy on the Berkshire Downs held a powerful magic for Scott: and the Cerne Abbas giant obviously fascinates J. C. Powys. Such natural phenomena as the caves of Wookey Hole seem to assume legendary ritual by their own right: for belief in witchcraft persisted up to the eighteenth century. The well is another mistress of ceremonies and well-dressing retains a local vogue. The friendly spirit from which garlands and gifts may elicit cures or prophecies merits recognition. Although its supernatural powers are passed over, the *Gazetteer* of 1738 pays tribute to this water genius: "About two miles and a half from Malvern Hills is another Spring, which the old People thereabouts call Holy-Well, on the side of a low Hill in an arable Field, which besides its healing Qualities, has an extraordinary Efficacy, in clearing the Skin from Sun-burnings and Freckles; and adds as much Lustre as agrees with concealed Art and Modesty: for after washing two or three Mornings, it makes the Skin as smooth as Glass." About the same time Dr. William Stukely made his antiquarian tours through England publishing an *Itinerarium Curiosum* and gaining for himself the by-name of the "Arch-Druid." His curiosity was, nevertheless, an advancement on that gaping wonder of which Coryate's friend Peacham wrote:

"Why do the rude vulgar so hastily post in a madnesse
To gaze at trifles, and toyes not worth the viewing?
And thinke them happy, when may be shew'd for a penny
The Fleet-streete Mandrakes, that heavenly motion of Eltham,
Westminster monuments, and Guildhall huge Corinæus,
That horne of Windsor (of an Unicorne very likely)
The cave of Merlin, the skirts of old Tom a Lincolne."

In its wider sense the term relic includes all remains of a bygone age of society. Abbeys, towers, Gothic mansions, almshouses belong in spirit and purpose to *le temps perdu*. In reviewing the changing face of England it is proper to recall that the desolate abbey of Disraeli's lyrical description might also be seen by the practical eye of General Tilney as a desirable country retreat. In Carabas Castle, a pretentious mansion superannuated by its size and expense, Thackeray finds an object of satire, whereas Trollope in Ullathorne Court found only enrichment of architectural beauty with the passing of three centuries. From the bastions of Kenilworth Scott conjured historical romance, but had the temper of his times been different he might have seen it thus: "The castelle standeth on the toppe of an hille, right stately, and hath a mighty diche, and hille warkes agayne withoute the diche. . . . The kepe is exceeding fair and strong, and in the waullis of this castelle be certein strong tower. . . . One thing in the waullis of this castelle is much to be notid that is that they be embatelid on both the sides. So that if the area of the castelle were won by cumming in at the other of the two greate gates of the castelle, yet the kepers of the waullis might defende the castelle." Leland's interest in Rockingham had the technicality of an observer close in period to his subject. It is perhaps necessary to stand at such a distance as Hardy from Maiden Castle, before the social implications of similar relics can be isolated.

Ritual in more recent times has changed in form, if not greatly in spirit. A new suit or a Spring hat takes the place of May's greenery for urban celebrants: countrymen beribbon their horse's mane and sport a nosegay buttonhole. Usage long preserved the characteristic procedure of hiring fairs and the manner of the itinerant higgler, as it enabled the Goose-fair to outlive its prime in Nottingham or the pensioner to receive gifts of food and lodging at Barchester. The gradual loss of ceremonial and feast-day holidays in favour of seasonal vacations, however, has removed many of the occasions of communal activity. The newer mode, new in comparison with the rites thus replaced, is manifest in the annual pilgrimage to the sea-side or the national interest in the opening of the cricket season. The sea-side resort and especially the holiday camp offer to all and sundry that sense of participation vouchsafed to our ancestors by the elegant procedure at Bath, Matlock and Harrogate. This tradition may be seen developing from Humphrey Clinker's sea-bathing at Scarborough to Louisa Musgrove's visit to Lyme Regis: it is scarified by Lamb after his experience of Hastings, but enjoyed afresh by Kilvert at Beer.

Again, and as often in country life, the irrepressible new has its roots deep in the folk-custom of an older England.

The Village Witch

As I was walking with my friend Sir Roger by the side of one of his woods, an old woman applied herself to me for my charity. Her dress and figure put me in mind of the following description in Otway:

"In a close lane as I pursu'd my journey
I spy'd a wrinkled hag, with age grown double,
Picking dry sticks, and mumbling to herself.
Her eyes with scalding rheum were gall'd and red;
Cold palsy shook her head; her hands seem'd wither'd;
And on her crooked shoulders had she wrapt
The tatter'd remnant of an old strip'd hanging,
Which serv'd to keep her carcase from the cold:
So there was nothing of a piece about her.
Her lower weeds were all o'er coarsely patch'd
With different colour'd rags, black, red, white, yellow,
And seem'd to speak variety of wretchedness."

As I was musing on this description, and comparing it with the object before me, the knight told me, that this very old woman had the reputation of a witch all over the country, that her lips were observed to be always in motion, and that there was not a switch about her house which her neighbours did not believe had carried her several hundreds of miles. If she chanced to stumble, they always found sticks or straws that lay in the figure of a cross before her. If she made any mistake at church, and cried amen in a wrong place, they never failed to conclude that she was saying her prayers backwards. There was not a maid in the parish that would take a pin of her, though she should offer a bag of money with it. She goes by the name of Moll White, and has made the country ring with several imaginary exploits which are palmed upon her. If the dairy-maid does not make her butter come so soon as she would have it, Moll White is at the bottom of the churn. If a horse sweats in the stable, Moll White has been upon his back. If a hare makes an unexpected escape from the hounds, the huntsman curses Moll White. "Nay," says Sir Roger, "I have known the master of the pack, upon such occasion, send one of his servants to see if Moll White had been out that morning."

This account raised my curiosity so far, that I begged my friend Sir Roger to go with me into her hovel, which stood in a solitary corner under the side of the wood. Upon our first entering, Sir Roger winked to me, and pointed at something that stood behind the door, which upon looking that way, I found to be an old broom-staff. At the same time he whispered me in the ear to take notice of a tabby cat that sat in the chimney corner, which, as the old knight told me, lay under as bad a report as Moll White herself; for besides that Moll is said often to accompany her in the same shape, the cat is reported to have spoken twice or thrice in her life, and to have played several pranks above the capacity of an ordinary cat.

I was secretly concerned to see human nature in so much wretchedness and disgrace, but at the same time could not forbear smiling to hear Sir Roger, who is a little puzzled about the old woman, advising her as a justice of peace to avoid all communication with the devil, and never to hurt any of her neighbours' cattle. We concluded our visit with a bounty, which was very acceptable.

I have been the more particular in this account, because I hear there is scarce a village in England that has not a Moll White in it. When an old woman begins to doat, and grow chargeable to a parish, she is generally turned into a witch, and fills the whole country with extravagant fancies, imaginary distempers, and terrifying dreams. In the mean time, the poor wretch that is the innocent occasion of so many evils begins to be frightened at herself, and sometimes confesses secret commerces and familiarities that her imagination forms in a delirious old age. This frequently cuts off charity from the greatest objects of compassion, and inspires people with a malevolence towards those poor decrepit parts of our species, in whom human nature is defaced by infirmity and dotage.

JOSEPH ADDISON *The Spectator*, 1711

Somerset Celebrities

FOUR miles from Glastonbury, lies the little city of Wells, where is one of the neatest, and, in some respects, the most beautiful, cathedrals in England, particularly the west front of it, is one complete draught of imagery, very fine, and yet very antient.

This is a neat, clean city, and the clergy, in particular, live very handsomly; the Closs, or part of the city, where the Bishop's Palace is, is very properly called so; for it is walled in, and lock'd up like a little fortification, and has a ditch round it.

The dignified clergy live in the inside of it, and the prebendaries, and canons, which are very numerous, have very agreeable dwellings, and live very pleasantly. Here are no less than seven-and-twenty prebends, and nineteen canons, belonging to this church, besides a dean, a chancellor, a precentor, and three arch deacons; a number which very few cathedrals in England have, besides this.

Dugdale, in his *Monasticon*, tells us, that the church of Wells has given to the kingdom, one Cardinal, six High Chancellors, five High Treasurers, one Lord Privy Seal, one Lord President of Wales, one Secretary of State, all of them bishops of this diocess; the county is the diocess, and contains three hundred and eighty-eight parishes, and the arch deaconries are of Wells, Bath, and Taunton.

The city lies just at the foot of the mountains called Mendip Hills, and is itself built on a stony foundation. Its manufacture is chiefly of stockings, as is mentioned already; 'tis well built, and populous, and has several good families in it; so that there is no want of good company there.

Near this city, and just under the hills, is the famous, and so much talk'd of Wokey Hole, which, to me, that had been in Pool's Hole, in the Peak of Derby, has nothing of wonder or curiosity in it; the chief thing I observ'd in this, is, what is generally found in all such subterraneous caverns; namely, That the water dropping from the roof of the vault, petrifies, and hangs in long pieces like isicles, as if it would, in time, turn into a column to support the arch. As to the stories of a witch dwelling here, as of a gyant dwelling in the other (I mean in Pool's Hole) I take them to be equally fabulous, and worth no notice.

In the low country, on the other side Mendip Hills, lies Chedder, a village pleasantly situated under the very ridge of the mountains; before the village is a large green, or common, a piece of ground, in which the whole herd of the cows, belonging to the town, do feed; the ground is exceeding rich, and as the whole village are cowkeepers, they take care to keep up the goodness of the soil, by agreeing to lay on large quantities of dung for manuring, and inriching the land.

The milk of all the town cows, is brought together every day into a common room, where the persons appointed, or trusted for the management, measure every man's quantity, and set it down in a book; when the quantities are adjusted, the milk is all put together, and every meal's milk makes one cheese, and no more; so that the cheese is bigger, or less, as the cows yield more, or less, milk. By this method, the goodness of the cheese is preserved, and, without all dispute, it is the best cheese that England affords, if not, that the whole world affords.

Here is the deep, frightful chasm in the mountain, in the hollow of which, the road goes, by which they travel towards Bristol, and out of the same hollow, springs a little river, which flows with such a full stream, that, it is said, it drives twelve mills within a quarter of a mile of the spring; but this is not to be understood, without supposing it to fetch some winding reaches in the way; there would not, otherwise, be room for twelve mills to stand, and have any head of water above the mill, within so small a space of ground. The water of this spring, grows quickly into a river, and runs down into the marshes, and joins another little river called Axe, about Axbridge, and thence into the Bristol Channel, or Severn Sea.

Daniel de Foe *A Tour through England*, 1724

At the Sea-side

At the other end of Scarborough are two public rooms, for the use of the company who resort to this place in the summer, to drink the waters, and bathe in the sea; and the diversions are pretty much on the same footing here as at Bath. The Spa is a little way beyond the town, on this side, under a cliff, within a few paces of the sea; and thither the bathers go every morning *en déshabille;* but the descent is by a great number of steps, which invalids find very inconvenient. Betwixt the well and the harbour, the bathing machines are ranged along the beach, with all their proper utensils and attendants. You have never seen one of these machines. Image to yourself a small, snug, wooden chamber, fixed on a wheel-carriage, having a door at each end, and, on each side, a little window above, a bench below. The bather, ascending into this apartment by wooden steps, shuts himself in, and begins to undress; while the attendant yokes a horse to the end next the sea, and draws the carriage forwards, till the surface of the water is on a level with the floor of the dressing room; then he moves and fixes the horse to the other end. The person within, being stripped, opens the door to the seaward, where he finds the guide ready, and plunges headlong into the water. After having bathed, he re-ascends into the apartment by the steps which had been shifted for that purpose, and puts on his clothes at his leisure, while the carriage is drawn back again on the dry land; so that he has nothing further to do but to open the door and come down as he went up: should he be so weak or ill as to require a servant to put off and on his clothes, there is room enough in the apartment for half-a-dozen people. The guides who attend the ladies in the water are of their own sex; and they and the female bathers have a dress of flannel for the sea; nay, they are provided with other conveniences for the support of decorum. A certain number of the machines are fitted with tilts, that project from the seaward ends of them, so as to screen the bathers from the view of all persons whatsoever. The beach is admirably adapted for this practice, the descent being gently gradual, and the sand soft as velvet; but then the machines can be used only at a certain time of the tide, which varies every day; so that sometimes the bathers are obliged to rise very early in the morning. For my part, I love swimming as an exercise, and can enjoy it at all times of the tide, without the formality of an apparatus.

TOBIAS SMOLLETT *Humphrey Clinker*, 1770

Christmas

NOTWITHSTANDING the frostiness of the morning, the sun in his cloudless journey had acquired sufficient power to melt away the thin covering of snow from every southern declivity, and to bring out the living green which adorns an English landscape even in mid-winter. Large tracts of smiling verdure contrasted with the dazzling whiteness of the shaded slopes and hollows. Every sheltered bank, on which the broad rays of the sun rested, yielded its silver rill of cold and limpid water, glittering through the dripping grass; and sent up slight exhalations to contribute to the thin haze that hung just above the surface of the earth. There was something truly cheering in this triumph of warmth and verdure over the frosty thraldom of winter; it was, as the squire observed, an emblem of Christmas hospitality, breaking through the chills of ceremony and selfishness, and thawing every heart into a flow. He pointed with pleasure to the indications of good cheer reeking from the chimneys of the comfortable farm-houses, and low thatched cottages. "I love," said he, "to see this day well kept by rich and poor; it is a great thing to have one day in the year, at least, when you are sure of being welcome wherever you go, and of having, as it were, the world all thrown open to you; and I am almost disposed to join with Poor Robin, in his malediction on every churlish enemy to this honest festival:

'Those who at Christmas do repine,
And would fain hence dispatch him,
May they with old Duke Humphry dine,
Or else may Squire Ketch catch 'em.'"

The squire went on to lament the deplorable decay of the games and amusements which were once prevalent at this season among the lower orders, and countenanced by the higher; when the old halls of castles and manor-houses were thrown open at daylight; when the tables were covered with brawn and beef, and humming ale; when the harp and carol resounded all day long, and when rich and poor were alike welcome to enter and make merry. "Our old games and local custome," said he, "had a great effect in making the peasant fond of his home, and the promotion of them by the gentry made him fond of his lord. They made the times merrier, and kinder, and better; and I can truly say with one of our old poets:

'I like them well—the curious preciseness
And all-pretended gravity of those
That seek to banish hence these harmless sports,
Have thrust away much ancient honesty.'

The nation," continued he, "is altered; we have almost lost our simple true-hearted peasantry. They have broken asunder from the higher classes, and seem to think their interests are separate. They have become too knowing, and begin to read newspapers, listen to alehouse politicians and talk of reform. I think one mode to keep them in good humour in these hard times would be for the nobility and gentry to pass more time on their estates, mingle more among the country people, and set the merry old English games going again."

We had not been long home when the sound of music was heard from a distance. A band of country lads, without coats, their shirt sleeves fancifully tied with ribands, their hats decorated with greens, and clubs in their hands, were seen advancing up the avenue, followed by a large number of villagers and peasantry. They stopped before the hall door, where the music struck up a peculiar air, and the lads performed a curious and intricate dance, advancing, retreating, and striking their clubs together, keeping exact time to the music; while one, whimsically crowned with a fox's skin, the tail of which flaunted down his back, kept capering round the skirts of the dance, and rattling a Christmas box, with many antic gesticulations.

The squire eyed this fanciful exhibition with great interest and delight, and gave me a full account of its origin, which he traced to the times when the Romans held possession of the island, plainly proving that this was a lineal descendant of the sword dance of the ancients. "It is now," he said, "nearly extinct, but he had accidentally met with traces of it in the neighbourhood, and had encouraged its revival; though, to tell the truth, it was too apt to be followed up by the rough cudgel-play and broken heads in the evening."

After the dance was concluded, the whole party was entertained with brawn and beef, and stout home-brewed.

WASHINGTON IRVING *The Sketch Book*, 1820

The Cobb

THE young people were all wild to see Lyme. Captain Wentworth talked of going there again himself; it was only seventeen miles from Uppercross: though November, the weather was by no means bad.

After securing accommodations, and ordering a dinner at one of the inns, the next thing to be done was unquestionably to walk directly down to the sea. They were come too late in the year for any amusement or variety, which Lyme as a public place might offer. The rooms were shut up, the lodgers almost all gone, scarcely any family but of the residents left; and as there is nothing to admire in the buildings themselves, the remarkable situation of the town, the principal street almost hurrying into the water, the walk to the Cobb, skirting round the pleasant little bay, which, in the season, is animated with bathing-machines and company; the Cobb itself, its old wonders and new improvements, with the very beautiful line of cliffs stretching out to the east of the town, are what the stranger's eye will seek; and a very strange stranger it must be, who does not see charms in the immediate environs of Lyme to make him wish to know it better. The scenes in its neighbourhood, Charmouth, with its high grounds and extensive sweeps of country, and still more, its sweet, retired bay, backed by dark cliffs, where fragments of low rock among the sands make it the happiest spot for watching the flow of the tide, for sitting in unwearied contemplation; the wooded varieties of the cheerful village of Up Lyme: and, above all, Pinny, with its green chasms between romantic rocks, where the scattered forest-trees and orchards of luxuriant growth declare that many a generation must have passed away since the first partial falling of the cliff prepared the ground for such a state, where a scene so wonderful and so lovely is exhibited, as may more than equal any of the resembling scenes of the far-famed Isle of Wight: these places must be visited, and visited again to make the worth of Lyme understood.

There was too much wind to make the high part of the new Cobb pleasant for the ladies, and they agreed to get down the steps to the lower, and were all contented to pass quietly and carefully down the steep flight, excepting Louisa: she must be jumped down them by Captain Wentworth. In all their walks he had had to jump her from the stiles; the sensation was delightful to her. The hardness of the pavement for her feet made him less willing upon the present occasion; he did it, however. She was safely down, and instantly to shew her enjoyment, ran up the steps to be jumped down again. He advised her against it, thought the jar too great; but no, he reasoned and talked in vain, she smiled and said, "I am determined I will": he put out his hands; she was too precipitate by half a second, she fell on the pavement on the Lower Cobb, and was taken up lifeless! There was no wound, no blood, no visible bruise; but her eyes were closed, she breathed not, her face was like death. The horror of that moment to all who stood around!

JANE AUSTEN *Persuasion*, 1817

Kenilworth Castle

AT length the princely Castle appeared, upon improving which, and the domains around, the Earl of Leicester had, it is said, expended sixty thousand pounds sterling, a sum equal to half a million of our present money.

The outer wall of this splendid and gigantic structure enclosed seven acres, a part of which was occupied by extensive stables, and by a pleasure garden, with its trim arbours and parterres, and the rest formed the large base-court or outer yard of the noble Castle. The lordly structure itself, which rose near the centre of this spacious enclosure, was composed of a huge pile of magnificent castellated buildings, apparently of different ages, surrounding an inner court, and bearing in the names attached to each portion of the magnificent mass, and in the armorial bearings which were there blazoned, the emblems of mighty chiefs who had long passed away, and whose history, could Ambition have lent ear to it, might have read a lesson to the haughty favourite who had now acquired and was augmenting the fair domain. A large and massive keep, which formed the citadel of the Castle, was of uncertain though great antiquity. It bore the name of Cæsar, perhaps from its resemblance to that in the Tower of London so called. Some antiquaries ascribe its foundation to the time of Kenelph, from whom the Castle had its name, a Saxon King of Mercia, and others to an early era after the Norman Conquest. On the exterior walls frowned the scutcheon of the Clintons, by whom they were founded in the reign of Henry I.; and of the yet more redoubted Simon de Montfort, by whom, during the Barons' wars, Kenilworth was long held out against Henry III. Here Mortimer, Earl of March, famous alike for his rise and his fall, had once gaily revelled in Kenilworth, while his dethroned sovereign, Edward II., languished in its dungeons. Old John of Gaunt, "time-honoured Lancaster," had widely extended the Castle, erecting that noble and massive pile which yet bears the name of Lancaster's Buildings; and Leicester himself had outdone the former possessors, princely and powerful as they were, by erecting another immense structure, which now lies crushed under its own ruins, the monument of its owner's ambition. The external wall of this royal Castle was, on the south and west sides, adorned and defended by a lake partly artificial, across which Leicester had constructed a stately bridge, that Elizabeth might enter the Castle by a path hitherto untrodden, instead of the usual entrance to the northward, over which he had erected a gatehouse or barbican, which still exists, and is equal in extent, and superior in architecture, to the baronial castle of many a northern chief.

Beyond the lake lay an extensive chase, full of red deer, fallow deer, roes, and every species of game, and abounding with lofty trees, from amongst which the extended front and massive towers of the Castle were seen to rise in majesty and beauty. We cannot but add, that of this lordly palace, where princes feasted and heroes fought, now in the bloody earnest of storm and siege, and now in the games of chivalry, where beauty dealt the prize which valour won, all is now desolate. The bed of the lake is but a rushy swamp; and the massive ruins of the Castle only serve to show what their splendour once was, and to impress on the musing visitor the transitory value of human possessions, and the happiness of those who enjoy a humble lot in virtuous contentment.

SIR WALTER SCOTT *Kenilworth*, 1821

Bramley Maying

ACROSS two fields more, and up a quiet lane, and we are at the Maying, announced afar off by the merry sound of music, and the merrier clatter of childish voices. Here we are at the green—a little turfy spot, where three roads meet, close shut in by hedgerows, with a pretty white cottage, and its long slip of a garden at one angle. I had no expectation of scenery so compact, so like a glade in a forest; it is quite a cabinet picture, with green trees for the frame. In the midst grows a superb horse-chestnut, in the full glory of its flowery pyramids, and from the trunk of the chestnut the May-houses commence. They are covered alleys built of green boughs, decorated with garlands and great bunches of flowers, the gayest that blow—lilacs, guelder-roses, peonies, tulips, stocks—hanging down like chandeliers among the dancers; for of dancers, gay, dark-eyed young girls in straw bonnets and white gowns, and their lovers in their Sunday attire, the May-houses were full. The girls had mostly the look of extreme youth, and danced well and quietly like ladies—too much so; I should have been glad to see less elegance and more enjoyment; and their partners, though not altogether so graceful, were as decorous and as indifferent as real gentlemen. It was quite like a ballroom, as pretty and almost as dull. Outside was the fun. It is the outside, the upper gallery of the world, that has that good thing. There were children laughing, eating, trying to cheat, and being cheated, round an ancient and practised vendor of oranges and gingerbread; and on the other side of the tree lay a merry group of old men, in coats almost as old as themselves, and young ones in no coats at all, excluded from the dance by the disgrace of a smock-frock. Who would have thought of etiquette finding its way into the May-houses! That group would have suited Teniers; it smoked and drank a little, but it laughed a great deal more. There were a few decent, matronly-looking women, too, sitting in a cluster; and young mothers strolling about with infants in their arms; and ragged boys peeping through the boughs at the dancers; and the bright sun shining gloriously on all this innocent happiness. Oh! what a pretty sight it was! worth losing our way for—worth losing our dinner—both which events happened; whilst a party of friends, who were to have joined us, were far more unlucky; for they not only lost their way and their dinner, but rambled all day about the country, and never reached Bramley Maying.

MARY MITFORD *Our Village*, 1832

Hastings

I LOVE town, or country; but this detestable Cinque Port is neither. I hate these scrubbed shoots, thrusting out their starved foliage from between the horrid fissures of dusty innutritious rocks; which the amateur calls "verdure to the edge of the sea." I require woods, and they show me stunted coppices. I cry out for the water-brooks, and pant for fresh streams, and inland murmurs. I cannot stand all day on the naked beach, watching the capricious hues of the sea, shifting like the colours of a dying mullet. I am tired of looking out of the windows of this island-prison. I would fain retire into the interior of my cage. While I gaze upon the sea, I want to be on it, over it, across it. It binds me in with chains, as of iron. My thoughts are abroad. I should not so feel in Staffordshire. There is no home for me here. There is no sense of home at Hastings. It is a place of fugitive resort, an heterogeneous assemblage of sea-mews and stock-brokers, Amphitrites of the town, and misses that coquet with the Ocean. If it were what it was in its primitive shape, and what it ought to have remained, a fair honest fishing-town, and no more, it were something—with a few straggling fishermen's huts scattered about, artless as its cliffs, and with their materials filched from them, it were something. I could abide to dwell with Meschek; to assort with fisher-swains and smugglers. There are, or I dream there are, many of this latter occupation here. Their faces become the place. I like a smuggler. He is the only honest thief. He robs nothing but the revenue—an abstraction I never greatly cared about. I could go out with them in their mackarel boats, or about their less ostensible business, with some satisfaction. I

53 A view of Scarborough, *ca.* 1820
From a drawing by W. Boot

54 Fountains Abbey, Yorkshire
After W. Richardson, 1843

can even tolerate those poor victims to monotony, who from day to day pace along the beach, in endless progress and recurrence, to watch their illicit countrymen—townsfolk or brethren perchance—whistling to the sheathing and unsheathing of their cutlasses (their only solace), who under the mild name of preventive service, keep up a legitimated civil warfare in the deplorable absence of a foreign one, to show their detestation of run hollands and zeal for old England. But it is the visitants from town, that come here to *say* that they have been here, with no more relish of the sea than a pond perch, or a dace might be supposed to have, that are my aversion. I feel like a foolish dace in these regions, and have as little toleration for myself here, as for them. What can they want here? if they had a true relish of the ocean, why have they brought all this land luggage with them? Or why pitch their civilised tents in the desert? What mean these scanty book-rooms—marine libraries as they entitle them—if the sea were, as they would have us believe, a book "to read strange matter in?", what are their foolish concert-rooms, if they come, as they would fain be thought to do, to listen to the music of the waves? All is false and hollow pretension. They come, because it is the fashion, and to spoil the nature of the place.

CHARLES LAMB *The Last Essays*, 1833

The Abbey Church

ABOUT half a mile from Marney, the dale narrowed, and the river took a winding course. It ran through meads, soft and vivid with luxuriant vegetation, bounded on either side by rich hanging woods, save where occasionally a quarry broke the verdant bosom of the heights with its rugged and tawny form. Fair stone and plenteous timber, and the current of fresh waters, combined, with the silent and secluded scene screened from every harsh and angry wind, to form the sacred spot that in old days Holy Church loved to hallow with its beauteous and enduring structures.

Over a space of not less than ten acres might still be observed the fragments of the great abbey: these were, towards their limit, in general moss-grown and mouldering memorials that told where once rose the offices and spread the terraced gardens of the old proprietors; here might still be traced the dwelling of the lord abbot; and there, still more distinctly, because built on a greater scale and of materials still more intended for perpetuity, the capacious hospital, a name that did not then denote the dwelling of disease, but a place where all the rights of hospitality were practised; where the traveller from the proud baron to the lonely pilgrim asked the shelter and the succour that never were denied, and at whose gate, called the Portal of the Poor, the peasants on the Abbey lands, if in want, might appeal each morn and night for raiment and for food.

But it was in the centre of this tract of ruins, occupying a space of not less than two acres, that, with a strength that had defied time, and with a beauty that had at last turned away the wrath of man, still rose if not in perfect, yet admirable, form and state, one of the noblest achievements of Christian art—the Abbey church. The summer vault was now its only roof, and all that remained of its gorgeous windows was the vastness of their arched symmetry, and some wreathed relics of their fantastic frame-work, but the rest was uninjured.

From the west window, looking over the transept chapel of the Virgin, still adorned with pillars of marble and alabaster, the eye wandered down the nave to the great orient light, a length of nearly three hundred feet, through a gorgeous avenue of unshaken walls and columns that clustered to the skies. On each side of the Lady's chapel rose a tower. One which was of great antiquity, being of that style which is commonly called Norman, short and very thick and square, did not mount much above the height of the western front; but the other tower was of a character very different. It was tall and light, and of a Gothic style most pure and graceful; the stone of which it was built, of a bright and even sparkling colour, and looking as if it were hewn but yesterday. At first, its turretted crest seemed injured; but the truth is, it was unfinished; the workmen were busied on this very tower the day that old Baldwin Greymount came as the king's commissioner to inquire into the conduct of this religious house. The abbots loved to memorise their reigns by some public work, which should add to the beauty of their buildings or the convenience of their subjects; and the last of the ecclesiastical lords of Marney, a man of fine taste and a skilful architect, was raising this new belfry for his brethren when the stern decree arrived that the bells should no more sound. And the hymn was no more to be chaunted in the Lady's chapel; and the candles were no more to be lit on the high altar; and the gate of the poor was to be closed for ever; and the wanderer was no more to find a home.

BENJAMIN DISRAELI *Sybil*, 1845

A Superannuated Mansion

AT the entrance of the park, there are a pair of great gaunt mildewed lodges—mouldy Doric temples with black chimney-pots, in the finest classic taste, and the gates of course are surmounted by the *chats bottés*, the well-known supporters of the Carabas family. The gates were passed. A damp green stretch of park spread right and left immeasurably, confined by a chilly grey wall, and a damp long straight road between two huge rows of moist, dismal lime-trees, leads up to the Castle. In the midst of the park is a great black tank or lake, bristling over with rushes, and here and there covered over with patches of pea-soup. A shabby temple rises on an island in this delectable lake, which is approached by a rotten barge that lies at roost in a dilapidated boat-house. Clumps of elms and oaks dot over the huge green flat. Every one of them would have been down long since, but that the Marquis is not allowed to cut the timber.

I forgot to say the house is in full view all the way—except when intercepted by the trees on the miserable island in the lake—an enormous red-brick mansion, square, vast and dingy. It is flanked by four stone towers with weathercocks. In the midst of the grand façade is a huge Ionic portico, approached by a vast, lonely, ghastly staircase. Rows of black windows, framed in stone, stretch on either side, right and left—three storeys and eighteen windows of a row. You may see a picture of the palace and staircase, in the "Views of England and Wales," with four carved and gilt carriages waiting at the gravel walk, and several parties of ladies and gentlemen in wigs and hoops, dotting the fatiguing lines of the stairs.

But these stairs are made in great houses for people *not* to ascend. The first Lady Carabas (they are but eighty years in the peerage), if she got out of her gilt coach in a shower, would be wet to the skin before she got half-way to the carved Ionic portico, where four dreary statues of Peace, Plenty, Piety and Patriotism, are the only sentinels. You enter these palaces by back-doors.

Well—I rang the bell at a little low side-door; it clanged and jingled and echoed for a long, long while, till at length a face, as of a housekeeper, peered through the door, and, as she saw my hand in my waistcoat pocket, opened it. Unhappy, lonely housekeeper, I thought. Is Miss Crusoe in her island more solitary? The door clapped to, and I was in Castle Carabas.

"The side entrance and 'All," says the housekeeper. "The halligator hover the mantelpiece was brought home by Hadmiral St. Michaels, when a Capting with Lord Hanson. The harms on the cheers is the harms of the Carabas family." The hall was rather comfortable. We went clapping up a clean stone backstair, and then into a back passage cheerfully decorated with ragged light-green Kidderminster, and issued upon

"THE GREAT 'ALL.

"The great 'all is seventy-two feet in length, fifty-six in breadth, and thirty-eight feet 'igh. The carvings of the chimlies, representing the buth of Venus, and 'Ercules, and Eyelash, is by Van Chislum, the most famous sculpture of his hage and country. The ceiling, by Calimanco, represents Painting, Harchitecture and Music (the naked female figure with the barrel horgan) introducing George, fust Lord Carabas, to the Temple of the Muses. The winder ornaments is by Vanderputty. The floor is Patagonian marble; and the chandelier in the centre was presented to Lionel, second Marquis, by Lewy the Sixteenth, whose 'ead was cut hoff in the French Revelation."—And so this worthy woman went on, from one room into another, from the blue room to the green, and the green to the grand saloon, and the grand saloon to the tapestry closet, cackling her list of pictures and wonders: and furtively turning up a corner of brown holland to show the colour of the old, faded, seedy, mouldy, dismal hangings.

At last we came to her Ladyship's bedroom. In the centre of this dreary apartment there is a bed about the size of one of those whizgig temples in which the Genius appears in a pantomime. The huge gilt edifice is approached by steps, and so tall, that it might be let off in floors, for sleeping-rooms for all the Carabas family. An awful bed! A murder might be done at one end of that bed, and people sleeping at the other end be ignorant of it. Gracious powers! fancy little Lord Carabas in a nightcap ascending those steps after putting out the candle!

The sight of that seedy and solitary splendour was too much

for me. I should go mad were I that lonely housekeeper—in those enormous galleries—in that lonely library, filled up with ghastly folios that nobody dares read, with an inkstand on the centre table like the coffin of a baby, and sad portraits staring at you from the bleak walls with their solemn mouldy eyes. No wonder that Carabas does not come down here often. It would require two thousand footmen to make the place cheerful.

A single family has no more right to build itself a temple of that sort than to erect a Tower of Babel.

WILLIAM MAKEPEACE THACKERAY *The Book of Snobs*, 1847

Stonehenge

LEAVING the bridge, I ascended a gentle acclivity, and presently reached what appeared to be a tract of moory undulating ground. It was now tolerably light, but there was a mist or haze abroad which prevented my seeing objects with much precision. I felt chill in the damp air of the early morn, and walked rapidly forward. In about half an hour I arrived where the road divided into two, at an angle or tongue of dark green sward. "To the right or the left?" said I, and forthwith took, without knowing why, the left-hand road, along which I proceeded about a hundred yards, when, in the midst of the tongue of sward formed by the two roads, collaterally with myself, I perceived what I at first conceived to be a small grove of blighted trunks of oaks, barked and gray. I stood still for a moment, and then, turning off the road, advanced slowly towards it over the sward; as I drew nearer, I perceived that the objects which had attracted my curiosity, and which formed a kind of circle, were not trees, but immense upright stones. A thrill pervaded my system; just before me were two, the mightiest of the whole, tall as the stems of proud oaks, supporting on their tops a huge transverse stone and forming a wonderful doorway. I knew now where I was, and, laying down my stick and bundle, and taking off my hat, I advanced slowly, and cast myself—it was folly, perhaps, but I could not help what I did—cast myself, with my face on the dewy earth, in the middle of the portal of giants, beneath the transverse stone.

The spirit of Stonehenge was strong upon me!

And after I had remained with my face on the ground for some time, I arose, placed my hat on my head, and, taking up my stick and bundle, wandered around the wondrous circle, examining each individual stone, from the greatest to the least; and then, entering by the great door, seated myself upon an immense broad stone, one side of which was supported by several small ones, and the other slanted upon the earth; and there in deep meditation, I sat for an hour or two, till the sun shone in my face above the tall stones of the eastern side.

George Borrow *Lavengro*, 1851

Hiram's Hospital

In the year 1434 there died at Barchester one John Hiram, who had made money in the town as a woolstapler, and in his will he left the house in which he died and certain meadows and closes near the town, still called Hiram's Butts, and Hiram's Patch, for the support of twelve superannuated wool-carders, all of whom should have been born and bred and spent their days in Barchester; he also appointed that an alms-house should be built for their abode, with a fitting residence for a warden, which warden was also to receive a certain sum annually out of the rents of the said butts and patches.

From that day to this the charity has gone on and prospered —at least the charity had gone on, and the estates had prospered. Wool-carding in Barchester there was no longer any; so the bishop, dean, and warden, who took it in turn to put in the old men, generally appointed some hangers-on of their own; worn-out gardeners, decrepit grave-diggers, or octogenarian sextons, who thankfully received a comfortable lodging and one shilling and fourpence a day, such being the stipend to which, under the will of John Hiram, they were declared to be entitled. Formerly, indeed,—that is, till within some fifty years of the present time,—they received but sixpence a day, and their breakfast and dinner was found them at a common table by the warden; such an arrangement being in stricter conformity with the absolute wording of old Hiram's will: but this was thought to be inconvenient, and to suit the tastes of neither warden nor bedesmen, and the daily one shilling and fourpence was substituted with the common consent of all parties, including the bishop and the corporation of Barchester.

Such was the condition of Hiram's twelve old men when Mr. Harding was appointed warden; but if they may be considered to have been well-to-do in the world according to their condition, the happy warden was much more so. The patches and butts which, in John Hiram's time, produced hay or fed cows, were now covered with rows of houses; the value of the property had gradually increased from year to year and century to century, and was now presumed by those who knew anything about it, to bring in a very nice income; and by some who knew nothing about it, to have increased to an almost fabulous extent.

Hiram's Hospital, as the retreat is called, is a picturesque building enough, and shows the correct taste with which the ecclesiastical architects of those days were imbued. It stands on the banks of the little river, which flows nearly round the cathedral close, being on the side furthest from the town. The London road crosses the river by a pretty one-arched bridge, and, looking from this bridge, the stranger will see the windows of the old men's rooms, each pair of windows separated by a small buttress. A broad gravel walk runs between the building and the river, which is always trim and cared for; and at the end of the walk, under the parapet of the approach to the bridge, is a large and well-worn seat, on which, in mild weather, three or four of Hiram's bedesmen are sure to be seen seated. Beyond this row of buttresses, and further from the bridge, and also further from the water which here suddenly bends, are the pretty oriel windows of Mr. Harding's house, and his well-mown lawn. The entrance to the Hospital is from the London road, and is made through a ponderous gateway under a heavy stone arch, unnecessary, one would suppose, at any time, for the protection of twelve old men, but greatly conducive to the good appearance of Hiram's charity. On passing through this portal, never closed to any one from six a.m. till ten p.m., and never open afterwards, except on application to a huge, intricately hung mediæval bell, the handle of which no uninitiated intruder can possibly find, the six doors of the old men's abodes are seen, and beyond them is a slight iron screen, through which the more happy portion of the Barchester elite pass into the Elysium of Mr. Harding's dwelling.

ANTHONY TROLLOPE *The Warden*, 1855

Backwater

MONDAY, 7 August.

I walked over the white chalk cliff towers roofed with green, to the village of Beer which lies in a long deep narrow chine recessed in a little bay between two great cliffs, so that as you approach it by land you cannot see this village of 1,200 people till you come quite close to it, and neither can the village in the chine be seen from Seaton or even from the sea unless you are exactly opposite the mouth of the chine. Beer is a sort of little Spanish colony. Many of the people are of Spanish blood and still show their descent by their swarthy complexions. Legend says that a vessel of the Spanish Armada was wrecked at Beer. Another tradition states that a Spanish ship went ashore there in later times and left a colony of Spaniards there who intermarried with the natives and made their mark. It was pleasant walking upon the short fine elastic turf along the edge of the vast precipitous white chalk cliffs and a fresh sweet breeze stole in over the sea. The sea below was dotted with rowing boats full of excursionists, tiny by the vast distance. As we came down into the long deep narrow chine we saw on the beach below a small crowd of people round a fisherman who was selling crabs just caught, by Dutch auction, naming a high price himself and gradually lowering it till he got a bid. The crowd presently melted away and two or three fishermen were left round the creel or crab basket, one of them kneeling on the shingle "nicking" the crab's claws, i.e. cutting the spring muscle of the claw, as he told us, thus rendering the claw powerless and preventing the crabs from biting each other's legs as they would otherwise when all struggling and crawling together in a heap in the crab basket.

We walked back up the street of the long narrow village nestling in its chine, where the ducks were gobbling fish offal in the open gutters, down which flows a swift little stream in which the fish are cleaned, and into which the house drains empty. Near the top of the village stands the strange old Church, dark and close, quaint and irregular, where the old fishermen howl the hymns on Sundays and where a former Vicar buried, says tradition, under the pulpit becomes perceptible to delicate organs on summer Sunday evenings. The Church clock sat at 10 o'clock, stopped may be, as the Vicar of St. Ives says the St. Ives Church clock is often stopped, by the smell of the fish. At many cottage doors sat pale nice looking girls making Honiton lace, their fingers flying and the pins and bobbins rattling over the pillows in the girls' laps. I stopped to look at one girl sitting just inside a cottage door embowered with nasturtiums and other creepers. A kind voice bade me enter. It looked cool and tempting in the shade of the porch, but it was getting late and I was obliged to go on up the blazing road.

FRANCIS KILVERT *Diary*, 1871

The Waits

Shortly after ten o'clock, the singing-boys arrived at the tranter's house, which was invariably the place of meeting, and preparations were made for the start. The older men and musicians wore thick coats, with stiff perpendicular collars, and coloured handkerchiefs wound round and round the neck till the end came to hand, over all which they just showed their ears and noses, like people looking over a wall. The remainder, stalwart ruddy men and boys, were mainly dressed in snow-white smock-frocks, embroidered upon the shoulders and breasts, in ornamental forms of hearts, diamonds and zigzags. The cider-mug was emptied for the ninth time, the music-books were arranged and the pieces finally decided upon. The boys in the meantime put the old horn-lanterns in order, cut candles into short lengths to fit the lanterns; and a thin fleece of snow having fallen since the early part of the evening, those who had no leggings went to the stable and wound wisps of hay round their ankles to keep the insidious flakes from the interior of their boots.

Old William Dewy, with the violoncello, played the bass; his grandson Dick the treble violin; and Reuben and Michael Mail the tenor and second violins respectively. The singers consisted of four men and seven boys, upon whom devolved the task of carrying and attending to the lanterns, and holding the books open for the players. Directly music was the theme, old William ever and instinctively came to the front.

"Now mind, naibours," he said, as they all went out one by one at the door, he himself holding it ajar and regarding them with a critical face as they passed, like a shepherd counting out his sheep. "You two counter-boys, keep your ears open to Michael's fingering, and don't ye go straying into the treble part along o' Dick and his set, as ye did last year; and mind this especially when we be in 'Arise, and hail.' Billy Chimlen, don't you sing quite so raving mad as you fain would; and, all o' ye, whatever ye do, keep from making a great scuffle on the ground when we go in at people's gates; but go quietly, so as to strik' up all of a sudden, like spirits."

"Farmer Ledlow's first?"

"Farmer Ledlow's first; the rest as usual."

"And, Voss," said the tranter terminatively, "you keep house here till about half-past two; then heat the metheglin and cider in the warmer you'll find turned up upon the copper; and bring it wi' the victuals to church-porch, as th'st know."

THOMAS HARDY *Under the Greenwood Tree*, 1872

A Love-carriage

NEVER in all my days did I see a corn harvest like that one. We started swiving, that is reaping, at the beginning of August-month, and we left the stooks standing in the fields till it should be time for the love-carriage, for the weather was so fine that they took no harm. It was the custom, if a farmer hadna much strength about him, that he should fix on a day for the neighbours to come and give a hand in the lugging of the grain. But up to that time, the weather being so good, we worked alone. It was up in the morning early, and no mistake!

At last the day of the love-carriage came, and a tremendous blue day it was, with a sky like a dark bowl—Worcester china colour. We'd got fifty people coming, no less, counting the women-folk. I was up afore dawn getting all ready, setting the china, both ours and what we'd borrowed, on the trestles in the orchard, helping Gideon to put the casks of beer in the yard, ready for the men to fill their harvest bottles, and fetching water from the well for the tea. The orchard was a sight to see when the trestles were set out (for I could put all ready with no fear of rain on such a day) with the mugs and platters of many colours, and the brown quartern loaves, and the big pats of butter stamped with a swan, and the slabs of honeycomb, dough cakes, gingerbread, cheese, jam and jelly, let alone the ham at one end of each trestle and the round of beef at the other. Even Gideon didna begrutch the food on this day. For it was one of the laws you couldna break, that at a love-carriage everybody must have his bellyful.

It was very early when the waggons began to roll into the fold, with a solemn gladsome sound, and each with its own pair of horses or oxen. Each farmer brought his own men and his own waggon, and sometimes he brought two. The teams were decked out with ribbons and flowers, and some had a motto as well, such as, "Luck to our Day," or "God bless the Corn." It was a fine thing to see the big horses, with great manes on their fetlocks, groomed till they shone like satin, stepping along as proud as Lucifer, knowing very well how long the waggoner had been, a-plaiting their ribbons. The oxen were good to see, also, for their horns were all bedecked, and about their necks were thick chains of Sweet William and Travellers' Joy and corn. Miller came among the first, with his gig and the old coach horse, the best he had, poor man. And very good work they did, too, for it's surprising what a deal you can get onto a gig if you put a set of wings on top.

So we went out under the blue sky to lug home the corn, the big waggons with solid wheels rolling over the stubble, Granfeyther Callard shouting "*Jiggin!*" when he meant "*Haw-woop!*" being quite tipsy with enjoyment, and causing a great confusion, the horses not knowing what to do. The rest of us followed on, strung out over the fields in bright colours, children and dogs running hither and thither, while in the rickyard the men told off to make the stacks put the logs in place ready for the stacks to be built on, got all prepared against the first waggon came back loaded high with grain, and then stood leaning on their pikels, talking over the work of the coming day, each man as busy about the planning of it all as if the harvest was his'n, and each man as glad of the grain as if he was to have the selling of it. For that was the manner of the love-carriages in time past.

MARY WEBB *Precious Bane*, 1924

Country Fair

THE square was crowded with the booths of merchants, most of them selling crockery, decorative china, usually pink and gold, or cakes, fruit and hard-bake, all three glistening with stickiness. Some booths sold linen shirts and cloth caps. Four shows were busy; a merry-go-round with a steam organ which played "White Wings"; a smaller merry-go-round, with a steam organ and cymbals, which played "Cheer, Boys, Cheer"; a smaller merry-go-round, with a trumpeter and drummer, who played what sounded like selections from "Annie Laurie," and a double stand of swingboats in full swing, with the swingers singing to all three. Further along were rifle saloons, with their noise of spitting, cracking, and tingling; Aunt Sally shies, with their men bawling:

"Rollo-bowlo-pitch.
Three shies a penny at your old Aunt Sally,
For a coconut or a good cigar,
For a good cigar or a coconut.
Come rollo-bowlo-pitch,"

and the yell of a cheap-jack who stood on a wagon selling pudding-basins, which he smashed to fragments from time to time when bidding was slack. "Tuppence the basin," he was shouting. "All-English pudding-basin for anybody's beef-steak and kidney pudding; come, tuppence, or I'll smash it, tuppence, or I smash it. What, you won't pay tuppence? You shan't have it cheaper. The all-English pudding-basin as used in our Royal Queen Victoria's kitchen at Windsor Palace, Windsor? Who says tuppence? Who says tuppence? Who says tuppence? Well, if you won't then . . . Smash"; and smash the basin went on the cobble-stones.

It was a holiday in Hilcote and the district near-by. The yards of all the inns were full of the traps of farmers: all the square was crowded. In the northern side of the square, close to the church, there was a hiring stand, where a few men and women hung about still, hoping to be hired; usually these were what were known as the Hilcote Hard Bargains, who had not been able to get along with those who had hired them there at Michaelmas. George had a look at them.

Further along the same pavement there were booths (as there had been for 350 years) for the sale of country things and country skill. A man sat there mending china, using the dancing-ball drill of Ancient Egypt, and sometimes inviting his watchers to try if they could work it. A woman, a little further along, mended rush-bottom or straw-bottom chairs while the owners waited. A turner sold the wooden cups and plates which he had made: these were still used by the very poor, though cheap tin had marred the market for them. Near him two women offered lace, once much made thereabouts, now falling out of life as fingers and eyesight failed among the makers. Another woman sold the old original Hilcote pies, being the boat of St. Nicholas in ginger-bread, stuffed with currants and spice. When George reached this part of the square the shows were lighting their flares and the women at the booths their lanterns, so that a warm light, as well as the glow of sunset, fell upon flowers and faces.

JOHN MASEFIELD *The Hawbucks*, 1929

A Dickensian Type

THE higgler was a common phenomenon in the district, and in time I came to know him well. With a blistered spring-cart

55 The Market Hall at Brackley, Northamptonshire
From a drawing of ca. 1830

56 Market Scenes in the Early Nineteenth Century
After W. H. Pyne

57 A Country Fair, 1822

After W. H. Pyne

and a hoppety old pony, he jogged along staring at the country. He would have a load of anything, from chicken-crates to worn motor-tyres. Seeing a farmer, he would draw up and comment on the nearest crop, and then ask: "Anything to sell?" Much of his trade was probably due to the farmer's love of "a deal." He cannot resist being drawn into a verbal fencing over prices. The prices creep closer, and suddenly the farmer finds he has sold some cockerels over which he started to haggle just for the fun of the game.

When the higgler has done a deal with a farmer he regards a bag of chaff as his perquisite. He also asks the farmer to sell him a truss of clover hay (stover) or some mangolds. In this way he keeps his horse. Usually he has an acre or two of land (who hasn't in Suffolk?), and he begs some seed at a nominal price. He is often irritating, but just as often amusing. He retails gossip as he trundles about. The market is his club, lots marked "Sundries" his rallying-points. There is more joy in the higgler's heart over sixpence made by buying a thing and selling it again than over one-and-sixpence earned at a straightforward job. He scrapes a living snatching at minute profits. The word DEAL is written on his heart. He often wears a stiff coat of antique fashion, with many flapped pockets and tight trousers giving him a Dickensian appearance. He carries one-pound notes crushed like waste paper in his trousers pocket, and silver rolled up in them. They are unravelled one by one on completion of a deal. Whatever the faults of the higgler, he is a cash customer, and usually pays on the nail. The compensations of his hacking life are an illusion of independence and the spice of possibility. Those cockerels he bought for four shillings apiece may make five-and-six in the market. Or they may make three-and-nine. The successful among them is the judicious risker. He buys boldly, prepared to chance a loss. The farmer likes him for it; he admires a sport and wishes him a good profit. If a farmer sells something to a "little man," he wants him to get something out of it. It is almost a matter of honour.

ADRIAN BELL *Corduroy*, 1930

Custom

THERE used to linger on, in those days, a yearly festival known as Oyster Fair. It appears that, long before the Danes gave the hamlet its present name, when the whole valley from Seaton to Easthampton was one great estuary, the wretched aborigines, who lived chiefly on fresh-water oysters, used to hold some sort of festival on or near the sandy beach now represented by the Seaton road where it runs through Eastwick. Whether it was the last catch or first catch of those now obsolete molluscs, we shall never know, but it is certain that Blagovarius, in his *Itinerary*, records the pagan festival, which consisted in his day of a procession carrying nets and paddles, and cooking oysters on an altar, with incidents usual to such occasions.

After Blagovarius came Saxon and Dane and centuries of darkness. The next record we have is of the Christian festival, presided over by the Abbot of Holme (that great grey ruin that still stands a few miles down the river). The estuary had been cramped down by water-mills to the present navigable river channel running between rich meadows; the oysters had disappeared. The business had become an annual tribute of fish brought from Seaton and landed at Eastwick for the benefit of the Lord Abbots, on whose escutcheon (*see* Johann's *Memorials*) the three oyster-shells still figure meaningless.

But oh! impermanence of all things human. The Lord Abbot of Holme, twice a prince (once spiritually, once temporally), went the same way as Blagovarius with his Roman road from Eyecastra or Achester, as he called Easthampton, to Porta Seatonensis. The Abbey of Holme is now but a great mass of crumbling stone in a meadow, part windmill, part cowshed. Three oyster-shells carved in the stone of an arch forty feet high are slowly washing out, and the once magnificent church is left to bats and the wind of heaven.

Amid all this, one thing remained permanent—the actual average human material. Never quite succumbing to climate and famine, to flood and disease, surviving the assaults of wild beasts and wilder men, outliving Roman and Northerner, Abbot and Adventurer, the labourers and bargees of Eastwick cling to their tiny bit of existence, between the river and the heathery hill; and with them, never written down by them, hardly spoken of, lived on the idea of a festival—a holiday—a respite from the monotonous round of earning enough to eat, that should occur about midsummer; and to this they held. Nothing would induce them to work on the twenty-fourth of June. They still called it Oyster Fair—though the slow river that gleamingly reflected the church tower had contained no oysters for eight hundred years.

R. H. MOTTRAM *Our Mr. Dormer*, 1927

Index